Washington Is Burning

Washington Is Burning

Corruption and Lies
in the Age of Trump

Andrew Cockburn

VERSO

London • New York

First published by Verso 2026
The author and publisher are grateful to the following publications in which
appeared earlier versions of the chapters reproduced herein: *Harper's Magazine*
(chapters 1–8, 13, and 18–23); *London Review of Books* (chapters 9–11 and 14);
Responsible Statecraft (chapters 15–17); *New Statesman* (Chapter 12)

The manufacturer's authorized representative in the EU for product safety (GPSR)
is LOGOS EUROPE, 9 rue Nicolas Poussin, 17000, La Rochelle, France
contact@logoseurope.eu

The moral rights of the author have been asserted

1 3 5 7 9 10 8 6 4 2

Verso
UK: 6 Meard Street, London W1F 0EG
US: 207 East 32nd Street, New York, NY 10016
versobooks.com

Verso is the imprint of New Left Books

ISBN-13: 978-1-83674-177-0
ISBN-13: 978-1-83674-180-0 (US EBK)
ISBN-13: 978-1-83674-179-4 (UK EBK)

British Library Cataloguing in Publication Data
A catalogue record for this book is available from the British Library

Library of Congress Cataloging-in-Publication Data

Names: Cockburn, Andrew, 1947– author
Title: Washington is burning : the corruption, lies, and ignorance that
  fuel the flames / Andrew Cockburn.
Description: London ; New York : Verso, 2026. | Summary: "Andrew Cockburn
  reveals the inner workings of Trump's Washington - a grotesque carnival
  of corruption. Cockburn sets fire to US pieties, focusing on the
  spectacular greed at the heart of the nation's political system"—
  Provided by publisher.
Identifiers: LCCN 2025043215 (print) | LCCN 2025043216 (ebook) | ISBN
  9781836741770 | ISBN 9781836741800 US ebk
Subjects: LCSH: Political corruption—United States—History | Political
  culture—United States—History | Public contracts—Corrupt
  practices—United States—History | Public-private sector
  cooperation—Corrupt practices—United States—History |
  Avarice—Political aspects—United States—History
Classification: LCC JK2249 .C63 2026 (print) | LCC JK2249 (ebook)
LC record available at https://lccn.loc.gov/2025043215
LC ebook record available at https://lccn.loc.gov/2025043216

Typeset in Sabon by MJ & N Gavan, Truro, Cornwall
Printed and bound by CPI Group (UK) Ltd, Croydon, CR0 4YY

For Declan, Otis, Artemis, and Daisy

Contents

Introduction

Revenge and Plunder

Empires are at their most interesting when they start tumbling into final decline. Edward Gibbon's long account of the Roman Empire's terminal experience takes on added drama when the barbarians finally break through the walls of the capital and sack it. Their leader "who no longer dissembled his appetite for plunder and revenge," according to Gibbon, delivered the imperial city "to the licentious fury of the tribes of Germany and Scythia," who swiftly embarked on an orgy of rapine and looting.

There are parallels aplenty with the second coming of Donald Trump, especially from the viewpoint of his defeated opponents. He made no bones about his appetite for revenge, decreeing punishment for erstwhile prosecutors, proponents of the "Russia collusion" conspiracy theory, and others who had sparked his ire. Plunder was certainly there for the taking, as evidenced by the millions of dollars extracted from tech oligarchs crowded at Trump's back when he took the oath to defend the constitution. One of these courtier-oligarchs, Amazon's Jeff Bezos, even went so far as to proffer a $40 million gratuity to Melania Trump for a documentary about her activities in the White House. The conquering president's wealthier supporters slavered at the promise of indulgent regulation of their business practices along with reduced taxes on their enormous incomes. Necessary savings would be levied from the less fortunate. Prison corporation stocks soared in happy anticipation of rich pickings from prospective mass incarceration of immigrants.

Legal safeguards against pillaging by financial profiteers, notably the crypto industry, were swept away. Defense corporations and their military partners rejoiced at the prospect of even more of the national treasure being shoveled their way, including billions promised for a reinvigoration of fanciful missile defense programs dubbed "Golden Dome" to guard American skies. Lobbyists savored the riches soon to be showered on them as corporations and nation-states set to feel the lash of Trump's edicts scrambled to buy influence with Trump's courtiers in hopes of averting punishment or securing advantage.

Ancient Romans viewed the takeover of their city as approximate to the end of the world. Swathes of American society, especially among the Democratic Party establishment, the bureaucracy, and the mainstream media, felt the same way. But the seeds of the barbarian triumph, planted over decades, had sprouted ever more healthily in recent years. Democrats might have fretted that Trump was fulfilling his promise to be a "dictator on day one," but the means to that end were ready at hand. For example, soon after he first became president in 2017, Trump had been briefed on a raft of emergency powers, including secret "presidential emergency action documents" awaiting deployment in locked and guarded government filing cabinets. As described in "The Enemies Briefcase," Trump's boast during his first term that "I have the right to do a lot of things that people don't even know about," was all too accurate. The "things" include imposing martial law, suspending habeas corpus, seizing control of the internet, imposing censorship, and incarcerating alleged subversives. Once upon a time Richard Nixon had ignited general alarm when he proclaimed: "When the president does it, that means that it is not illegal." But little was done. On the contrary, Congress soon expanded presidential extra-constitutional powers, passing the International Emergency Economic Powers Act in 1977, which enabled a president to declare national emergencies "to deal with any unusual and extraordinary threat"—a potent tool deployed by Trump in laying waste to international trade with tariffs. It also empowered him or any president to sanction countries, businesses, and individuals without warning, without furnishing evidence, and, effectively, without appeal. As Trump's press secretary Karoline Leavitt boldly asserted in her first briefing, the president "is the executive of the executive branch, and, therefore, he has the power to fire anyone in the executive branch that he wishes to." Along the way, presidents have also exercised the self-appointed right, to wiretap Americans at will (Bush Jr.), rain bombs on countries around the world (Clinton), and assassinate American citizens (Obama).

The steady shredding of constitutional impediments to one-man rule from the Oval Office would not have been possible without congressional cooperation, usually in the form of determined inaction. Fearful of offending powerful interests in the military and intelligence establishments, Congress had acquiesced in the steady erosion of constitutional protections, notably its own supposedly exclusive right to declare war. The military-industrial complex has faced no obstacle in its decades-long inflation of threats to extract ever-increasing sums from lawmakers with little dissent. Nor had Wall Street or corporate America overall ever faced significant pressure to rein in their depredations.

The stories in this collection highlight many of the ways in which the rot has accumulated. It is not possible, for example, to understand the role of the Democratic Party in paving the way for Trump without understanding the prime requirement of party leaders, which has been to maintain control over their own organization, a prize rendered ever more attractive by the torrent of money channeled to the leadership's partners, the campaign consultant industry. In pursuit of this goal, even winning elections is of secondary concern, while considerations of national interest, let alone reform, are of comparatively minimal interest. It follows that anyone seeking to intrude on this control has to be ruthlessly eliminated. The unremitting offensive against progressive forces unleashed against the 2016 Sanders campaign provides ample confirmation of this thesis, from the party hierarchy's suppression in 2017 of a popular progressive candidate, then-congressman Keith Ellison, for party chairman in favor of a colorless party hack, to the imposition of Joe Biden, despite his record of failed campaigns, as presidential nominee in 2020, to the manipulation of Democratic primaries for the benefit of the visibly senile Biden in 2024. At a local level, bosses pursued the same course, notably in Philadelphia, where an entrenched machine has happily pocketed funding from wealthy right-wing Republican donors.

This sorry process culminated in the Biden administration's enthusiastic participation in Israel's genocidal assault on Gaza, casually overriding laws precluding military support for countries committing gross violation of human rights as well as the expressed opposition, manifested in serial opinion polls, by the Democratic rank-and-file. In a public display of its lack of concern for laws, voters' inclinations, and simple humanity, party leaders refused to allow a Palestinian-American to speak at their nominating convention in August 2024 and firmly suppressed the slightest demonstration of support for the Palestinian cause. As I noted in *Harper's*, this echoed, to the very day, the Democratic Party's rejection of an integrated delegation from Mississippi at the Democratic 1964 convention sixty years before. The reckoning came in November, when Trump swept to victory, thanks in large part through abstention by previously loyal Democratic voters, repulsed by the party leadership's adamant support for the ongoing slaughter.

Politics do not normally get discussed in this way, at least not in the mainstream media (where Gaza as a major contributory factor to the Democratic defeat was seldom mentioned). Those whose view of the world is shaped by official channels are accordingly encouraged in the belief that our parties are motivated by ideology, that our foreign policy is governed by considerations of the national interest, that our lavishly financed system of national defense is a necessary and effective precaution against fearsome threats, that corporations strive to protect the environment. But these presumptions are largely false. To cite some examples, examined in greater depth in following chapters: John F. Kennedy did not believe Soviet missiles in Cuba posed a significant threat to the United States, and his principal concern during the October 1962 missile crisis was to win the imminent midterm elections; UN weapons inspectors told the Clinton administration that Iraq had no weapons of mass destruction, but Clinton suppressed the news for fear of criticism that he had "let Saddam off the hook" and thereby bears much responsibility for the Iraq War. High-ranking generals welcomed escalation in Afghanistan because "it will do us good at budget time." The Pentagon's insistence on buying ever more expensive and highly complex equipment, such as the startlingly deficient K-46 aerial refueling tanker, has produced a steadily shrinking and increasingly ineffective force. Successive administrations successfully diverted blame for 9/11 from Saudi Arabia to protect arms sales to that country while the CIA partnered with Al-Qaeda to install a fundamentalist Islamic regime in Syria. The US fights a war on drugs while actively supporting regimes controlled by drug traffickers, as in Honduras. The nuclear industry saved itself from financial oblivion by promoting the notion that it provides "clean power" as an answer to climate change, despite undeniable evidence to the contrary, while the Monsanto corporation was aided by fear of invasive species in its efforts to sell ever more toxic glyphosate weed killer. Older Americans consigned to nursing homes are increasingly subjected to the tender mercies of private equity profiteers, one reason why they died, alone, in their thousands during the Covid pandemic. The hefty damage payments consequent on police killings of innocent people is a boon to the multi-billion-dollar municipal bond market.

These and other manifestations of our system at work all deserve attention, though considered reflection about such matters will be subsumed while the barbarian is inside the gates of Washington, figuratively burning down the city. But the system may endure, as it did after 1814, when Admiral Cockburn marched into the city. Trump would doubtless not approve the precedent, since Cockburn's army was diverse, made up of former slaves he had freed, armed, and trained who were happy participants in burning the White House. When Francis Scott Key, a fervent supporter of slavery, wrote "The Star-Spangled Banner" he added lines implicitly denouncing Cockburn's liberating activities. But these lines are never sung nowadays, and they name bridges after Key. There is no reference to Cockburn or his army of freed slaves in the Museum of African American History in Washington, DC.

1

Washington Is Burning

On a sunny Saturday in June, thousands gathered on the National Mall in Washington, DC, to sing "The Star-Spangled Banner." This year marks the two-hundredth anniversary of Francis Scott Key's composition, officially adopted as the national anthem in 1931 following news that leftist members of the Erie, Pennsylvania, city council were opening meetings with a rousing chorus of "The Internationale." As the melody rang out over the grass and along Constitution Avenue, it echoed off neighboring memorials and galleries, including the partly built National Museum of African American History and Culture a block and a half down the street.

Although preceded by a lengthy program of musical performances, the anthem itself got short shrift. As usual, only the familiar opening verse was sung, because of various ideological stumbling blocks in subsequent verses—most especially the third, with its fervent hope that

> No refuge could save the hireling and slave
> From the terror of flight, or the gloom of the grave.

For myself, the words always evoke a glow of family pride, because Key's malign desire that fleeing slaves should find no refuge was directly inspired by the actions of my distinguished relative Admiral Sir George Cockburn of the Royal Navy. Two hundred years ago this August, he fought his way to the White House at the head of an army partly composed of slaves he had freed, armed, and trained and torched the place, along with the Capitol and much of official Washington. In the course of a two-year campaign, he rescued as many as 6,000 slaves, and despite Key's hopeful verse, not to mention angry demands from the US government, he sailed them away to freedom.

Obviously, the admiral qualifies as one of the great emancipators, and I am proud to claim a connection. In a recent conversation with Dr. Lonnie Bunch, who is overseeing the creation of the African American museum as its director, I suggested that he include George Cockburn in a Hall of the Righteous, cheek by jowl with Abraham Lincoln and William Lloyd Garrison. He was nice enough to hear me out, although he made it clear that his intention is not to produce a Black version of the nearby Holocaust Memorial Museum, with its Wall of Rescuers, but something far broader in scope. The real challenge, Bunch told me, is to avoid a "rosy view of the past. Romanticized memory is not history." Workers have already installed a 1930s guard tower from the Louisiana State Penitentiary and a Jim Crow–era railroad car.

To maintain a rosy view of the War of 1812, it is best to concentrate on the tattered banner and its mythic survival amid British rockets and bombs. There is less romance in the full story. It was a war of aggression, launched by President James Madison in hopes of conquering Britain's Canadian colony, thought to be easy prey while the British were distracted by their life-and-death struggle with Napoleon. Not for the last time, expert opinion expected a walkover. "The acquisition of Canada this year, as far as the neighborhood of Quebec, will be a mere matter of marching," wrote Thomas Jefferson soon after war was declared. A fellow ringleader of the war party, Henry Clay, assured Congress that "the militia of Kentucky are alone [able] to place Montreal and Upper Canada at your feet."

As with more recent enterprises, things did not go as planned, especially since the military was woefully unprepared and led by incompetent commanders. The Canadian expedition ended in disaster and large portions of Maine and Michigan fell under enemy occupation. By the time the British agreed to call it a day, the bitterly divided United States was war-weary and on the verge of bankruptcy.

By then George Cockburn was the most hated man in (white) America, vilified in the press as the "great bandit." The scion of a Scottish landed family ruined by his speculator father, he had entered the navy at the age of fourteen. From then on, he was almost continually at sea—and, once war with France broke out in 1793, frequently in combat. This conflict, initially waged against revolutionary France and then against Napoleon, was essentially the first world war, fought across much of the globe and offering plenty of opportunities for a tough, ambitious professional such as Cockburn. At twenty-three, he was already a captain, in command of a 215-man frigate. Horatio Nelson, Britain's greatest naval hero, would soon praise the young officer's "zeal, ability, and courage, which shine conspicuous on every occasion which offers."

By 1813, when he first arrived in Chesapeake Bay, Cockburn was forty-one years old and a rear admiral. His mission was straightforward: to inflict as much damage as possible on this economic heartland, thereby dissuading prowar Democratic-Republicans (as opposed to antiwar Federalists) from their rash attack on the British Empire. "I have no hesitation," he wrote to a superior officer, "in pronouncing that the whole of the shores and towns within this vast bay, not excepting the capital itself, will be wholly at your mercy, and subject if not to be permanently occupied, certainly to be successively insulted [raided] or destroyed at your pleasure."

This ruthless scheme, which Cockburn was to follow to the letter, would have been absolutely impossible without first-class intelligence operatives to alert his raiding parties to enemy forces and guide them around the tortuous shoreline. Fortunately, volunteers for such a mission soon appeared: slaves. At first they were single men, eagerly welcomed by the British as the pilots and guides they needed. But the numbers quickly grew as entire families made their way to the ships. At this point the invaders made a crucial decision: they would accept any slave—man, woman, or child—and guarantee they would not be handed back to their owners.

It was a shrewd assault on the young republic, which at the time was really two nations: a free people, intoxicated by their new democracy, and an enslaved people, ill-fed, clad in rags, and routinely brutalized. In fact, the revolution had in many ways made the lives of enslaved Americans even worse. For example, among the goals of Virginian Founding Fathers such as Jefferson had been the breakup of big landed estates. Whereas in colonial times such estates passed to a single heir (the eldest), they could now be divided equally among siblings. This meant that slave families, too, were increasingly broken up. In his pathbreaking history *The Internal Enemy: Slavery and War in Virginia, 1772–1832*, Alan Taylor points out that "the revolution had produced a tragic contradiction by promoting greater equality for white men while weakening the security of black families." In addition, observes Taylor, "by diffusing slave ownership, the new laws also broadened public support for slavery." A nascent movement in favor of emancipation that had flickered during the years of the Revolution soon died away.

In Taylor's view, family separation was the most onerous of all the miseries inflicted on enslaved Blacks. Perpetually indebted Virginia and Maryland planters were happy to breed and sell surplus bodies, regardless of family ties, to the expanding cotton plantations of the deep South. So enslaved Black men, especially those living within easy reach of the coast, led their families to the British in large numbers.

The British understood very well that slavery was their enemy's Achilles' heel, and when Cockburn and his fleet returned to the Chesapeake in the spring of 1814 after wintering in Bermuda, he was determined to take full advantage. His orders read:

> Let the landings you make be more for the protection of the desertion of the Black Population than with a view to any other advantage. ... The great point to be attained is the cordial Support of the Black population. With them properly armed & backed with 20,000 British Troops, Mr. Madison will be hurled from his throne.

On May 29, horrified planters had their first look at the next stage of the British scheme. A raid on Pungoteague, on Virginia's Eastern Shore, featured the Colonial Marines, a regiment of former slaves now armed and trained on Tangier Island, Cockburn's base in the middle of the bay. The rags in which their owners clothed them had been replaced by bright red uniforms, and they were eager for battle, rapidly putting the defending militia to flight. "I was highly pleased with the conduct of the Colonial Marines," reported the raid's commander, "every Individual of which Evinced the greatest eagerness to come to Action with their former masters."

Cockburn, delighted with his recruits, noted happily that they excited "the most general & undisguised alarm" among the populace. He was certainly correct. "Our negroes are flocking to the enemy from all quarters, which they convert into troops, vindictive and rapacious—with a most minute knowledge of every bye path," wrote an American commander in early August. "They leave us as spies upon our posts and our strength, and they return upon us as guides and soldiers and incendiaries."

Raids along the coast in the spring and summer of 1814 left dozens of towns, plantations, and stores burned, with livestock and freshly harvested tobacco carried away. Yet these were merely precursors to Cockburn's ultimate plan to strike at the heart of the enemy by raiding Washington itself. This, he calculated, would be a devastating psychological blow, discrediting the Madison administration and drawing enemy troops away from Canada. Furthermore, the Americans had burned York, as Toronto was called in those days, so this could be billed as justified retaliation.

To enlist the support of his superiors, Cockburn invited the cautious army commander, General Robert Ross, along on a night raid to demonstrate the feebleness of the American defenses. He somehow forgot to mention that he had raided the same place three nights before, driving off the militia and cowing the local residents. The brass were duly convinced. "Traditionally, the British fighting in America are portrayed as the blundering redcoats, prey to light-footed Americans sniping from behind trees," Taylor told me. "But Cockburn was the resourceful, innovative, and flexible commander in this war, and a superb tactician. In fact, he was just the kind of commander that we admire today."

The advance on Washington, with the Colonial Marines very much to the fore, was launched in the third week of August. As Cockburn had predicted, the American defenses were in a sorry state; a hurriedly assembled militia was swiftly routed on August 24 at Bladensburg, on the outskirts of the capital. Francis Scott Key, who as a militia officer had been busy offering unsolicited advice to the commanding general, was among those stampeding back to the city and beyond. Only an improvised US naval artillery unit, partly manned by free Blacks, made a stand.

Most significantly, the American collapse was accelerated by a rumor among the troops that a slave revolt had broken out in their rear. Walter Smith, a brigadier general of the District of Columbia militia, summarized the abiding paranoia in the ranks: "Each man more feared the enemy he had left behind, in the shape of a slave in his own house or plantation, than he did anything else." The sight of the Colonial Marines, charging in the British vanguard, cannot have been reassuring.

With Washington now at his mercy, Cockburn contented himself with destroying public buildings, such as the Capitol, military installations, and the offices of the *National Intelligencer*, a newspaper that had been regularly abusing him. His ultimate goal was the White House, from which President Madison had fled a few hours before, followed by his wife, Dolley. Cockburn took possession accompanied not only by some of his officers but also by a squad of Colonial Marines—men who only a few months before had been items of property, subject to disposal at the whim of their owners. The admiral and his party first helped themselves to a dinner ordered by Dolley in expectation of an American victory and collected souvenirs (Cockburn took the First Lady's chair cushion, remarking lewdly that it would be a reminder of "her seat"). Then they piled up the furniture and set fire to the building.

Following the subsequent failed attack on Baltimore that inspired Key's verses, Cockburn moved south to harry the Georgia planters and rescue more slaves, recruiting many of them. The motive for his rescue work clearly went beyond military expediency—he continued to encourage fugitives up to the last days of the war, and indeed into the peace. Despite angry

American insistence that the peace treaty mandated the return of all property (meaning, especially, former slaves), Cockburn bluntly refused to hand them over and shipped everyone off to Bermuda. Most eventually settled in Canada, but the Colonial Marines accepted an offer of land in Trinidad. Settled in villages, each under the command of their company sergeants from the old regiment, they were known as the Merikens. Their descendants live there to this day.

Memories of the time when invaders had freed and armed the slaves and brought the republic to the brink of collapse persisted among both slaves and the slave owners who dominated government policy in the ensuing decades. Fearful that the threat might one day reappear, the United States commissioned coastal fortifications as a defense against the Royal Navy. One of these was Fort Sumter, ultimately the flash point for the war that ended slavery once and for all. Meanwhile, the Colonial Marines and the significance of their role were gradually eased out of official history. Francis Scott Key, on the other hand, went on to a long career as a powerful crony of President Andrew Jackson, a mentor to Chief Justice Roger Taney of *Dred Scott* fame, and, as district attorney for the capital, an energetic prosecutor of abolitionists.

In Washington, there are many reminders of that amazing summer of 1814 just beneath the surface, starting with the scorch marks still present under the white paint on the Executive Mansion. Last May, examining a bridge over the Anacostia River in the eastern part of the city, I realized I had found another. The original bridge, a wooden affair, had been burned a few days before the Battle of Bladensburg, thanks to the firm conviction of the American commander, General William Winder, that the admiral and his fearsome force would definitely advance this way. Meanwhile, Cockburn had chosen an unexpected approach from the northeast, so the destruction was for nothing.

Nowadays the modern bridge links two cities. To the west is the new, prosperous Washington, adding residents at a rate of 1,000 per month—most of them young and well educated, reviving long-neglected neighborhoods, thronging the local restaurants, and propelling a real estate boom. To the east is Anacostia, comprising Ward Seven and Ward Eight of the District of Columbia. The area is largely poor and overwhelmingly Black. Ward Seven has one sit-down restaurant—a Denny's—and one grocery store. Median household income for families with children in Ward Eight is $26,700, as opposed to a soaring $88,233 for the city overall and its inner suburbs. Most of the 10 percent of Washingtonians trapped in "deep poverty," defined as 50 percent of the poverty level, live here. So do a large proportion of the city's 60,000 "returned citizens"—people who have done jail time and whose felony convictions are a permanent barrier to anything but menial jobs.

The headliners at the event in May that brought me to the bridge, which was being renamed in honor of Ethel Kennedy, were definitely from the well-heeled Washington. Mrs. Kennedy had earned the honor thanks to her years of unpublicized help for people living in these eastern neighborhoods. On hand was an impressive cross section of the local power scene: Mayor Vincent Gray, US Attorney General Eric Holder (who had just helped Gray lose his re-election bid by unveiling a corruption probe), and House Minority Whip Steny Hoyer, as well as a platoon of Kennedys. Guests and speakers gathered under a tent on a greensward beside the river, within sight of a luxuriantly wooded island.

It was a beguilingly pastoral scene. Yet a knowledgeable eye could discern that we were in a poor African American neighborhood. In the background stood a derelict coal-fired power plant, long slated for demolition, which for generations has been depositing toxic PCBs into the inviting water, now too dangerous for anyone to swim in, let alone eat its fish. The forested island across the river has for years been used as a dumping ground for garbage. Such features are part of a nationwide phenomenon, in which four out of five toxic-waste dumps are in Black neighborhoods. (The largest concentration of uncontrolled toxic waste in the United States is on the South Side of Chicago.) "It's not an accident," declared Robert Kennedy Jr., the principal speaker at the event, "that this coal-burning power plant was put in this neighborhood." He also cited the facility's history of PCB pollution and its "uncontrolled mercury discharge raining down on this community."

Among those present and paying tribute as grateful beneficiaries of Mrs. Kennedy's help were current and former members of the Earth Conservation Corps: inner-city teenagers and young adults dedicated to cleaning up the filthy river so that wildlife, including bald eagles and ospreys, might once again nest along its banks. A simple statistic tells much about the lives of its youthful membership. Since the organization's founding in 1989, twenty-three of them have died—"killed," as longtime corps leader Bob Nixon observed to me, by "extreme poverty." He recalled names. There was, for example, nineteen-year-old Jerome Scott, a budding ornithologist misdiagnosed with mono by the District of Columbia General Hospital and sent home to die suddenly of untreated leukemia, and Diamond Teague, a straight-A student shot for no apparent reason as he sat on his doorstep, Gerald "Tink" Huelett, stabbed for ten dollars, and Benny Jones, beaten to death with a lead pipe for sitting on the wrong park bench. Almost all the murders remain unsolved.

The 1968 riots—the second burning of Washington—ironically destroyed scores of Black-owned businesses while boosting white flight to the suburbs. Then came the crack epidemic, which swept through the capital's Black community in the 1980s and 1990s. "This was a totally different neighborhood when I was growing up," said David Smith, a corps veteran, as we toured his home district of Deanwood. "Before crack, people would play ball in the streets, leave their doors unlocked. That all ended with crack. Suddenly everyone had bars on their windows, steel doors. Shootings all the time. It pretty much destroyed the community."

Crack may have finally receded, but the marijuana laws have helped keep the prisons full—of Black people. An ACLU map depicting the location of all DC-area marijuana arrests in 2010 makes this strikingly clear. Black neighborhoods were dramatically stippled with dots, while Ward Two, a white neighborhood and home to two major colleges, was a virtual blank. (Earlier this year, the ACLU spearheaded a successful drive to decriminalize marijuana in the district.)

Smith is acutely conscious of the history that is being erased by the march of gentrification, as represented by the formerly Black H Street neighborhood, just west of the Kennedy Bridge, with its new streetcar line, bars, restaurants, freshly laid sidewalks, and fancy street lamps. Now its residents are predominantly white. Four years ago, an initiative by the neighborhood council to ban chicken wings in a newly opened 7-Eleven (on grounds that the bones attract rats and choke dogs) fell just a few votes short of passing.

Fueled by the national security spending and corporate lobbying that followed 9/11, the flood of (mostly white) newcomers to the city appears irreversible. Indeed, Washington's Black community slipped below 50 percent of the population in 2011 for the first time in half a century. Neighborhoods that for years never saw a white face have been transformed almost overnight. As Bob Nixon remarked to me, the "murder line," a macabre indicator of gentrification, "moves further east every year." One day soon it may extend all the way into Prince George's County, Maryland, which thirty years ago was poor, white, and festooned with Confederate flags, and today has a Black majority.

Smith took me on a tour of *his* Washington, one that is fast disappearing. Heading east on the freeway, we passed Nationals Park, a showcase of the city's transformation. The imposing stadium, home to the Washington Nationals baseball team, opened in 2008 in what was formerly the poverty-stricken and crime-ridden Navy Yard district. "They moved people out when they started building, but told them they could come back when the place was rebuilt," Smith remarked as we sped by. "But you had to be creditworthy and earn ninety-thousand dollars a year. So very few ever came back."

Nowadays Navy Yard is everything a developer or city official could desire: $500,000 condos, a Marriott hotel, an enviable corporate address just a few blocks from the Capitol. The old community has largely dispersed, although no one could tell me exactly where they had gone. Laneisha McCauley, a high school student from one of the few families that did return, wrote a prizewinning essay a few years ago recalling her lost neighborhood, where "African American children crammed the sidewalks playing Double Dutch" and there was always "a hand outstretched to reach mine."

Moving east of the river and down into Ward Eight, we surveyed Barry Farm, a district built for freedmen following the Civil War, generating profits that financed nearby Howard University. Now the area is run-down, partly abandoned, and a target for developers. We passed the sprawling, half-built complex destined to be a multibillion-dollar headquarters for the Department of Homeland Security, billed as a pump primer for the Ward Eight economy. Gesturing at the high walls, Smith observed that almost all the jobs would be reserved for college graduates with security clearances—not much of a prospect for returned citizens, or for almost anyone else from the neighborhood.

Eventually we picked up Reverend Edwin Jones of the Living Faith Baptist Church. Like Smith, the pastor lamented that young African Americans in Washington have little sense of their community's rich history. How many would even know that Nannie Helen Burroughs Avenue, the street running past Jones's church, is named for a trailblazing civil rights activist?

Together we drove over to Woodlawn Cemetery, the final stop on our tour. Spread over twenty-two acres of rolling hillside, it's a picturesque, even romantic spot. Yet many headstones of Reconstruction-era Black senators, congressmen, and writers have been vandalized or semi-obscured by grass and weeds, which the pastor and other volunteers have been laboriously beating back.

Smith, who comes from a family with profound ties to the civil rights struggle over five generations, is himself focused on memorializing another historical episode—a spectacular slave escape—which he believes can serve as an inspiration to young people in his community. More than three decades after the Colonial Marines stormed into the capital, local abolitionists hatched a plan to publicize the ongoing role of Washington as a major center for the slave trade. Among the planners was Paul Jennings, formerly James Madison's enslaved valet, who had fled the White House in 1814 just ahead of Cockburn's forces. By 1848, having recently bought his freedom from a reluctant Dolley, he was working as a butler for the powerful Senator Daniel Webster and was deeply involved in the Underground Railroad.

On the night of April 15, seventy-seven men and women slipped away from the houses of their masters. (One of them, fifteen-year-old Mary Ellen Stewart, was the property of Dolley Madison.) They made their way to the *Pearl*, a sixty-five-foot schooner hired by Jennings and his fellow conspirators, which was moored at the Seventh Street Wharf. Once loaded, the ship moved down the Potomac, headed for the Chesapeake and ultimately New Jersey, a free state.

Tragically, the wind turned against them and they had to anchor for the night at Point Lookout, Maryland, where the river empties into the bay. In the meantime, a party of infuriated owners, having awakened to find their slaves gone, set off in a steamboat, catching up to the *Pearl* at Point Lookout. The fugitives were brought back and handed over to slavetraders, who speedily split them up and sold most of them to plantations in the Deep South. (A fortunate few, including Stewart, were eventually bought by antislavery activists and set free.)

In its immediate goal, then, the scheme was a failure. Nevertheless, it did succeed in its wider purpose—within two years, the slave trade (if not slavery itself) would be outlawed in Washington. The incident also galvanized public opinion throughout the country, and ultimately inspired Harriet Beecher Stowe to write *Uncle Tom's Cabin*.

Smith is executive director of the nonprofit Pearl Coalition, which is building a replica of the original schooner. His hope is that the ship, and the history it represents, will continue to have a galvanizing effect. "The *Pearl* is important for the young because it connects them with a forgotten past, and their responsibility to see that history does not repeat itself," he told me. At the very least, the *Pearl* can serve as a counterpoint to Francis Scott Key's eponymous memorial, Key Bridge, which spans the Potomac far upriver from Anacostia. A plaque at the Georgetown end hails Key, the prosecutor of abolitionists and the aspiring scourge of runaway slaves, as "active in antislavery causes." As far as history goes, it doesn't get much rosier than that.

Harper's Magazine, September 2014

2

The Enemies Briefcase

Secret Powers and the Presidency

A few hours before a presidential inauguration ceremony, the prospective president receives an elaborate and highly classified briefing on the means and procedures for blowing up the world with a nuclear attack, a rite of passage that a former official described as "a sobering moment." Secret though it may be, we are at least aware that this introduction to apocalypse takes place. At some point in the first term, however, experts surmise that an even more secret briefing occurs, one that has never been publicly acknowledged. In it, the new president learns how to blow up the Constitution.

The session introduces "presidential emergency action documents," or PEADs, orders that authorize a broad range of mortal assaults on our civil liberties. In the words of a rare declassified official description, the documents outline how to "implement extraordinary presidential authority in response to extraordinary situations"—by imposing martial law, suspending habeas corpus, seizing control of the internet, imposing censorship, and incarcerating so-called subversives, among other repressive measures. "We know about the nuclear briefcase that carries the launch codes," Joel McCleary, a White House official in the Carter administration, told me. "But over at the Office of Legal Counsel at the Justice Department there's a list of all the so-called enemies of the state who would be rounded up in an emergency. I've heard it called the 'enemies briefcase.'"

These chilling directives have been silently proliferating since the dawn of the Cold War as an integral part of the hugely elaborate and expensive Continuity of Government (COG) program, a mechanism to preserve state authority (complete with well-provisioned underground bunkers for leaders) in the event of a nuclear holocaust. Compiled without any authorization from Congress, the emergency provisions long escaped public discussion —that is, until Donald Trump started to brag about them. "I have the right to do a lot of things that people don't even know about," he boasted in March, ominously echoing his interpretation of Article II of the Constitution, which, he has claimed, gives him "the right to do whatever I want as president." He has also declared his "absolute right" to build a border wall, whatever Congress thinks, and even floated the possibility of delaying the election "until people can properly, securely, and safely vote."

"This really is one of the best-kept secrets in Washington," Elizabeth Goitein, the co-director of the Liberty and National Security Program at New York University's Brennan Center for Justice, told me. "But though the PEADs are secret from the American public, they're not secret from the White House and from the executive branch. And the fact that none of them has ever been leaked is really quite extraordinary." Goitein and her colleagues have been working diligently for years to elicit the truth about the president's hidden legal armory, tracing stray references in declassified documents and obscure appropriations requests from previous administrations. "At least in the past," said Goitein, "there were documents that purported to authorize actions that are unconstitutional, that are not justified by any existing law, and that's why we need to be worried about them."

Part of what makes the existence of PEADs so alarming is the fact that the president already has a different arsenal of emergency powers at his disposal. Unlike PEADs, which are not themselves laws, these powers have been obligingly granted (and often subsequently forgotten) by Congress. They come into force once a president declares a state of emergency related to whatever crisis is at hand, though the link is often tenuous indeed. For example, to fight the war in Vietnam, Lyndon Johnson used emergency powers originally granted to Harry Truman for the Korean War. As Goitein has written, the moment a president declares a "national emergency"—which he can do whenever he likes—more than one hundred special provisions become available, including freezing Americans' bank accounts or deploying troops domestically. One provision even permits a president to suspend the ban on testing chemical and biological weapons on human subjects.

Thinly justified by public laws, these emergency powers have become formidable instruments of repression for any president unscrupulous enough to use them. Franklin Roosevelt, for example, invoked emergency powers when he incarcerated 120,000 Americans of Japanese ethnicity. One of them, Fred Korematsu, a twenty-three-year-old welder from Oakland, California, refused to cooperate and sued. His case reached the Supreme Court, which duly ruled that the roundup of US citizens had been justified by "military necessity." Justice Robert Jackson, one of three dissenters, wrote that though the emergency used to justify the action would end, the principle of arbitrary power sanctified by the court decision "would endure into the future, a loaded weapon ready for the hand of any authority that can bring forward a plausible claim of an urgent need."

Jackson's warning now rings louder than ever, given the spectacle of a president who revels in displays of arbitrary power. His boasts are clearly not idle, and have duly elicited a chorus of alarmed protest, amplified by the prospect of an election that could certify his grip on power for (at least) another four years. In the event of his displacement, sooner or later, by a more conventional chief executive pledged to respect our laws and institutions, we might hope that Congress would move aggressively to assert the Constitution and close all the secret loopholes Trump so cherishes. After all, this has happened before. Half a century ago, a president was caught acting lawlessly, sparking national outrage and prompting a reckoning with how extensively arbitrary presidential power had eaten away at Americans' freedoms. Back then, Congress seemed resolved to prevent such abuses from happening again. But the attempt was brief; the impulse rapidly faded. Given the threats facing what is left of our liberty today, it is important to look at what happened, and why.

∾

In the 1970s, the Colorado senator Gary Hart served on the famed Church Committee, which probed and exposed CIA assassinations, FBI operations to subvert and destroy the civil-rights movement (including efforts to drive Martin Luther King Jr. to suicide), and other secret, scandalous initiatives. These shocking revelations, including close ties to organized crime, revealed the terrifying extent of unbridled presidential power, with the use of secret police—the FBI and CIA—as personal instruments. Given Hart's time on the committee, one would expect him to be intimately familiar with the secret powers of the president. Yet when he read an April 10 op-ed in the *New York Times* by Goitein and her colleague Andrew Boyle headlined TRUMP HAS EMERGENCY POWERS WE AREN'T ALLOWED TO KNOW ABOUT, he was caught by surprise. "It snapped my head back," he told me.

Even though Hart, now retired and living in the Rocky Mountains, was deeply immersed in matters of national security and intelligence for decades, he had not heard about the extraordinary powers that Goitein and Boyle were describing. Throughout his work on the Church Committee, he said, "We did not come across, did not examine, the so-called secret powers put in place in anticipation of a nuclear attack." He was shocked to learn not only that they existed, but that they had expanded in recent years. "One would have thought that, with the end of the Cold War in the early nineties, the secret powers would have been put on the shelf somewhere," he said. After reading the op-ed, Hart called several "close friends" who had formerly occupied "very, very senior" defense and security posts. Some responded with claims of ignorance. Others refused to talk at all. "People I know well, who had to know about these powers, simply refused to even send an email back saying 'I can't talk about it,'" said Hart. "They just clammed up."

When Hart assumed office in 1975, Washington was still reverberating from the twin earthquakes of Watergate and the Vietnam War. Americans had learned that a president could use his power in ways both shocking and criminal. Richard Nixon had flouted the law with an easy conscience, commissioning burglaries and directing a cover-up. His defense, as he later described it, was that "when the president does it, that means that it is not illegal." The

Vietnam disaster had spurred Congress to pass the War Powers Act a year and a half earlier, overriding a presidential veto with a two-thirds majority in both houses. Authored by the liberal Republican congressman Paul Findley, the act barred the president from going to war without authorization from Congress (or so its sponsors believed). Now, as Hart's tenure began, the Capitol was being further rocked by revelations of a vast and illegal domestic spying operation and the first hints of an assassination program. In response, Congress created two committees to investigate the CIA—one headed by the young and ambitious Senator Frank Church of Idaho, the other eventually led by Representative Otis Pike, a tough ex-Marine from New York.

Over the next year, the committees found copious evidence that presidents and their agents had routinely strayed outside the Constitution. As the Senate committee's chief counsel, F.A.O. "Fritz" Schwarz Jr., told me, he and his colleagues initially assumed that they would simply be investigating Nixon's wrongdoings and CIA "improprieties." But it soon became clear that the rot went far deeper. "It wasn't only a Nixon problem," he said. "It was not only a CIA problem. The abuses of power go back to at least Franklin Roosevelt." Roosevelt, they found, had commissioned FBI chief J. Edgar Hoover to uncover evidence of "subversion" (without defining what that meant) in the lead-up to World War II, requesting that such investigations be limited "insofar as possible" to "aliens." Along with Hoover and Attorney General Homer Cummings, FDR agreed that the investigations should be kept secret from Congress.

As he learned how the FBI had also attempted to destroy the civil rights movement, Schwarz came to believe that, compared with the CIA, "the FBI was the greater danger to American democracy," especially when deployed in the political service of a chief executive. Johnson, for example, had directed a "special squad" in the FBI to spy and report on opposition groups during the 1964 Democratic National Convention. "It's a tendency among presidents to say, 'Gosh, we have these resources, let's use them,'" said Schwarz. "If you have power, you can get more."

While the two intelligence committees generated exciting headlines (though Pike's discovery that the most frequent CIA covert action was to interfere in other countries' democratic elections passed almost entirely without comment), a third committee was probing equally momentous issues in quiet obscurity. In 1972, a number of senatorial elders, including the Republican Charles Mathias of Maryland, having noted the use of antediluvian emergency powers to prosecute the disastrous Vietnam War, had instituted the Special Committee on the Termination of the National Emergency. Co-chaired by Church and Mathias, its task was to unearth and revoke those emergency powers that were authorized by Congress and subsequently forgotten.

The first problem faced by the committee was to find out what emergency powers existed. "This," read a 1973 report, "has been a most difficult task." Nowhere in government was there a complete catalogue detailing these emergency laws, which were buried within the vast body of laws passed since the first Congress. "Many were aware that there had been a delegation of an enormous amount of power, but of how much power no one knew," the committee said. Then, just when the staff had resigned themselves to poring over all eighty-seven volumes of the Statutes at Large—the record of all laws and resolutions passed by Congress —they discovered a shortcut. As part of the Continuity of Government program, "The Air Force had digitized the whole thing," Patrick Shea, a Church aide who worked as a staffer on the committee, told me recently. "They had it on computer tape, buried inside a mountain—NORAD headquarters—outside Colorado Springs, in case there was a nuclear war."

Using the digitized records, aides searched for keywords that might have been used when describing "extraordinary powers": "war," "national defense," "invasion," and "insurrection." The opening paragraph of the committee's initial report made their findings clear:

A majority of Americans alive today have lived all of their lives under emergency rule. For forty years, freedoms and governmental procedures guaranteed by the Constitution have, in varying degrees, been abridged by laws brought into force by states of national emergency.

In addition to Johnson's use of Truman's Korean War powers, the committee noted that FDR had relied on an old wartime measure, introduced by Woodrow Wilson in 1917, to close the banks in 1933 in response to the Great Depression. To his amusement, Shea even discovered that a Civil War–era emergency law enabling cavalry on the Western plains to buy forage for their horses had been used to skirt Congress in financing the war in Vietnam.

Before the committee's investigation, no one had realized that "temporary" states of emergency could become permanent. "Because Congress and the public are unaware of the extent of emergency powers," it found, "there has never been any notable congressional or public objection made to this state of affairs. Nor have the courts imposed significant limitations." The drafters of these emergency powers, whoever they were, "were understandably not concerned about providing for congressional review, oversight, or termination of these delegated powers." By way of comparison, the report cited a 1952 opinion by Justice Jackson, in which he described the emergency powers granted by the constitution of the Weimar Republic. Instituted following World War I, it was expressly designed to secure citizens' liberties "in the Western tradition." However, it also empowered the president to unilaterally suspend any and all individual rights in the interest of public safety. After various governments had made temporary use of this provision, read Jackson's account, "Hitler persuaded President Von Hindenburg to suspend all such rights, and they were never restored."

The committee concluded that a president could "seize property and commodities, seize control of transport and communications, organize and control the means of production, assign military forces abroad, and restrict travel"—a state of affairs that the committee reasonably described as "dangerous." As ominous as the committee's discoveries may have been, however, they received scant media attention, lacking the sex appeal of assassination plots, poison dart guns, or White House liaisons with the Mafia. When I asked Shea why else these revelations might have attracted such little notice, he told me that Church "wasn't so anxious for publicity" in 1973, when the emergency committee was first set up. It was only after Church had been given control of the intelligence committee and had decided to run for the 1976 Democratic nomination, said Shea, that he wanted "all the publicity he could get." (To secure the assignment, Church had falsely promised the Senate leadership that he would not run.) As for Mathias, who had helped sound the alarm about emergency powers in the first place, Shea told me that he "always liked to stay in the background. He was the soul of discretion. There were people like that in the Senate in those days."

By 1974, the emergencies committee had drafted a bill that ended most existing emergencies and mandated the automatic termination of new ones after six months. Yet the bill's passage was continually delayed, and its contents were steadily watered down, thanks in large part to what Jerry Brady, a former chief of staff on the committee, recalled as "pretty vigorous pushback from the president and others at the White House."

We now know, thanks to declassified archives, that the administration kept tight supervision over the committees' work, and that Henry Kissinger urged unyielding resistance. As he exclaimed during a meeting with President Gerald Ford and others in May 1975: "It is an act of insanity and national humiliation to have a law prohibiting the president from ordering an assassination." The White House deputy chief of staff, Dick Cheney, whose most distinguishing feature, according to another senior Ford aide, were his "snake-cold eyes, like a Cheyenne gambler's," also attempted to thwart the investigations behind the scenes. After reviewing thousands of declassified documents, the National Security Archive reported in 2015 that Cheney ultimately decided which documents requested by Church and his staff should be handed over, and that "CIA accommodation measures were explicitly designed to keep Church Committee investigators away from its most important records." (Among those assigned to this task in the CIA legislative office was a young conservative lawyer named William Barr.)

Little wonder, then, that the effort "to terminate the national emergency" failed. The bill did manage to abolish existing states of emergency. (This provision was supposed to kick in after six months, though it was pushed back to two years.) But automatic suspension of new emergencies, as originally proposed, gave way to a requirement that Congress should meet twice a year "to consider a vote" on termination. Its force thus quietly diluted, the bill finally became law in 1976, whereupon Congress swiftly forgot about it, never once meeting to vote on whether to end states of emergency. The provision allowing Congress to end them through a "concurrent resolution" that did not require a president's signature was obviated by a Supreme Court decision in 1983, and any such resolution has required a veto-proof majority ever since.

So total was Congress's failure to follow through on limiting emergency powers that in 1977 it actually voted to expand them. That year, it passed the International Emergency Economic Powers Act, which enables the president to declare national emergencies "to deal with any unusual and extraordinary threat" that "has its source in whole or substantial part outside the United States." The law empowers presidents to sanction countries, businesses, and individuals without warning, without furnishing evidence, and, effectively, without appeal. As I previously reported in *Harper's Magazine,* the Office of Foreign Assets Control, which operates under the 1977 law, can freeze an American's bank account while offering nothing more than a vague explanation.

The intelligence committees, whose revelations had been far more dramatic than those of the emergencies committee, had no more success in curbing executive authority. Congress avoided pinning responsibility on presidents for ordering assassinations— Church apparently feared that antagonizing the Kennedy family by publicizing JFK's role in such plots would imperil his presidential hopes. (The Pike Committee staff took a more hard-nosed view: "We laughed when Church described the CIA as a 'rogue elephant,'" one former staffer, Greg Rushford, told me. "We knew they were the president's guys.") The net result of the inquiries was the creation of permanent secret committees in the House and Senate to provide "oversight" of the intelligence agencies. "If they were going to do something that had potential blowback, they had to let us know ahead of time," Hart, who was a member of the new Senate oversight committee, told me.

"I don't recall in my original years there that we ever vetoed an operation. But they did notify us of things they were going to do."

The new House committee appeared no more inclined to make waves. "We're the oversight committee—we commit oversights," joked Richard Anderson, a CIA analyst who joined the committee in 1978. As with the international economic powers legislation, Congress dutifully provided a measure, the Foreign Intelligence Surveillance Act (FISA), that purported to rein in the executive's power to spy on citizens while merely legalizing it. Passed with a large bipartisan majority, the law set up a court composed of eleven judges to secretly grant "warrants" for wire-taps and burglaries. The ACLU's chief legislative counsel, Jerry Berman, protested that the proposed law "broadly authorizes intrusive investigations of American citizens. It takes away the inherent power of the president to do these things, but then gives him the express power to do them, with all the flexibility that he had before." A simple statistic from the FISA court suggests that Berman's concerns were well founded: of 33,900 applications for FISA warrants between 1979 and 2012, precisely 11 were rejected.

The ensuing decades demonstrated in grim relief just how limited the successes of the 1970s had been. Ronald Reagan presided over a wide-ranging covert operation in Nicaragua using money generated by secret arms sales to Iran and simultaneously conducted an illegal domestic propaganda campaign to generate support. When the Iran-Contra scandal was exposed, Congress professed outrage and went through the motions of an investigation that not only shrank from targeting Reagan himself or revealing the full scope of his minions' misdeeds (including rehearsals for mass roundups of "subversives"), but ensured that the principal perpetrators escaped punishment entirely. George H. W. Bush attacked Panama without congressional approval (but fortified by a legal opinion from Assistant Attorney General William Barr) only a few years later, while Clinton would do the same in Serbia. George W. Bush used congressional authorization for military force against Al-Qaeda after 9/11 to occupy Iraq, illegally wiretapping Americans all the while. Barack Obama broke new extra-constitutional ground in ordering the execution by drone of a US citizen. None suffered more than brief censure, and all are now remembered with respect, even reverence.

Donald Trump can expect no such indulgence, nor does he seem to want it. As the seventeenth-century French moralist François de La Rochefoucauld wrote, "Hypocrisy is the tribute vice pays to virtue." Trump, never troubling to disguise his disregard for the law, is clearly no hypocrite. His evident lack of scruples—along with the primal terror induced by the prospect of a second term—is the very reason that the long-dormant issue of emergency presidential powers has now come to the fore.

In June, McCleary and Mark Medish, a senior National Security Council director under Clinton, joined Hart and former senator Tim Wirth to warn in *Politico* that in the event of "a national emergency on the grounds of national security, the president would have more than 120 statutory emergency powers" at his disposal, potentially enabling him to postpone the election. "It looks as though a rolling coup is underway, with Trump and his confederates testing the waters for ways to scupper the election," Medish told me recently. Democratic leaders are meanwhile cautious, he said, "about doing anything that might demoralize voters by drawing too much attention to unconventional election threats," which they feel would risk depressing the vote.

As McCleary pithily remarked, when the president decides to ignore it, the Constitution turns out to be "no more than a gentleman's agreement." But there is little sign that Congress is prepared to treat executive power—both secret and otherwise—as a fundamental problem that will endure when or if Trump retreats to Mar-a-Lago. Admittedly, the Democrats sought to bring down Trump over his maladroit dealings with Ukraine, but the initiative died a predictable death. The days of bipartisan revolt against unchecked presidential power are long gone. "It was a time that is unlikely to be duplicated anytime soon," Jack Boos, who served as counsel for the Pike Committee, told me sadly. "We had a major scandal and a weakened presidency. It was a perfect storm that many thought could be exploited and turn the whole place upside down. But that was naïve, always was."

Even if the prospective nightmare of Trump disrupting or ignoring the election goes away, the "loaded weapon" that Justice Jackson warned about will still be to hand. The enemies briefcase will still hold its list. Who knows whose names will be on it?

Harper's Magazine, November 2020

Postscript. For a brief, shining moment during the Biden administration it appeared that Congress might move to claw back unconstitutional powers ceded to the president. Senator Mike Lee, a conservative Republican from Utah, introduced the Article One Act in 2021, which would make any national emergency declared by a president lapse automatically after thirty days. The bill garnered bipartisan support in both houses. "Right now, Presidents can tap into emergency powers without any meaningful political check, time limit, or public rationale," declared co-sponsor Steve Cohen, Democratic congressman from Memphis. But party leaders showed little interest, and once it became clear that Trump, rather than Biden, would occupy the White House, Lee and other Republicans lost interest. One of Trump's first acts in 2025 was to declare the import of fentanyl and other drugs a national emergency, justifying the imposition of tariffs on China, Canada, and Mexico. The trajectory of Trump's sweeping evisceration of legal restraint indicated he had taken the lesson of that secret briefing fully to heart.

3

Party Walls

Who Party Leaders Really Work For

Conventional wisdom holds that our political moment is, in Joe Biden's words, "not normal." Thus, the usual political lessons to be drawn from such historical events as the New Deal or US entry into the world wars are supposedly irrelevant now. This is surely a dangerous misconception, especially when promoted by those who remember the past incorrectly. That is why the work of Walter Karp, a passionate scholar of American political history who offered a bracing antidote to the popular beliefs of his own era, is so useful today.

A generation ago, Karp served as a contributing editor of this magazine. In the words of his friend and longtime editor Lewis Lapham, he was "a stormy petrel of a man, small and excitable, delighting in the rush of his words and the energy of his ideas" who "believed that in America it is the people who have rights, not the state, and that the working of a democratic republic requires a raucous assembly of citizens unafraid to speak their minds." For more than a decade, beginning in 1978, he focused on abuses of power in Washington for *Harper's Magazine*, deriding Democrats who collaborated with Ronald Reagan, the elected officials behind failing school systems, and Capitol Hill controls on the press. While he lived before the limitless political spending and the egregiously partisan Supreme Court that mark our political landscape, Karp's pungent analyses are entirely relevant at a time when true representation seems far removed from the minds of politicians.

Karp firmly believed that the actions of party leaders can be explained only if one understands that they are primarily motivated by the pursuit and retention of power; any suggestion that national interest, or even ideology, drives their decisions he considered delusional. Karp once wrote that "we can judge the character of public men only by what they actually do," which all too often involved betraying the platform that got them elected, almost always to further their own political fortunes. In his estimation, Democrats and Republicans therefore had much in common; by prioritizing their own rule, the two parties operated on a principle of collusion—"for without it neither party organization could long survive."

Karp's analysis of the actions and motives of the Democratic presidents Franklin D. Roosevelt, John F. Kennedy, and Lyndon B. Johnson provide illuminating examples of his approach. Though each had been enthusiastically elected on the promise of far-reaching reform, they all took steps that effectively frustrated their professed reformist intent. Having kept afloat the system threatened by a Depression-ravaged populace, Roosevelt largely abandoned further reforms in his second term on the grounds that gathering war clouds in Europe mandated concentration on "national security." A generation later, Kennedy, possessed of a congressional majority inclined to reform, announced that he would introduce no major legislation without the cooperation of the Senate Republican leader Everett McKinley Dirksen, who duly blocked measures supposedly dear to the president's heart, such as a civil rights bill, thus saving Kennedy from alienating the Southern racist wing of the Democratic Party. When it came to Johnson, Karp wrote, one could presume that he sent more troops to Vietnam in hopes that it would "kill reform," "distract the citizenry from domestic concerns," and "provide the means to suppress dissenters and insurgents in the name of wartime unity."

Overall, Karp argued, the enduring goal of our dominant political institutions is to maintain control of the parties, a goal that can supersede even their supposed objective of winning elections. "The whole purpose of party organizations at every political level," he wrote in his 1973 book *Indispensable Enemies*, "is to sift out, sidetrack and eliminate men of independent political ambition, men whom the party bosses cannot trust." Karp predicted that his analysis would be deemed "grossly 'conspiratorial'" or "paranoid." He rebutted any critics thus:

> When it can be established that a number of political acts work in concert to produce a certain result, the presumption is strong that the actors were aiming at the result in question. When it can be shown, in addition, that the actors have an interest in producing those results, the presumption becomes a fair certainty. No conspiracy theory is required.

Those who argued the contrary were suggesting that, regardless of their actions, those in high office are essentially "men of goodwill," which he deemed a "farfetched theory indeed."

Events this year confirm that Karp's theories remain roundly applicable. The Democratic response to the overturning of *Roe v. Wade* serves as a prime example. When the Supreme Court issued its ruling in *Dobbs v. Jackson Women's Health Organization*, eliminating the constitutional right to abortion, it rapidly became clear that party leadership had readied no campaign to capitalize on the outrage triggered by the court's Catholic fanatics, despite the opinion's leak seven weeks prior. Reacting to complaints from the abortion rights movement—a key component of the Democratic base—the White House communications director Kate Bedingfield told the *Washington Post* that "Joe Biden's goal in responding to *Dobbs* is not to satisfy some activists who have been consistently out of step with the mainstream of the Democratic Party." Her remark, undoubtedly representing Oval Office sentiment, would have come as no surprise to Karp. Nor would the reports that, following Kansas voters' rejection of a proposed abortion ban by an eighteen-point landslide, White House advisers reportedly urged a position of "modesty and nuance."

Ever since Bernie Sanders's 2016 campaign, Democratic Party leadership has made it abundantly clear that eliminating the leftist insurgency is perhaps its highest priority. Examples abound, ranging from the brutal tactics deployed to prevent the popular progressive congressman Keith Ellison's election as party chairman in 2017, to the full-court press assembled against

Sanders in favor of nominating Biden in 2020. Earlier this year, the Democrats, reaping the consequences of their lackluster choice, resigned themselves to a crushing defeat in the midterms. But then West Virginia senator Joe Manchin voted to pass the Inflation Reduction Act, replete with climate funding; gas prices fell, thanks in part to Vladimir Putin selling large quantities of oil despite sanctions; and Biden, appealing to younger, progressive voters, canceled a portion of the $1.6 trillion federal student loan debt burdening millions of graduates. These developments enabled Biden and his team to gain favor with progressives, but they in no way indicate a leftward shift that will last beyond November. Karp, for his part, would likely predict the opposite.

In keeping with his gloomy assessment of our political leaders, Karp described them in trenchant terms: "oligarchs" and "bosses" servicing "machines." Such language is generally absent in the more decorous prose of punditry today, as is any echo of Karp's thesis that all political decisions, even when labeled as acts of statesmanship, are adopted to serve the interests of the relevant players. Oligarchs, bosses, and machines are rampant in today's political system. On the "left," one need look no further than the Democratic Congressional Campaign Committee, the body that oversees election efforts for the House of Representatives.

Its chair, always a Democratic House member chosen by party leadership, selects the DCCC's executive director and other senior staff. This little-known group exercises immense power in deciding which campaigns receive the party's blessing and, no less importantly, who gets campaign consultancy work—ever more lucrative regardless of who wins. The list of recent executive directors and their subsequent employment support Karp's depiction of such machines as self-perpetuating: In 2005, Rahm Emanuel, then a congressman and chairman of the DCCC, hired the political consultant John Lapp as executive director ahead of the 2006 midterms. At a time of rising discontent with the Bush administration, the team sought out centrist candidates supportive of the disastrous Iraq War. The Democrats won the House, by thirty-one seats, for which Emanuel took full credit. But many of the winning candidates were those—such as Steve

Cohen in Memphis and John Yarmuth in Louisville—to whom the Emanuel-Lapp team had refused support.

While Emanuel went on to serve as chief of staff to Barack Obama—whose progressive campaign platform was soon neutered with the help of "moderates" ushered into Congress by Emanuel—Lapp co-founded the political consultancy Ralston Lapp Media. In 2010, the firm reaped $3 million in contracts from the DCCC and House Democrats, where the executive director was now Lapp's former deputy Jon Vogel. Following the party's losses in the 2010 midterms amid the Tea Party surge, Vogel set up MVAR Media, which continues to gain lucrative DCCC contracts. Vogel was succeeded by Robby Mook, who later ran Hillary Clinton's 2016 presidential campaign. Despite frustration over his inept performance, Mook retained party favor. By 2019, he was running House Majority PAC, the independent expenditure arm of the Democratic House leadership, founded by Ali Lapp, wife of John.

Chuck Rocha, a Democratic consultant, summarized the issue bluntly. "Many of the firms that are servicing the DCCC are made up of the former executive directors who used to run the DCCC," he said. "Once you run it as an executive director, then you become a media consultant, and the DCCC will hire you then to work on all of these races across the country." For much of the period discussed above, the DCCC leadership has been determinedly white and overwhelmingly male—this for a party utterly reliant on black, Hispanic, and women voters. Complaints grew from minority lawmakers, as well as from consultants like Rocha, after which Lucinda Guinn, who identifies as Latina, was appointed as executive director in 2019. Following the party's poor showing in the 2020 congressional races, Guinn left the job to become a partner at Ralston Lapp, which had billed the DCCC more than $760,000 over the course of the campaign. Rocha concedes that the leadership situation has improved somewhat, especially on the Senate side, but maintains that problems persist. When he met with four different Latino or Black congressional candidates this summer, he told me, they claimed that the list of approved consultants given them by the DCCC did not include any Black- or brown-majority-owned consulting firms.

There is a financial imperative to these arrangements. Consultants are rewarded for failure partly thanks to the importance of media buying to their business model. Media buyers charge a hefty commission in the form of kickbacks from TV networks and other media companies. The consultant wings of party machines are therefore naturally disposed to favor paid media, as opposed to grassroots efforts propelled by enthusiastic volunteers. Much of the time, Democratic grassroots campaigns are led by progressives—those mobilizing the exact voters Karp once described as unwanted "active citizens."

While the Democrats regularly provide textbook confirmation of Karp's relevance, the Republicans' record appears more complicated, given that their insurgency has seemingly triumphed. Mitch McConnell and the establishment he represents have long struggled to quell the mutiny that flowered in the 2010 election and continued through Donald Trump's presidency. The effort continues to falter, partly thanks to the Democratic establishment's failure to convict Trump, no matter the production value of the January 6 hearings. (However, criminal charges related to the alleged theft of documents could yield different results.) Part of the insurgents' success may be attributed to a factor that Karp did not anticipate: the enabling of dark-money mega-donors, such as the Koch brothers and tech entrepreneur Peter Thiel, thereby loosening party control over finances, a vital tool for enforcing discipline. Nevertheless, the beleaguered leadership has done its best to combat what former House Speaker John Boehner derides in his memoir *On the House* as a "freak show" of "lunatics" overly endowed with independent political ambition and difficult to control. Boehner and his colleagues attempted to corral the upstarts into the Republican Study Committee under leadership they selected. Among other efforts to stem the tide, they recruited a primary opponent to run against the Michigan congressman Justin Amash, an irksomely principled member of the conservative faction—the exact kind of meddling Karp would expect from party leadership. Nevertheless, Amash won, and in 2015 Boehner was overthrown as House Speaker by the Freedom Caucus.

The year before, disaffected Republican voters in central Virginia defeated the House majority leader Eric Cantor, an oligarch if ever there was one, in a primary upset. The victor, the conservative college professor David Brat, outspent forty times over by his well-heeled opponent according to some calculations, ran a populist grassroots campaign focused on the federal deficit, opposition to "crony capitalists" in politics, and immigration. Few outside the district had paid much attention. One who did was Donald Trump, who arrived via helicopter at a Brat fundraiser around six weeks before he himself unveiled his presidential run. "Dave Brat is onto something," he told organizers.

The Republican establishment reacted with fury to the defeat of one of its favorite sons. "They really hated Brat," recalls a former Republican staffer who requested anonymity, "especially after he was a ringleader in overthrowing Boehner." In 2016, Brat's constituency was redistricted, losing Hanover, a Republican county. The machinations that led to this rearrangement were complicated, involving a legal battle over statewide Republican gerrymandering, but Brat supporters had little doubt about who was behind it. "It was all part of [the leadership's] effort to take Dave Brat out," Dale Swanson, co-founder of the district's Conservative Women's Coalition, told me.

Yet, for all the furor, the Republican insurgency never quite achieved its stated goals. Obamacare was never repealed, even when Republicans held power in Congress and in the White House under Trump. The Kochs, who had funded Freedom Caucus campaigns with the expectation that the recipients would honor pledges to shrink government spending, watched unfaithful beneficiaries vote to raise the debt ceiling and swell the deficit. Even with Trump's arrival at the White House, apparently the culminating insurgent triumph, followers' hopes remained unfulfilled. Wall Street and corporations still ruled the roost. "It's still a government of the people, not for the people," Swanson complained to me, "a government repping lobbyists, not us." Trump's diatribes against McConnell, the ultimate Republican establishment leader—"a broken-down hack" with "a crazy wife" —denote his failure to subdue the establishment. A striking number of GOP candidates, however, owe their primary victories to Trump's endorsement. A Republican civil war may be the Democrats' best hope for victory in the midterms and beyond—especially if establishment leaders continue to oppose candidates who could actually win.

In their shared determination to exclude dissidents, both parties inevitably drive many such to secede and operate independently. This does not shield them, however, from the meddling of major party leaders. This year, for example, Texas Republicans brought suit, albeit unsuccessfully, to exclude a raft of Libertarian candidates from the ballot. Democrats have been equally ruthless in their efforts to banish at least one Green Party candidate seeking election: Matthew Hoh, a Marine combat veteran who quit a Foreign Service career in 2009 to protest America's war in Afghanistan, who is campaigning for a Senate seat in North Carolina. His platform is unreservedly progressive; among other leftist positions, he promotes universal health care, workers' rights, and an end to America's aggressive militarism. In North Carolina, as in many other states, minor parties are often enjoined to gather a set number of signatures from registered voters spread across a specified number of congressional districts, which are then validated by county election boards before routine certification by the state Board of Elections. The state board, made up of five members, is appointed by the governor, currently Roy Cooper, a Democrat, and consists of three Democrats and two Republicans.

Although the North Carolina Greens fulfilled the deliberately cumbersome requirements for signatures supporting a minor party petition—the bulk of which were certified by election board officials—the State Board of Elections refused to validate them. They claimed, on the day before the statutory deadline to file as a candidate, that some of the signatures could be fraudulent and required further investigation. At the virtual board meeting, the Greens' attorney asked whether any of the potentially tainted signatures were among those already verified by the county election boards, at which point the chairman, a Democrat, curtly declined to answer, then muted the attorney's microphone. It took a federal appeals court decision to finally allow Hoh's name on the ballot. Meanwhile, both state and federal Democratic groups participated in several lawsuits against the North Carolina Greens that were overseen by the Elias Law Group, a go-to law firm for the Democrats, generally acclaimed for its efforts to counter Republican voter suppression initiatives and Trump's election fraud charges. The Greens have alleged that Elias operatives targeted voters on the Greens' ballot petition, often falsely identifying themselves as Green Party officials, in order to persuade them to withdraw their names. Such insidious subterfuge would fit well with Karp's proposition that "the grassroots political activity of the citizenry and its inseparable adjunct, the entry into political life of non-organization politicians, is a constant threat to party organizations."

Karp's political prognoses tend to be most vividly demonstrated in races within a given party. Take Philadelphia. The city has been a showcase for urban renewal in recent decades, complete with gentrification, an attrited public school system, and austerity in public services—attributes that leftists deride as free-market neoliberalism. These developments also run alongside gross inequality and outright poverty, notably among the majority Black population, which suffers a poverty rate double that of white residents. The city has long been a Democratic fiefdom, and despite changing demographics—the current mayor is white, for the first time since 2000—the City Council is majority Black. "The political machine is still Democrat," the Philadelphia activist Robert Saleem Holbrook told me. "Old-school Democrats: pro-development, pro-gentrification, pro-charter school, paying lip service to unions only at election time."

Lately, however, a threat to the machine has emerged. In recent elections, Philadelphians have been voting for progressives in both city and state races. Anthony H. Williams, a state senator for the past twenty-four years, had, until this year, never faced a serious opponent. Responding to a union activist endorsed by the Democratic Socialists of America, Paul Prescod, running against him, Williams called the news "insulting." To fight the challenge, he garnered hefty financial support not only from his Democratic colleagues, but also from Republican mega-donor Jeffrey Yass, a former professional gambler who made his billions as a Wall Street trader and is currently the richest man in Pennsylvania;

Yass pours his money into his favorite free-market causes in the United States—especially when it comes to so-called school choice. Williams's response perfectly confirms Karp's point about the dedicated self-interest of party machines: "Don't criticize me because of where I get money to run a campaign," he told a reporter. "You want me to tie both hands behind my back and hamper myself to run an effective election? I'm not going to do that." Williams won the Democratic primary in May, ensuring his re-election this fall, though Prescod received almost 40 percent of the vote. "Think about that," Holbrook said. "The Democratic machine was willing to go to Republican PACs to hold off a progressive challenger."

The machine also put considerable energy into an effort to derail another unwelcome progressive candidate. Summer Lee, a Democratic Socialist and a longtime supporter of Sanders, challenged and defeated an incumbent Democratic state representative in Pittsburgh in 2018 with 68 percent of the vote, becoming the first Black woman from western Pennsylvania to sit in the statehouse. Two years later, she won re-election. A vocal proponent of universal health care, the Green New Deal, Palestinian rights, and criminal justice reform, Lee announced her intent to run for Congress in a district that historically favors Democrats. To oppose her, the party recruited Steve Irwin, a rich white attorney who attracted a torrent of money, not least from pro-Israel PACs such as AIPAC's United Democracy Project and Democratic Majority for Israel—a lobby that has been an especially useful ally in beating back progressive challengers this cycle.

Some in Lee's circle discerned a more underhanded effort to derail her election. During her primary race, Pennsylvania's state and congressional districts were being redrawn, and political parties and citizen groups had submitted redistricting proposals. The mapping issue was ultimately decided by the state Supreme Court, where liberals hold the majority, and where justices had previously thrown out a former map, put in place by the Republican legislature and an example of egregious gerrymandering. The court-blessed map has been generally commended as bipartisan, but it did exhibit one curious feature: Lee's home address was cut out of the district in which she intended to run, along with other portions of her voter base. This rearrangement was mostly a detriment to Lee, having far less of an effect on her primary opponents, and thereby generating suspicion among her campaign staff that she had been deliberately targeted. At the very least, Karp would likely have seen the redistricting as a thumb on the scale.

Lee won her primary race, and is expected to win the general. Meanwhile, in this year's Senate Democratic primary, the city machine endorsed Conor Lamb, a corporate-friendly congress-man beloved by the national party. Lamb ran unsuccessfully against John Fetterman, the state's lieutenant governor. Fetter-man, a Sanders supporter, ran on a progressive social platform, supporting government-funded health care, legalized cannabis, and a reformed immigration system. (Fetterman has dodged attacks from pro-Israel PACs, having promised to "lean in" and strengthen relations with Israel.) His success, as well as Lee's, surely gives the lie to the mantra that "progressives can't win." If successful, they pose a potential threat to establishment control. They can, however, be warded off by invoking existential menace. This "indispensable enemy" was one of Karp's central concepts: a potent opponent that justifies shameful compromises and betrayals of the sort seen in the FDR, Kennedy, and Johnson presidencies.

Trump has been the most indispensable of enemies for the Democrats, so corrupt and clownish that Clinton hoped he would be her opponent in 2016. That hope has endured, as Biden's September speech in Philadelphia once again confirmed, with its dark invocations of "Donald Trump and MAGA Repub-licans" who "embrace anger," "thrive on chaos," and live "not in the light of truth but in the shadow of lies." Meanwhile, his own Democratic allies had been pouring millions of dollars into Trump-backed primary campaigns around the country, from Colorado to New Hampshire, in a cynical effort to further split Republican factions. This strategy may yield success, especially since it has dawned on Democrats that support of abortion rights is a winning ticket. But an indispensable enemy can turn into something much more dangerous. It may evolve into a figure less fallible than Trump: a sharper, more presentable candidate such as the Florida governor Ron DeSantis, capable of summoning the MAGA army while maintaining support from supposedly moderate Republicans. Democrats still strive to suppress their own insurgents, but the day may come when they regret following their instincts. Of course, by then it may be too late. Just ask Hillary Clinton.

Harper's Magazine, November 2022

Postscript. In the years after this article was published, the Democratic Party continued to confirm the validity of this analysis, carelessly wishing for Trump, the ever-indispensable enemy, to be the Republican candidate in 2024, while at the same time ruthlessly suppressing any possibility of a genuine contest for the Democratic nomination. When Biden's senility became impossible to conceal, party bosses imposed Kamala Harris, with disastrous results.

4

Down the Tube

Television, Turnout, and the Election-Industrial Complex

"I never met a politician who started out to be a fundraiser," remarked Mike McKenna, a Republican energy lobbyist and recipient of constant pleas for cash from lawmakers. For years, he has watched them dial for dollars and endure nightly gatherings convened for the extraction of donations—"grim affairs," in his phrase—because they have been convinced such efforts are vital for survival at the polls. "Most of them run for office because they want to achieve something," he told me. "But once they get there, they spend their time raising money. I don't know a single one who enjoys it." Ironically, he explained over a beer on Washington's K Street, most of the money they raise is wasted, especially on expensive TV campaigns that do nothing to move voters. The principal effect of these labors, he insisted, is to "feed the consultant class."

My companion was referring to the strategists, pollsters, TV ad-makers, media buyers, direct-mail specialists, broadcasters, and other subcategories of what we should properly call the election-industrial complex. Amid an economy that has bumped along since the 2008 crash, this industry has enjoyed a staggering growth curve, barely matched in percentage terms even by its military counterpart, as candidates and campaigns rattle their begging bowls ever more furiously with each cycle.

Such manic spending is driven by a core belief of modern American politics: the votes can be bought if the check is big enough. "You now have the potential of two hundred people deciding who ends up being elected president every single time," Barack Obama told a select group of donors gathered in Medina, Washington, in February 2012. "I mean, there are five or six people in this room *tonight* [who] could simply make a decision, 'This will be the next president,' and probably at least get a nomination." Obama's audience, which included several billionaires, had each paid $17,900 into his re-election coffers to attend. According to Ken Vogel, indefatigable chronicler of political money flows, the president's jeremiad contained the obligatory reference to the brothers Koch and their famously bottomless war chest—an ever-reliable bogeyman, of course, for Democratic fundraisers.

Thanks in part to such invocations, the 2012 election generated a shade under $7 billion for the industry, an all-time record. A single Republican consulting firm, Crossroads Media, collected no less than $248 million during the campaign, even though it was on the losing side. But the $7 billion figure will almost certainly be dwarfed by the 2016 total, as indicated by just one astounding statistic: a week before this year's New Hampshire primary, the contending campaigns had already spent $100 million there on TV ads. In the previous election, by contrast, the campaigns had invested a mere fiftieth of that amount on TV at the same point.

Unquestioning faith in the power of money is occasionally shaken by a discordant note. This year, there was the public fiasco of Right to Rise USA, Jeb Bush's $118 million super PAC, which spent almost $65 million before the first primary vote was cast and yielded wretched showings in Iowa, New Hampshire, and South Carolina before the candidate finally pulled the plug. Scott Walker, the governor of Wisconsin, meanwhile rode into the race as the reputed candidate of the Koch brothers and their fabled billions, along with a $20 million super PAC, and swiftly vanished without a trace.

In contrast, Donald Trump soared ever higher in the polls while boasting that he had no need to raise money because he had plenty of his own (of which he spent comparatively little). Garnering free time on TV thanks to his entertainment value and skillful use of social media, Trump appeared to call the whole election-complex model into question, earning him "few friends in the campaign industry," according to a December article in the trade journal *Campaigns and Elections*. Yet the professionals remained unruffled, opining that as a billionaire celebrity, Trump was one of a kind, and anyway, he wouldn't last long once the polls opened. "I'm concerned for the country," the Democratic consultant Mark Mellman told *Campaigns and Elections* when asked about Trump's ascent. "I'm not concerned for the industry."

Mellman, two-time winner of the journal's 2014 award for "Best Bare-Knuckled Street Fight Victory," was right. Before too long, Trump fell into line, at least to the extent of spending heavily on TV. In addition, anti-Trump ads have generated much bonus revenue for the industry: Our Principles, a super PAC that has spent $3.3 million this election, was launched for the specific purpose of attacking him, while Right to Rise adorned an Iowa roadside with a billboard reading "DONALD TRUMP IS UNHINGED"—JEB BUSH. Otherwise, nothing has changed. The consultants continue to be amply fed, so Hillary Clinton must regularly exit the campaign trail to hunt for money—every two days, on average, in the month before the Iowa caucuses. Bernie Sanders's money-raising prowess generates admiring comment all around. Marco Rubio kowtows to the casino magnate Sheldon Adelson, who pumped a reputed $150 million into industry pockets during the 2012 contest, though his preferred candidates mostly lost anyway.

Although reformers lament the Supreme Court's contemporary loosening of restraints on campaign finance, the rise of the modern election industry can in fact be dated to post-Watergate efforts to *rein in* campaign spending. New rules imposed accounting requirements, which effectively mandated the services of professionals, while limits on party spending fostered an explosion in PACs—each of which, naturally, required a consultant. Decade after decade, the industry kept growing. Meanwhile, a spate of recent legal decisions—most notably the Supreme Court's 2010 *Citizens United* ruling but also a lower court's *SpeechNow. org v. Federal Election Commission*—inaugurated the age of "independent expenditures": industry-speak for super PACs, to which corporations and individuals can donate without restraint. This has ensured a potentially limitless income stream, all shared among a relatively small number of individuals and firms.

In further benefit to the consultant class, these entities are not allowed to communicate with the candidates they claim to support. Chuck Rocha, a Democratic consultant catering mostly to minority candidates, summarized the advantages of this enforced independence: "It's like living under the golden arches—no need to talk to the candidate, no need to talk to the staff, just put up a bunch of TV ads, sit back, and let the money roll in." Even better, at least as far as the industry is concerned, is the magnetic effect super PACs exert on wealthy but ignorant donors. As Trevor Potter, the former chairman of the Federal Election Commission, explained to me, "You went from a handful of firms to a vast playing field with people all over the country, with enormous sums of money being spent—and being spent by people who are unsophisticated in the ways of politics."

Curious to learn more about industry economics, I sought insider wisdom from Mark McKinnon, an affable Texan who has directed an impressive number of election victories, including George W. Bush's media campaigns in 2000 and 2004. Obligingly, he briefed me on how the arrival of unsophisticated players has so greatly benefited the professionals: "The people who produce the media and buy the media get a refund from the television stations. In the old days, that was a fifteen percent rebate. For the longest time we would make deals with the campaign and say, 'Don't worry about this, you don't have to actually pay us, because we're getting compensated by commission.' It never seemed like real money to the campaign, because they didn't have to write a check to us, it just came back to us from the TV station, even though in reality it was their money. Meanwhile, the stations were making us rich." He hastened to add that no such commissions were extracted by his firm, Maverick Media, during the Bush campaigns.

Nowadays, candidates have gotten wiser, and they bargain for smaller commissions. Nevertheless, McKinnon pointed out, skyrocketing budgets can easily compensate for reduced commissions. As for super PACs, he added, they tend to have zero oversight. The candidates they ostensibly support, after all, are legally barred from communicating with them. To make matters clear, he sketched out a hypothetical case in which a media consultant with connections to a presidential candidate is not interested in working directly for his campaign—because campaigns spend so much money in unremunerative areas, such as travel and staff salaries. Instead, our hypothetical consultant enlists colleagues and sets up a super PAC.

"You can do it in five minutes with three people," McKinnon said. "You set it up and you have a treasurer and a whatever. That's my two buddies and me. Then we go to a couple of [the candidate's] wealthy friends and say, 'Hey, do you want to elect your friend? Well, we've got a super PAC here. You can give five, ten, fifteen, twenty million dollars, and really have an impact on this race.' The donor doesn't know anything about what we do or how we do it. We're going to go full commission and pay ourselves really well, because nobody's negotiating with us. For all the donor knows, fifteen percent is the standard deal, because that's what he's being told. This is sort of like saying, 'Okay, you guys. The bank is open, there's no cameras. There's no security. Take as much as you need.'"

With this scenario in mind, it's worth examining where all the money has gone in the current presidential race. The $118 million collected for Jeb Bush's Right to Rise USA (by fundraisers working, of course, on commission) certainly endeared him to the consultant class. But if the election-industrial complex likes Jeb, it must *love* Ben Carson. The soft-spoken neurosurgeon's campaign committee and super PACs had taken in more than $64 million as of the first week of February, of which they spent some $57 million—most of it on raising more money. In the first three months of 2014, for example, the National Draft Ben Carson for President Committee alone raised $2.4 million, outstripping even Hillary Clinton's cash-harvesting operations during the same period. It spent half of this sum on firms associated with Bruce Eberle, noted for his fundraising work with Black conservatives like Carson and the briefly high-flying Herman Cain, candidates who are unlikely to win elections but entirely likely to excite the generosity of low-income donors.

A sample of what those donors were buying landed on my doormat in Washington earlier this year. Given that Obama won 90 percent of the city's votes in 2012, it might seem that the dollar or so it cost to produce and deliver the elaborate Carson mailer—especially to a household that has never sent a nickel to a conservative Republican candidate—was a waste. But Jon Coley, a direct-mail specialist deemed by many a master of the art, told me that the mailer I received was by no means a waste to the consultant. "The more you mail, the more money you make," he explained on the phone from his pickup while patrolling his cattle farm in Wellington, Alabama. "No more work goes into mailing a hundred and fifty thousand people than fifty thousand people—and there's a markup per piece."

Carson's flailing enterprise is far from the only proof that a losing campaign can be nearly as profitable as a winning one. After Newt Gingrich pulled out of the 2012 race, a firm called TMA Direct brought in an additional $1 million by renting out his and other donor lists. Another firm, Granite Lists, currently offers the 69,552 names on Scott Walker's list for a mere $8,694—a great deal, says the company, for "conservative candidates, organizations, and antiunion causes." The more capacious universe of Mitt Romney donors, meanwhile, can be rented for $131,468.

A practice known as "rev-share" makes the lists even more valuable for the campaigns—and the consultants—that originally compiled them. Many rental agreements specify that a sizable fraction of some initial sum raised by the list—or, indeed, the entire sum—must be paid to the original owner. Thereafter, the renter is free to use the list exclusively for his own benefit. Everyone wins (Granite's standard brokerage commission is 20 percent) except the unwitting donor, whose money may have found its way to a candidate he or she despises. As Vincent Harris, a digital strategist for the Rand Paul campaign, told *Politico*: "Sometimes 60 percent, 70 percent, 100 percent of your donation is going into the pocket of some consultant." Some consultants, he added, have become millionaires by this means alone.

Profitable as such shadowy transactions may be, they pale in comparison with the mother lode of television. Indeed, broadcasters themselves constitute an essential wing of the election-industrial complex. "Super PACs may be bad for America, but they're very good for CBS," crowed CEO Les Moonves in 2012, explaining that he expected election spending to boost his network's annual profits by $180 million. The 2016 election promises to be even more lucrative. As Trevor Potter observes, this titanic influx of cash presents a major conflict of interest, since the networks are simultaneously "supposed to be doing news reporting about spending and what's going on in the world of politics." Unsurprisingly, TV news reporters seldom dwell on the ineffectiveness of the ads that pay their salaries. But the bigger contradiction remains: quite simply, television does not deliver. There are exceptions to this rule—TV ads may be crucial in bringing an unknown candidate to the public's attention—but a growing body of academic research confirms it. In one 2008 experiment, for example, researchers studied voters subjected to heavy TV advertising, then compared their reactions with those of voters who had viewed little or none. They found that the first group was no more likely to vote than the second.

According to David Broockman, a political scientist at Stanford, multiple studies have demonstrated that such ads are essentially self-erasing. "There really is not much evidence that TV has a long-lasting effect on people's views," he told me. "Someone sees a TV ad on Monday afternoon, they change who they say they'll vote for on a survey on Tuesday, but by Wednesday, their view has snapped back to what it was on Monday morning before they saw the ad, because they've just forgotten it."

Faith in the power of political commercials goes back to the dawn of television. In 1952, the PR director for the Republican National Committee wrote that "TV offers the best, if the most expensive medium to carry the personalities of the candidates to the firesides of America." Soon, every campaign that could afford the expense was buying time, a development that naturally fostered a new class of consultants, salesmen, and self-anointed experts. Yet as Adam Sheingate points out in *Building a Business of Politics,* "The political use of television spread widely without much hard evidence that it was effective." In 1955, Herbert Simon, an economist and political scientist who would go on to win a Nobel Prize, conducted one of the earliest experiments to test the question. Anticipating the more recent studies cited above, he compared the votes of residents in Iowa counties that had television reception with the votes of residents in counties that did not—and found no difference between them.

Mark McKinnon suggested to me that the public may now be wearying of televised political ads, or increasingly immune to them, "like a host that gets used to a virus." Jeb Bush's recent debacle would seem to suggest the same conclusion. Yet there is little sign of change. Just as the defense industry successfully promotes ineffective but highly profitable weapons systems, the election industry keeps pushing this ineffective campaign tool on desperate candidates.

Might there be a better way to connect with voters? The election industry has shown little interest in testing its methods (another parallel with defense). Techniques tend to be a matter of lore or seat-of-the-pants instinct, the only constant being that they require lots of money. As McKinnon remarked, "What we do is pretty mystical to people." However, in 1998, two Yale political scientists, Donald Green and Alan Gerber, set out to change all that. Starting with local voters in New Haven, they began investigating what really persuades people to turn out and vote, something that Americans are exceedingly reluctant to do. (Turnout in American presidential elections—57.5 percent in 2012—is among the lowest in the world, and lower still in local elections.) This is a matter of crucial importance, given that most people's political inclinations tend to change little over time, even under barrages of campaign advertising. As commentators have learned to repeat ad infinitum, winning is largely about making sure your base shows up on Election Day.

Green and Gerber divided a homogeneous pool of voters in two. One group was subjected to a specific method of per-suasion—a mailing, say, or a phone call. The other group, the control, was left alone. Over time, the researchers broadened their experiment, overseeing hundreds of such studies across the country. Their conclusions about turnout echoed what Herbert Simon had demonstrated more than four decades before: TV, partisan mail, and robocalls had no effect at all.

Back in the nineteenth century, elections were festive, raucous affairs, often accompanied by free booze and entertainment supplied by the political parties, with saloons doubling as polling places. Turnout by the (all-male) electorate was consequently high. Then came the Progressive reformers, who put an end to the fun, instituting the secret ballot, ejecting party representatives from polling places, banning alcohol, and generally imposing what the historian Richard Bensel called a "morguelike atmosphere" on the proceedings. Subsequent initiatives, such as vote-by-mail—not to mention the impersonality of TV campaigning—have further alienated voters from the process. Reversing that alienation, Green and Gerber revealed, is the key to increasing turnout. One of their experiments even involved throwing "Election Day Festivals" close to polling places. These electoral fiestas lacked booze and brawls but offered plenty of other entertainment, including cotton-candy machines "expertly staffed by political-science professors." Voters had a good time, and turnout rose accordingly.

Of all the ways to get people to come out and vote tested by the academics, one emerged as the absolute gold standard. Talking to them face-to-face, the longer the better, turned out to have a dramatic effect. This is known in the trade as the "ground campaign" or "field operation," conducted by volunteers or paid staff, preferably from the neighborhood they are canvassing. It doesn't come free: the canvassers, even if they are volunteers, have to be housed, fed, trained, and transported. Yet the effect is infinitely more cost-effective than any traditional media-heavy approach.

Meanwhile, this truth has not entirely escaped professional notice. Democrats used a ground campaign instead of media to overturn Republican rule in Dallas in 2006. Dave Carney, the chief strategist for Texas governor Rick Perry, had flown in Green, Gerber, and their colleagues a year earlier to conduct experiments across the state. "Basically, we invested the cost of [one direct mailing] in our field operations," Carney later told a Texas newspaper. "The results blew our expectations." In his two presidential campaigns, Barack Obama pursued an energetic ground campaign in combination with a sophisticated "big data" targeting operation to identify, precisely, those voters who needed to be cajoled to the polling booth—though he also bought hundreds of millions of dollars' worth of TV time. Of the 2016 candidates, Ted Cruz and Bernie Sanders have most successfully embraced the ground-game approach, incorporating sophisticated digital technology to identify likely supporters for canvassing by ground teams.

For the most part, however, traditional campaigns have shown far less interest in engaging directly with voters. Paul Begala, the former Clinton operative turned television commentator, described a Democratic organizing drive in Republican states as "hiring a bunch of staff people to wander around Utah and Mississippi and pick their noses."

It is easy to understand why establishment groups might recoil from a volunteer-based, low-cost strategy. Not only does it offer little promise of revenue, it necessarily relies on people more committed and militant than those at the center may deem acceptable. When Donald Green organized those cotton-candy election festivals, for example, he collaborated with Working Assets (now called CREDO), a phone and credit-card company founded in 1985 with the aim of generating revenue for environmental and social progress. Michael Kieschnick, Laura Scher, and Peter Barnes, the activists who started the company, wanted to do more than merely raise money for good causes. They envisaged deploying CREDO's customer base to support reproductive rights, boost voter registration, and close coal plants. "We have been part of coalitions that have blocked a dozen plants so far," Kieschnick noted proudly in 2007. "Only a hundred or more to go."

In 2010, CREDO played a leading role in defeating Proposition 23, an initiative sponsored by oil interests to roll back emissions regulations in California, by recruiting 10,000 volunteers in a massive get-out-the-vote operation. Two years later, as Republicans and Democrats raked in post–Citizens United cash inevitably destined for TV buys, Kieschnick laid plans for a different mode of campaign. "We are starting a super PAC to defeat ten Tea Party Republicans," he told me at the time. None of the money would be spent on TV; he aimed to win by talking directly to voters.

Florida congressman Allen West, at the top of the target list, was a former Army lieutenant colonel sanctioned for his harsh interrogation techniques while deployed in Iraq. (Rabid and incoherent even by Tea Party standards, West declared that liberal women "have been neutering American men and bringing us to the point of this incredible weakness.") Others in Kieschnick's sights included Michele Bachmann, then a Minnesota congress-woman, and Dan Lungren, a former California attorney general who revived capital punishment in the state, fought for harsher drug laws, opposed gay marriage, and campaigned vigorously for cuts in Social Security and Medicare.

Experts predicted an easy win for West. For the race in his heavily Republican district, the congressman raised more than $19 million, plowing $8.8 million of this sum back into fundraising and spending another $7.2 million on media buys. Meanwhile, the CREDO team, in the words of its political direc-tor, Becky Bond, set out to build a "David-and-Goliath campaign where we used our volunteers ... to move more votes than their hundreds of super-PAC ads." The volunteers were largely women; many of them had been motivated by West's misogynistic tirades. The CREDO effort paid off, with West losing by 2,429 votes.

"I have never, ever met a candidate who did not profess a total commitment to old-fashioned voter contact," Kieschnick told me recently. "But if you look under the hood of the campaign, the candidates spend most of their time raising money for television ads. Candidates fear being told their opponents have an ad when they do not, even if it makes no difference. It is easy for consult-ants to raise money, for a fee, and then spend it on advertising, and get another fee. But where is the fee on volunteers?"

All together, five of CREDO's targets, including Lungren, were sent packing. The ten campaigns cost CREDO's super PAC a total of $2.5 million. Meanwhile, American Crossroads, a cash-glutted super PAC founded by Karl Rove, spent $105 million during the same year and managed to elect only one of its preferred candidates. After the extent of the organization's losses became clear, one disappointed hedge-fund donor even considered suing Rove, on the grounds that his "investment" had been fraudulently secured, until he learned that the law allowed for no such recourse.

The grassroots campaign that helped to evict West in 2012 grew out of long experience and a well-honed organization. Two years later, Eric Cantor, the majority leader of the House of Representatives and a leading candidate for Speaker, was thrown out of office because Ron Maxwell got mad.

A film director with a number of big-budget credits, including the 1993 epic *Gettysburg*, Maxwell lives on a mountaintop deep in rural Virginia, near Cantor's congressional district. Cantor "really got on my radar screen in the last year of the Bush Administration," Maxwell told me, "when Bush was pushing through all the [Wall Street] bailouts." Additional evidence of the politician's crony capitalism—his habit of "doing the bidding of the US Chamber of Commerce"—further dismayed Maxwell, as did Cantor's inveterate hawkishness and his support for immigrant amnesty, which the director saw as a corporate ploy to impoverish the American worker. The tipping point came in August 2013, when Cantor endorsed Obama's plan to bomb Syria. Maxwell gathered a group of friends and neighbors who largely shared his brand of conservative Republicanism and said, "You know, we've got to get rid of Eric Cantor."

The reaction, Maxwell told me, was muted. "It was, like, 'Ron's blowing off some steam here. Why would anybody take it seriously?'" Nevertheless, after probing the mood of the district over the next few months, Maxwell concluded that many Republicans shared his views. They objected to Cantor's policies—and were irked that the congressman, who believed his hold on the (artfully gerrymandered) district to be unshakable, was never around.

Casting about for a suitable candidate to oppose Cantor in the 2014 Republican primary—which is the de facto election in this GOP stronghold—Maxwell settled on Dave Brat, a conservative economics professor at Randolph-Macon College, a small school a few miles north of Richmond. Prospectively, it was a forlorn effort. The national Tea Party groups declined to endorse the quixotic insurgency. Maxwell himself was beating the bushes for funds, even from friends not necessarily sympathetic to Brat's agenda. His wife, who gave $1,000, was one of the largest donors: most donations were less than $200. Cantor was meanwhile rolling in money from such Wall Street behemoths as Goldman Sachs. By the time it was over, he had outspent his upstart opponent by a ratio of 41 to 1. One category of expenditure alone—$168,000 for steakhouse tabs—cost almost as much as Brat's entire campaign. Needless to say, Cantor's staff also blew huge sums on TV ads, many of which tarred Brat (bizarrely, for anyone exposed to his views on free-market economics) as a "liberal college professor."

Brat's grassroots ground campaign mirrored the effort of CREDO in 2012. As Maxwell told me, the upstart was "shaking hands, meeting people at Kmart, Costco, Kiwanis Club, Lions Club, PTAs, Little League, every night. All the volunteers were knocking on doors." There were no TV advertisements, he said: "Zero. There was no money for it. We were certainly worried about it, because before the Brat election, we were in a world where everybody thought TV matters."

For the election consultants and pundits alike, Cantor's ultimate victory was never in doubt: his pollster predicted he would win 60 percent of the vote. This confidence remained intact right up until the announcement that Brat had won, 56–44, abruptly closing down the incumbent's lavish celebration at a Richmond hotel.

Kieschnick, who retired from CREDO in 2015, believes that this strategy holds bright promise for the progressive element. Asked whether big money could ever be defeated, he told me, "Yes, but only because most of the One Percent—not all!—waste most of their money in politics on expensive but bad advertising and even more expensive consultants. Since the American people agree with us on most of the issues, it is an ongoing struggle between voter suppression, misinformation, and voter turnout. If we simply shifted half of the billions spent on television into ongoing, year-round, person-to-person engagement with voters, progressive candidates would dominate. But year after year, we raise more money and waste it."

Mike McKenna, who has spent his career working the other side of the aisle, has come to a similar conclusion. "If you can convince the politicians that they don't really need to spend their time raising all that money," he told me earnestly, "they'll carry you round Capitol Hill on their shoulders."

Harper's Magazine, April 2016

Postscript. Subsequent election cycles confirmed the warnings in this piece, culminating in the fiasco of the 2024 Kamala Harris campaign, which raised and spent $1.5 billion in fifteen weeks, most of it on a deluge of paid media, yielding little in terms of votes but a great deal to the bank accounts of relevant parties closely linked to the campaign.

5

Secretary of Nothing

John Kerry and the Myth of Foreign Policy

When former president Bill Clinton nominated Barack Obama for a second term at the 2012 Democratic National Convention in Charlotte, North Carolina, the hall was packed to the rafters with party dignitaries. One was conspicuous by her absence: Hillary Clinton, away on diplomatic business in East Timor. "For decades," she said by way of explanation, "secretaries of state have not attended political conventions because of the non-partisan nature of our foreign policy."

Politicians love being thought of as nonpartisan and above the murky fray. That must explain why so many of them want to be secretary of state, even though the office confers little power of patronage (its choicest appointments—ambassadorships—being sold off by the president to the highest bidder), a puny budget, and none of the authority that comes from the ability to kill people or make them rich.

Nevertheless, two people very definitely wanted to be secretary of state in the first Obama administration: Senator John F. Kerry of Massachusetts and Governor Bill Richardson of New Mexico. Both denied it, of course. But Democratic Party sources insist that Obama, locked in a bitter nomination battle with Hillary Clinton, offered both men the coveted post in hopes of gaining their support when he needed it.

Richardson, who had served the Clinton administration as secretary of energy and ambassador to the United Nations, was campaigning largely on the strength of his foreign policy experience. But as the Iowa caucuses approached, he lagged at around 8 percent in the polls—far behind Obama and Clinton, but with enough supporters to make him an object of desire for both campaigns.

The Clintons believed they were safe from a Richardson defection, because he had served in Bill Clinton's cabinet and furthermore indicated he would make no such alliance. What prize could Obama dangle to sever the ties of loyalty and friendship? The choice was clear. He reportedly contacted Richardson days before the Iowa vote and offered him the State Department—confidentially, it being considered unseemly to allot cabinet positions before the election. Richardson accordingly directed his caucus delegates to support Obama, to the fury of the Clintons. "I guess energy secretary and UN ambassador weren't enough for him," raged Bill Clinton as Obama won a decisive victory in Iowa on January 3. (Richardson insists the story is "totally false," a slander spread by Clinton loyalists.)

The battle moved on, and Hillary Clinton surged back in New Hampshire, meaning that Obama was now obliged to hook a bigger fish. Kerry, though defeated by George W. Bush in 2004, remained a powerful presence among the Democrats, not least because he controlled a lucrative donor list with 3 million email addresses. Obama already owed much to the senator, who had selected him to make what became a career-defining address at the 2004 convention. (A friend of mine, a delegate, bumped into Obama later that night while he and another delegate were strolling outside the hall. "That showed some charisma," said my friend's companion in congratulation. "*Some* charisma?" replied Obama, irked at the qualifier.)

Now Kerry delivered an equally important favor, endorsing Obama just days after his potentially terminal defeat in New Hampshire. Beforehand, he is reported to have elicited a firm promise that he would be appointed secretary of state in November. Kerry's chief of staff, David Wade, insists that "nothing like that ever happened, whatsoever." But again, Democratic Party sources argue that there was indeed a quid pro quo, with Obama contradicting his earlier pledge.

Richardson still thought the job was his. In late March, he

publicly endorsed Obama, causing the Clinton loyalist James Carville to pronounce him a "Judas." The press, meanwhile, remained unaware of Obama's warring commitments. In August, Richardson coyly admitted to the *Albuquerque Journal* that while "not launching a campaign" for the job, he did have hopes of selection for State. Kerry, running for reelection to the Senate, could not express such ambitions, though others touted his candidacy for Foggy Bottom.

As we know, with the election satisfactorily concluded, Obama awarded the coveted position to the defeated Hillary—relief from four years of Clinton rancor being clearly worth breaking a promise or two. Richardson, after withdrawing his nomination for secretary of commerce, dropped out of politics. Kerry, re-elected to the Senate, became chairman of the Senate Committee on Foreign Relations. Former occupants of that chair had used it to make trouble, the best-known example being William Fulbright, who held regular, probing hearings on Vietnam between 1966 and 1971. The April 22, 1971, session had been notable for the dramatic testimony of a young war hero turned dissident, John Kerry, who thereby launched his political career.

By 1985, Kerry was himself a senator and a junior member of the same committee, where he oversaw commendable investigations into the links between covert operations in Central America and the narcotics trade, as well as (in partnership with John McCain) the POW/MIA racket. But when he took over the leadership post, in 2009, Kerry stopped rattling cages. There would be no Fulbright-style hearings on Afghanistan. The reason, said a close political colleague, was that Kerry "wants to be secretary of state."

Four years later still, his time appeared to have come. Clinton was quitting the office in preparation, so all presumed, for a second run at the White House. But once again, it looked like politics would intervene. To a considerable degree, the Obama national-security team in the first term had been an Irish affair— "three cold, hard Irishmen," as one former State Department official recalled. This troika consisted of Tom Donilon, John Brennan (custodian of the drone-strike kill list), and Denis

McDonough (who gradually took control of the National Security Council machinery). All three had earned Obama's trust. Yet they had a potent rival in Susan Rice. Rice had reportedly had her eye on the post of national security adviser at the beginning of Obama's first term, but had settled for UN ambassador, in which capacity she had been a forceful voice for active engagement in the Libyan civil war. Now it seemed possible that she would succeed in her bid for the security adviser post—where she would present a major threat to the Irish junto. Donilon and McDonough (Brennan having gone to his reward as CIA director) floated a solution: send her off to be secretary of state.

"Why not?" says a State Department official who observed these maneuvers. "All the power is in the White House anyway, and *they* would pick her staff—the assistant secretaries and so on. She'd be surrounded by their people and couldn't make trouble." It was a reasonable scheme, but it fell apart after the jihadist group Ansar al-Sharia attacked the US Consulate in Benghazi, Libya, on September 11, 2012, killing Ambassador Chris Stevens and three other Americans. On television, Rice declared that the attack had been a spontaneous mob action—bringing down the wrath of Republicans, who accused her of engineering a cover-up and pledged to fight her confirmation for State. Obama gamely defended her, but Rice was soon forced to abandon her bid.

At long last, Obama fulfilled the promise he had made four years earlier and named Kerry to the post. Some suggested that the move had been impelled only by a prod from Kerry's old friend John McCain, who expressed irritation that a senior senator was being treated with such scornful indifference. After calling for "economic patriotism" during his confirmation hearing and hailing the "crippling sanctions" levied on Iran, Kerry was confirmed with enthusiastic bipartisan support. He now embarked on the final task of his career: constructing a legacy out of the unpromising materials of the Middle East peace process. Thus did Kerry begin flying countless miles back and forth to Israel and its occupied territories. His initial goal was merely to promote talks between Israeli and Palestinian negotiators. Before too many months had passed, however, locals began openly expressing derision at what they perceived as an empty exercise in political theater. Jeering at Kerry's efforts, the *Times of Israel* invoked the old saw that insanity is repeating the same action again and again in hopes of obtaining a different result.

Uri Avnery, the veteran Israeli peace activist, meanwhile mocked the very notion of negotiations "between an almighty occupying power and an almost totally powerless occupied people." The "full might of the United States" may well be behind Kerry, he wrote in his weekly column last June, but then added a crucial question: "Or is it?" Clearly, only Obama himself could impose a peace, which he was (and is) unlikely to attempt on behalf of anyone's legacy but his own.

Kerry, it seems, had fallen into the trap of believing in the existence of something called "foreign policy," divorced from domestic political interests. There is no such thing. Edwin O'Connor made exactly this point in his 1956 political novel, *The Last Hurrah*. "We're under the disadvantage of having to evolve a foreign policy that meets local requirements," explains Frank Skeffington, an old-fashioned machine boss running for reelection in an East Coast port city modeled on Boston. "When you come right down to it, there are only two points that really count." Skeffington held up two fingers. "One," he said, ticking the first, "*All Ireland must be free*. Two," he said, ticking the second, "*Trieste belongs to Italy*. They count. At the moment the first counts more than the second, but that's only because the Italians were a little slow in getting to the boats."

Pundits, of course, are fond of remarking that "all politics is local." They imagine they are quoting the late House speaker Tip O'Neill, though the maxim was coined by a journalist in 1932. O'Neill himself once defeated GOP opposition to a billion-dollar jobs bill by listing all the bridges and infrastructure in Republican leader Robert Michel's home district that would benefit from the legislation. But the idea that international politics follows the same rules, whether in democracies or dictatorships, and that all so-called foreign policy is actually a reflection of domestic factors, is too heretical to entertain—especially when it threatens a vast and flourishing intellectual industry.

Every year, thousands of young men and women graduate from the many schools of international relations around the United States, duly certified in the theory and practice of foreign policy and therefore qualified for a career slaloming between government, think-tanks, and academia. Though they will have pored over such seminal texts as Joseph Nye's *Presidential Leadership and the Creation of the American Era* and Robert Keohane's *After Hegemony: Cooperation and Discord in the World Political Economy*, none of them will have heard of Bernard H. Barnett, an attorney who died in Atlanta in 1987. That is a pity. If the study of Barnett's career formed even a tiny segment of any of the hundreds of international relations courses currently on offer, students might get an inkling of just how chimerical their discipline truly is.

Barney, as everybody called him, specialized in tax matters, especially those involving large corporations, with particular emphasis on the oil industry. From his original base in Louisville, Kentucky, where he took an ambitious young Republican named Mitch McConnell under his wing, Barnett's practice eventually extended to nine cities, the most important being Washington and Miami.

Apart from his legal gifts and aptitude as a businessman, Barnett was that rare thing in mid-twentieth-century America: a Jewish Republican. Not surprisingly, Republican politicians cherished his friendship, especially at election time, and eagerly harkened to his pleas on behalf of Israel.

Preferring to work "out of the limelight," as his son Charles told me recently, Barnett lent his name and public support to just a few uncontroversial entities, such as the United Jewish Appeal. Far more crucially, according to a source who knew him well, he crafted the legal framework for the American Israel Public Affairs Committee (AIPAC). The former Minnesota senator Rudy Boschwitz affectionately describes Barnett, whom he first met through the wealthy industrialist Max Fisher, as "a giant." "Max and Barney cut a very wide swath both in the halls of Congress and among a series of Republican presidents," Boschwitz told me, as they lobbied "strongly and effectively for the state of Israel in its young, formative years."

AIPAC's clout derives in large part from its ingenious structure, which enables it to operate simultaneously as a tax-exempt educational foundation, a lobbying operation, the coordinator of apparently independent local political action committees, and an unregistered foreign agent. By the end of the Carter administration, AIPAC had become a mighty political force, capable of swaying and even supervising the US government's actions in the Middle East.

Barnett's role in these developments was noted in high places, specifically by Richard V. Allen, Ronald Reagan's first national security adviser, who felt that Barnett's skills could profitably be deployed elsewhere. Campaigning in Miami in 1980, Allen had observed the viscerally anticommunist Cuban exile community, at the time racked with feuds and discord, and realized what formidable allies they could be—especially when dealing with a recalcitrant Congress controlled by Democrats.

"I approached the Cubans," Allen told me recently. "They were already Reagan supporters, but loosely organized. I suggested they organize themselves like AIPAC." To teach them just how to accomplish this, Allen recommended Barney Barnett. In no time at all, the Cuban American National Foundation was up and running, structured precisely along AIPAC lines, with separate research, funding, and lobbying operations, while local chapters around the country forged financially lubricated ties to individual members of Congress in both parties.

Allen's brainchild more than fulfilled its promise, not only lending support to Reagan's bellicose initiatives in Central America but also helping to ensure that Florida, carried by Jimmy Carter in the 1976 election, went overwhelmingly for Reagan in 1984. Barnett remained closely involved, housing CANF's Washington operation in his law office at 1000 Thomas Jefferson Street, close to the Georgetown waterfront. "We were at one end," recalls a lawyer who worked down the hall and was intimately familiar with the Barnett firm. "The Cubans were at the other, and there were a bunch of Israelis running in and out of a room in the middle with a high-security lock."

ᐬ

Barnett's passing was marked by brief and uninformative obituaries in the *New York Times* and the *Palm Beach Post*. (Jorge Mas Canosa, chairman of CANF, was one of the pallbearers at the funeral.) Yet the epitaph for this relative unknown could easily echo that of Christopher Wren, as inscribed on the great architect's tombstone in the floor of St. Paul's Cathedral: IF YOU SEEK HIS MEMORIAL, LOOK AROUND YOU.

Thanks to Barnett's ingeniously fashioned and highly efficient machine for distributing money to the campaign chests of legislators, no administration—and none but the most electorally suicidal of politicians—will dare defy AIPAC's injunctions. Israelis themselves are awed by the lobby's power. Uri Avnery vividly summed up the scene at AIPAC's 2008 annual conference in a blog post:

> All the three presidential hopefuls made speeches, trying to outdo each other in flattery. 300 Senators and Members of Congress crowded the hallways. Everybody who wants to be elected or reelected to any office, indeed everybody who has any political ambitions at all, came to see and be seen.

While the smaller and less affluent Cuban American community never attempted to match AIPAC's reach, they got what they needed: an ironclad veto on America's relations with Fidel Castro and, no less important, a powerful role in the local and national politics of their adopted nation. Jorge Mas Canosa, for example, dominated Miami politics for nearly two decades. As one of his associates told the *Miami Herald* in 1992, "I can't believe it. You sit there and watch him deal with [city] commissioners and he treats them like chauffeurs." (This source also told the reporter that he would "be destroyed" if quoted by name.) Meanwhile, candidates for higher office in venues far from Florida, such as Joseph Lieberman in Connecticut and Robert Torricelli in New Jersey, eagerly solicited Mas Canosa's endorsement. In return, they got a reliable partner proficient in trading votes and money (Torricelli alone collected $240,000) for power.

Needless to say, there is no mention of Barnett in those standard texts by Nye and Keohane, nor do AIPAC and CANF figure in the works of a towering eminence like the late Kenneth Waltz.

Yet history clearly demonstrates that *leaders*—whether demo-crats or dictators—consistently keep their eye fixed on their own domestic political advantage, a fact ignored by professors and policy analysts, though sometimes acknowledged by politicians themselves.

Alexander Hamilton, for example, commented in *The Federal-ist* no. 6 that innumerable wars originated "entirely in private passions; in the attachments, enmities, interests, hopes, and fears of leading individuals in the communities of which they are members." As a principal illustration of this important truth, he cited the case of Pericles, lauded as one of the greatest statesmen of classical Athens, who "in compliance with the resentment of a prostitute, at the expense of much of the blood and treasure of his countrymen, attacked, vanquished, and destroyed the city of the Samnians" before igniting the disastrous Peloponnesian War in order to extricate himself from political problems back home.

Alert to the realities of international politics, Hamilton would have had little trouble appreciating the story related to me a few years ago by a former senior British intelligence official, describ-ing how Greece came to join the European Union. According to this account, the British prime minister James Callaghan was hoping to promote Greece's application for membership in 1976 as a means of appeasing Labour's left-wingers, who were urging that the Greeks' recent ejection of their fascist military regime be rewarded. But the bureaucrats of the European Commission took a dim view of the application, on the entirely accurate grounds that Greece's economy was too backward to be allowed into the club.

Callaghan was despondent. At that point, the head of MI6, Sir Maurice Oldfield, appeared at 10 Downing Street to recommend that the prime minister phone French President Giscard d'Estaing and make a direct appeal to have the EC's verdict set aside. Cal-laghan made the call—and to his surprise received immediate and enthusiastic approval for the proposal. With the United Kingdom and France thus united, resistance in Brussels collapsed and the Greek application moved ahead. Later, Callaghan asked Oldfield for an explanation.

"It may be," replied the spy chief, "that a certain patriotic Greek lady has been denying the pleasures of her bed to a senior French official unless and until her country's application is accepted." The intelligence proved correct. The French president's private passion was satisfied, Greece joined the European Union and traded its drachmas for euros, and was thus launched on the road to its present state of beggary.

The historian Walter Karp also made clear the absurdity of the proposition that foreign and domestic policy are somehow separate, that presidents in trouble at home nevertheless conduct their foreign policy without regard for these difficulties. In his most important work, *The Politics of War* (1979), Karp illustrated his thesis by examining America's entry into World War I. At the time, President Woodrow Wilson made an artful attempt to persuade both contemporaries and future generations that he was leading the country into the European slaughter only with the greatest reluctance, and in the face of dire provocation. In fact, according to Karp's interpretation, Wilson—an unsavory egomaniac who brought Jim Crow to its apogee by segregating federal offices—was intent on dragging America into the war from the start, motivated by both personal ambition and urgent domestic political exigencies.

The erstwhile Princeton University president had ridden to the White House in 1912 on a reform ticket. Indeed, 70 percent of the votes in that year's election were cast for the two progressive candidates, in hopes of extirpating Wall Street's control of capital. "The privileged interests, the 'money trust,'" wrote Karp, "seemed about to receive their death blow."

However, Wilson's own political beliefs ran in quite the opposite direction. His public conversion to the cause of reform was of recent vintage, driven by the need to secure progressive Republican support, but he privately regarded the movement as an obnoxious outbreak of "ill-humors." So, to fulfill the bare minimum of the electorate's expectations, he put through Congress a limited program to restrain banking and big business.

Not everyone was deceived. Senator Robert La Follette of Wisconsin described the 1913 act establishing the Federal Reserve as a "big bankers' bill," while another progressive Republican lawmaker said Wilson's measures against the trusts had "not enough teeth to masticate successfully milk toast." Wilson realized that he had better find some way of diverting the popular mood for change before the people woke up to his true inclinations and voted him out of office. The solution, he confided to his friend and adviser Colonel Edward House, was to "impel" the nation to "great national triumphs" abroad.

The outbreak of the world war in 1914 presented Wilson with the perfect opportunity to jettison the populist agenda. He announced in November of that year that the reform era was at an end, his legislation having satisfactorily remedied all the people's grievances. Meanwhile, though publicly professing neutrality in the conflict, he spared no effort in assisting the British, notably in their campaign, illegal under international law and ruinous to Germany's civilian population, to blockade that country's food supply. Karp states flatly that from "autumn 1914 onward, the diplomacy of the United States would be conducted by Wilson and House not in the interests of America, not by the venerable traditions of the Republic," but only to secure for the messianic Wilson what his friend and flatterer House described as "the noblest part that has ever come to a son of man."

The part Wilson and his adviser had in mind was that of supervising the postwar peace, reshaping the world into a vaguely conceived "association of nations." But reaching that position required a prior, active role in the war itself, and Wilson's problem was that the American people wanted no part of it. Former president Theodore Roosevelt, himself eager for America to join the carnage, ruefully admitted in 1915 that an estimated 98 percent of Americans saw no reason whatsoever why they should become involved.

Eventually it was left to the British to relieve the president of his predicament, handing over an intercepted message from the German foreign minister to the German ambassador in Mexico with instructions to propose an alliance with the Mexican government should the United States enter the war—the famous Zimmermann telegram. Its public release had the desired effect, generating a wave of war hysteria and xenophobia in the press, which was in turn encouraged by the financiers and munitions profiteers who now formed the president's core constituency. Wilson got his war.

Following Germany's defeat, Wilson embarked on phase two of his overall plan: to play that "noblest part." But it all went wrong. Although the masses gave him an ecstatic greeting on his arrival in Europe to supervise the peace conference, the wily politicians at the head of the French and British governments were bent on advancing their own agendas. They proved notably uncooperative in framing Wilson's pet scheme, the League of Nations, as he had envisioned it. Returning home to secure the necessary domestic endorsement for the League, he faced an angry and vengeful populace. Wilson, as Karp puts it, had "deceived and betrayed his countrymen, had falsely maneuvered them into war, had robbed them of their peace, their hopes, and the lives of 116,708 of their sons." What sort of welcome did he expect?

In an acid summation near the end of his story, Karp notes: "Today, American children are taught in our schools that Wilson was one of our greatest Presidents. That is proof in itself that the American Republic has never recovered from the blow he inflicted on it." Dying at the hands of clumsy doctors in 1989, Karp was at least spared the rapturous applause that greeted the publication earlier this year of A. Scott Berg's best-selling *Wilson*, whose heroic protagonist lived "to renew ideals." The illusion of a freestanding foreign policy, which Karp worked so hard to banish, remains stubbornly intact.

Some might cite the contrary example of the Dulles brothers, John Foster and Allen, who wielded great power in the 1950s as heads of the State Department and the CIA, respectively, and who appear to have pursued a foreign policy of militant anticommunism devoid of domestic considerations. Yet they served at the pleasure of a master, President Eisenhower. So when Secretary Dulles urged an initiative contrary to Ike's political requirements, such as dispatching American troops to Vietnam in 1954, the boss had no hesitation in peremptorily quashing the idea.

In a similar vein, foreign policy treatises tend to dodge the role of oil corporations in directing US policy in the Muslim Middle

East, though accounts of the CIA's 1953 Iranian coup can hardly ignore the fact. Those same treatises also tiptoe around figures such as Bruce Jackson, vice president for international operations at Lockheed in the 1990s, who successfully lobbied for the expansion of NATO into Eastern Europe, even at the expense of the United States breaking a solemn promise to the Russians.

President Kennedy's handling of the Cuban missile crisis in 1962 might also appear to have been purely a foreign policy exercise. But the transcripts of Kennedy's meetings during the crisis indicate clearly that his prime consideration was the domestic political impact of allowing the Soviets to base missiles so close to the United States. On the other side of the crisis, Soviet premier Nikita Khrushchev appears to have authorized the missile deployment to patch over problems with his military, who were chafing both at a reduction in troop levels and at Khrushchev's failure to deliver promised production of ICBMs. Meanwhile, Kennedy had famously told the CIA he didn't want to know about Khrushchev's problems with his generals. Such domestic spats struck him as an irrelevant distraction.

Yet in a fascinating book on Soviet foreign policy of the era, *Public Policy in an Authoritarian State: Making Foreign Policy During the Brezhnev Years* (1993), Richard Anderson proves that the opposite was true. Such weighty developments as changing relations with Eastern European satellite states, or arms control talks with the West, often hinged on the domestic tug-of-war between the paramount leader Leonid Brezhnev and his rivals in the party hierarchy.

Obsessed with beating one another, Soviet officials consistently enacted foreign policies that damaged Soviet interests at home and abroad. Their American counterparts ignored what was going on in the Soviet Union because they were concentrating just as hard on their own electoral battles. They were caught flat-footed when the bickering in Moscow handed them victory in the Cold War, freeing Eastern Europe in 1989 and tearing apart the Soviet Union itself two years later. People, Anderson told me, think political campaigning is all about winning votes. But that ignores the copious evidence of continual skirmishing between Brezhnev and his peers: "To exercise power, you have to have supporters, whether they vote or not. Foreign policy is a way of buying support."

"It's ridiculous to talk about US foreign policy," adds Joel McCleary, who has had ample opportunity to ponder the matter over recent decades as a former Democratic Party official and international financial and political consultant. "It's a platonic form, without concrete substance. You could say there are US foreign policies," he continued. He cited his experience as an unofficial State Department envoy dispatched to Zimbabwe in 2002. "I was meant to be discussing a transition from Mugabe," he told me. "But when I got there, I found the Pentagon was using him for renditions, and he wasn't going anywhere."

McCleary, who had been studying the social life of bees when I called him, suggested that the only time the term "foreign policy" might have any validity is when all the various elements of power in Washington decide to move in the same direction, "like a swarm. Tonkin Gulf was a swarm. Iraq in 2003 was a swarm. Of course," he added, "swarms don't always lead to good results."

As he flew doggedly back and forth between the United States and Israel during the spring and summer of 2013, spending up to fourteen hours closeted with Israeli prime minister Benjamin Netanyahu (and almost as much with Palestinian Authority president Mahmoud Abbas), John Kerry was by no means part of a swarm. State Department officials fulminated that he was "running the place like his Senate office, with no connection to the rest of the building"—meaning that he was relying on a small coterie of advisers he had brought with him from Capitol Hill. Some noted that he seemed unaware of the ever greater importance of Asian powers.

"His view of Asia is thirty years out of date," one former senior official told me. "He doesn't realize how dynamic the region is. One thing the Israelis and Palestinians have in common is the fear that the Americans will turn all their attention to Asia. That's why they tell Kerry, 'We're so close to an agreement,' and he believes them!" Kerry's determination to make a personal impact regardless of political realities extended beyond his focus on the Israeli–Palestinian peace process. At one moment when he briefly turned his attention to Asia, for example, he considered cutting back the planned US missile defense program in the Pacific if China would help rid North Korea of nuclear weapons. He even hinted at a possible summit between the United States and Kim Jong Un.

Ignoring Obama's manifest determination to avoid any entanglement in the Syrian civil war, Kerry also plowed ahead with efforts to persuade the Russians to cooperate in ejecting the Assad regime, implicitly criticizing the president for not having done more. "This is a very difficult process, which we come to late," he observed stiffly at the beginning of June. Needless to say, none of this went down well in the Oval Office. "There's only room for one narcissist in this administration," quipped a former White House official. "If Obama disliked Richard Holbrooke, he *really* dislikes John Kerry."

Matters might have continued in this fashion, with Kerry jetting back and forth in futile isolation, had not a horrible tragedy in a Damascus suburb, vividly communicated by footage of dozens of dead and dying children, induced a seismic shift in the global political landscape. It was now politically impossible for Obama to ignore calls for some sort of military reaction, a course urged by both Kerry and Susan Rice, the habitual interventionist. It appeared that, once again, Washington was getting ready to swarm.

Yet Obama, ever the cautious politician, had no desire to leave a flank exposed to his Republican opposition by striking without their explicit endorsement, and so delayed the punitive attack on Syria pending congressional approval. Kerry eagerly joined the promotional effort, exhorting members of Congress not to ignore "our Munich moment" and comparing Syrian civilians to Jewish refugees being sent back to face Hitler's gas chambers.

In his derisive post on Kerry's peace process odyssey, Uri Avnery recalled an earlier and equally fruitless initiative by a long-forgotten UN envoy named Gunnar Jarring, who had shuttled back and forth between Israel and Egypt to no avail. Then came the surprise Egyptian attack across the Suez in October 1973 —and, as Avnery put it, "the whole political world started to move." Peace between the two countries ensued with remarkable speed, culminating in the Camp David Accords just five years later.

Obama's attempt to get congressional approval for the Syria strike may have been a similarly world-moving moment. I refer not to the request itself but to the American public's reaction. For years, our political leaders have taken for granted popular acquiescence in whatever drive-by shooting they have in mind, with "foreign policy" invoked as a handy rubber stamp. But that weekend in September, even as Kerry and Obama and Rice sought to whip Congress into line, the American people suddenly revealed that they, too, had a foreign policy. A wave of calls and emails swept over Capitol Hill, overwhelmingly denouncing the proposed attack. Even Barney Barnett's legacy, in the form of a mass AIPAC lobbying effort, could not prevail against this tide.

Then John Kerry finally found *his* long-awaited moment, with an offhand answer to an unexpected and unprompted question about Assad's options for avoiding a strike. As peace, not just with Syria but with Iran too, suddenly appeared an advantageous option, the secretary of state was swept along, growing tall in the theatrical role he had coveted for so long, though playing the part not as Talleyrand or Metternich, but as Chauncey Gardiner.

Harper's Magazine, December 2013

Postscript. The shining prospect of peace in Syria and with Iran swiftly faded. Kerry flew countless more miles in pursuit of the chimera of climate control, an effort as fruitless as his earlier efforts in the Middle East. Barney Barnett's legacy, in the form of AIPAC and the Florida Cuban lobby, has endured and flourished.

6

No Joe!

Joe Biden's Disastrous
Legislative Legacy

In the heart of the US Capitol there's a small men's room with an uplifting Franklin Delano Roosevelt quotation above the door. Making use of the facilities there after lunch in the nearby House dining room about a year ago, I found myself standing next to Trent Lott. Once a mighty power in the building as Senate Republican leader, he had been forced to resign his post following some imprudently affectionate references to his fellow Republican senator, arch-segregationist Strom Thurmond. Now he was visiting the Capitol as a lucratively employed lobbyist.

The bathroom in which we stood, Lott remarked affably, once served a higher purpose. History had been made there. "When I first came to Washington as a junior staffer in 1968," he explained, "this was the private hideaway office of Bill Colmer, chairman of the House Rules Committee." Colmer, a long-serving Mississippi Democrat and Lott's boss, was an influential figure. The committee he ruled controlled whether bills lived or died, the latter being the customary fate of proposed civil rights legislation that reached his desk. "On Thursday nights," Lott continued, "he and members of the leadership from both sides of the House would meet here to smoke cigars, drink cheap bourbon, play gin rummy, and discuss business. There was a chemistry, they understood each other. It was a magical thing." He sighed wistfully at the memory of a more harmonious age, in which our elders and betters could arrange the nation's affairs behind closed doors.

~

I don't know that Joe Biden, currently leading the polls for the 2020 Democratic presidential nomination, ever frequented that particular restroom, in either its bygone or contemporary manifestation, but it could serve as a fitting shrine to all that he stands for. Biden has long served as high priest of the doctrine that our legislative problems derive merely from superficial disagreements, rather than fundamental differences over matters of principle. "I believe that we have to end the divisive partisan politics that is ripping this country apart," he declared in the Rose Garden in 2015, renouncing a much-anticipated White House run. "It's mean-spirited. It's petty. And it's gone on for much too long. I don't believe, like some do, that it's naïve to talk to Republicans. I don't think we should look on Republicans as our enemies."

Given his success in early polling, it would seem that this message resonates with many voters, at least when they are talking to pollsters. After all, according to orthodox wisdom, there is no more commendable virtue in American political custom and practice than bipartisanship. Politicians on the stump fervently assure voters that they will strive with every sinew to "work across the aisle" to deliver "commonsense solutions," and those who express the sentiment eloquently can expect widespread approval. Barack Obama famously launched himself toward the White House with his 2004 speech at the Democratic National Convention proclaiming that there is "not a liberal America and a conservative America," only a "United States of America."

By tapping into these popular tropes—"The system is broken," "Why can't Congress just get along?"—the practitioners of bipartisanship conveniently gloss over the more evident reality: that the system is under sustained assault by an ideology bent on destroying the remnants of the New Deal to the benefit of a greed-driven oligarchy. It was bipartisan accord, after all, that brought us the permanent war economy, the war on drugs, the mass incarceration of Black people, 1990s welfare "reform," Wall Street deregulation and the consequent $29 trillion in bank bailouts, the 2001 Authorization for Use of Military Force, and other atrocities too numerous to mention. If the system is indeed broken, it is because interested parties are doing their best to break it.

Rather than admit this, Biden has long found it more profitable to assert that political divisions can be settled by men endowed with statesmanlike vision and goodwill—in other words, men such as himself. His frequent eulogies for public figures have tended to play heavily on this theme. Thus his memorial speech for Republican standard-bearer John McCain dwelled predictably on the cross-party nature of their relationship, beginning with his opening: "My name is Joe Biden. I'm a Democrat, and I loved John McCain." Continuing in that vein, he related how he and McCain had once been chided by their respective party leaderships for spending so much time in each other's company on the Senate floor, and referred fondly to the days when Senators Teddy Kennedy and James Eastland, the latter a die-hard racist and ruthless suppressor of civil rights bills, would "fight like hell on civil rights and then go have lunch together, down in the Senate dining room."

Clearly, there is merit in the ability to craft compromise between opposing viewpoints in order to produce an effective result. John Ritch, formerly a US ambassador and top aide on the Senate Foreign Relations Committee, worked closely with Biden for two decades, and has nothing but praise for his negotiating skills. "I've never seen anyone better at presiding over a group of politicians who represent conflicting egos and interests and using a combination of conciliation, humor, and muscle to cajole them into an agreed way forward," Ritch told me recently. "Joe Biden has learned the skills to get things done in Washington. And I've seen him apply it equally with foreign leaders."

The value of compromise, however, depends on what result is produced, and who benefits thereby. McCain's record had at least a few commendable features, such as his opposition to torture (though never, of course, war). But it is hard to find much admirable in the character of a tireless defender of institutional racism like Strom Thurmond. Hence, Trent Lott's words of praise—regretting that the old racist had lost when he ran as a Dixiecrat in the 1948 presidential election—had been deemed terminally unacceptable.

It fell to Biden to highlight some redeeming qualities when called on, inevitably, to deliver Thurmond's eulogy following the latter's death in 2003 at the age of one hundred. Biden reminisced with affection about the unlikely friendship between the deceased and himself. Despite having arrived at the Senate at age twenty-nine "emboldened, angered, and outraged about the treatment of African Americans in this country," he said, he nevertheless found common cause on important issues with the late senator from South Carolina, who had been wont to describe civil rights activists as "red pawns and publicity seekers."

One such issue, as Branko Marcetic has pitilessly chronicled in *Jacobin*, was a shared opposition to federally mandated busing in the effort to integrate schools, an opposition Biden predicted would be ultimately adopted by liberal holdouts. "The Black community justifiably is jittery," Biden admitted to the *Washington Post* in 1975 with regard to his position. "I've made it—if not respectable—I've made it reasonable for longstanding liberals to begin to raise the questions I've been the first to raise in the liberal community here on the [Senate] floor."

Biden was responding to criticism of legislation he had introduced that effectively barred the Department of Health, Education, and Welfare from compelling communities to bus pupils using federal funds. This amendment was meant to be an alternative to a more extreme proposal put forward by a friend of Biden's, hall-of-fame racist Jesse Helms (Biden had initially supported Helms's version). Nevertheless, the *Washington Post* described Biden's amendment as "denying the possibility for equal educational opportunities to minority youngsters trapped in ill-equipped inner-city schools." Edward Brooke of Massachusetts, then the sole African American senator, called Biden's measure "the greatest symbolic defeat for civil rights since 1964."

By the 1980s, Biden had begun to see political gold in the harsh antidrug legislation that had been pioneered by drug warriors such as Nelson Rockefeller and Richard Nixon, and would ultimately lead to the age of mass incarceration for Black Americans. One of his Senate staffers at the time recalls him remarking, "Whenever people hear the words 'drugs' and 'crime,' I want them to think 'Joe Biden.'" Insisting on anonymity, this former staffer recollected how Biden's team "had to think up excuses for new hearings on drugs and crime every week—any connection, no matter how remote. He wanted cops at every public meeting —you'd have thought he was running for chief of police."

The ensuing legislation might also have brought to voters' minds the name of the venerable Thurmond, Biden's partner in this effort. Together, the pair sponsored the 1984 Comprehensive Crime Control Act, which, among other repressive measures, abolished parole for federal prisoners and cut the amount of time by which sentences could be reduced for good behavior. The bipartisan duo also joined hands to cheerlead the passage of the 1986 Anti-Drug Abuse Act and its 1988 follow-on, which cumulatively introduced mandatory sentences for drug posses-sion. Biden later took pride in reminding audiences that "through the leadership of Senator Thurmond, and myself, and others," Congress had passed a law mandating a five-year sentence, with no parole, for anyone caught with a piece of crack cocaine "no bigger than [a] quarter." That is, they created the infamous dis-parity in penalties between those caught with powder cocaine (white people) and those carrying crack (Black people). Biden also unblushingly cited his and Thurmond's leading role in enact-ing laws allowing for the execution of drug dealers convicted of homicide, and expanding the practice of civil asset forfeiture, law enforcement's plunder of property belonging to people suspected of crimes, even if they are neither charged nor convicted.

Despite pleas from the NAACP and the ACLU, the 1990s brought no relief from Biden's crime crusade. He vied with the first Bush administration to introduce ever more draconian laws, including one proposing to expand the number of offenses for which the death penalty would be permitted to fifty-one. Bill Clinton quickly became a reliable ally upon his 1992 election, and Biden encouraged him to "maintain crime as a Democratic initiative" with suitably tough legislation. The ensuing 1994 Violent Crime Control and Law Enforcement Act, passed with enthusiastic administration pressure, would consign millions of Black Americans to a life behind bars.

In subsequent years, as his crime legislation, particularly on mandatory sentences, attracted efforts at reform, Biden began expressing a certain remorse. "I am part of the problem that I have been trying to solve since then, because I think the disparity [between crack and powder cocaine sentences] is way out of line," he declared at a Senate hearing in 2008. However, there is little indication that his words were matched by actions, especially after he moved to the vice presidency the following year. The executive director of the Criminal Justice Policy Foundation, Eric Sterling, who worked on the original legislation in the House as a congressional counsel, told me, "During the eight years he was vice president, I never saw him take a leadership role in the area of drug policy, never saw him get out in front on the issue like he did on same-sex marriage, for example. Biden could have taken a stronger line [with Obama] privately or publicly, and he did not."

While many Black Americans will neither forgive nor forget how they, along with relatives and friends, were accorded the lifetime stigma of a felony conviction, many other Americans are only now beginning to count the costs of these viciously repressive initiatives. As a result, criminal justice reform has emerged as a popular issue across the political spectrum, including among conservatives eager to burnish otherwise illiberal credentials. Ironically, this has led, in theory, to a modest unraveling of a portion of Biden's bipartisan crime-fighting legacy.

Last December, as Donald Trump's erratic regime was falling into increasing disarray, the political-media class briefly united in celebration of an exercise in bipartisanship: the First Step Act. Billed as a long overdue overhaul of the criminal justice system, the legislation received rapturous reviews for its display of cross-party cooperation, headlined by Jared Kushner's partnership with liberal talk-show host Van Jones. In truth, this was a very modest first step. It offered the possibility of release to some 2,600 federal inmates, whose relief from excessive sentences would require the goodwill of both prosecutors and police, as well as forbidding some especially barbaric practices in federal prisons, such as the shackling of pregnant inmates. Overall, it amounted to little more than a textbook exercise in aisle bridging, a triumph of form over substance.

In the near term, it's unlikely that there will be further bipartisan attempts to chip away at Biden's legislative legacy, a legacy that includes an inconsistent (to put it mildly) record on abortion rights. *Roe v. Wade* "went too far," he told an interviewer in 1974. "I don't think that a woman has the sole right to say what should happen to her body." For some years his votes were consistent with that view. He supported the notorious Hyde Amendment prohibiting any and all federal funding for abortions, and fathered the "Biden Amendment" that banned the use of US foreign aid for abortion research.

As the 1980s wore on, however, and Biden's presidential ambitions started to swell, he began to cast fewer antiabortion votes (with some exceptions), and as chairman of the Senate Judiciary Committee led the potent opposition to Judge Robert Bork's Supreme Court nomination. Then came Clarence Thomas. Even before Anita Hill reluctantly surfaced with her convincing recollections of unpleasant encounters with the porn-obsessed judge, Biden was fumbling his momentous responsibility of directing the hearings. As Jane Mayer and Jill Abramson report in *Strange Justice*, their book about the Thomas nomination battle, Biden's questions were "sometimes so long and convoluted that Thomas would forget what the question was." Biden prided himself on his legal scholarship, Mayer and Abramson suggest, and thus his questions were often designed "to show off [his] legal acumen rather than to elicit answers."

More damningly, Biden not only allowed fellow committee members to mount a sustained barrage of vicious attacks on Hill: he wrapped up the hearings without calling at least two potential witnesses who could have convincingly corroborated Hill's testimony and, by extension, indicated that the nominee had perjured himself on a sustained basis throughout the hearings. As Mayer and Abramson write, "Hill's reputation was not foremost among the committee's worries. The Democrats in general, and Biden in particular, appear to have been far more concerned with their own reputations," and feared a Republican-stoked public backlash if they aired more details of Thomas's sexual proclivities. Hill was therefore thrown to the wolves, and America was saddled with a Supreme Court justice of limited legal qualifications and extreme right-wing views (which he had taken pains to deny while under oath).

Fifteen years later, Biden would repeat this exercise in hearings on the Supreme Court nomination of Samuel Alito, yet another grim product of the Republican judicial selection machinery. True to form, in his opening round of questions, Biden droned on for the better part of half an hour, allowing Alito barely five minutes to explain his views. As the torrent of verbiage washed over the hearing room, fellow Democratic Senator Patrick Leahy sank his head in his hands.

Biden's record on race and women did him little damage with the voters of Delaware, who regularly returned him to the Senate with comfortable margins. On race, at least, Biden affected to believe that Delawareans' views might be closer to those of his old buddy Thurmond than those of the "Northeast liberal" he sometimes claimed to be. "You don't know my state," he told Fox as he geared up for his second attempt on the White House in 2006. "My state was a slave state. My state is a border state. My state has the eighth-largest Black population in the country. My state is anything [but] a Northeast liberal state." Months later, in front of a largely Republican audience in South Carolina, he joked that the only reason Delaware had fought with the North in the Civil War was "because we couldn't figure out how to get to the South. There were a couple of states in the way."

Whether or not most Delawareans are proud of their slave-holding history, there are some causes that they, or at least the dominant power brokers in the state, hold especially dear. Foremost among them is Delaware's status as a freewheeling tax haven. State laws have made Delaware the domicile of choice for corporations, especially banks, and it competes for business with more notorious entrepôts such as the Cayman Islands. Over half of all US public companies are legally headquartered there.

"It's a corporate whore state, of course," the anonymous former Biden staffer remarked to me offhandedly in a recent conversation. He stressed that in "a small state with thirty-five thousand bank employees, apart from all the lawyers and others from the financial industry," Biden was never going to stray too far from the industry's priorities. We were discussing bankruptcy, an issue that has highlighted Biden's fealty to the banks. Unsurprisingly, Biden was long a willing foot soldier in the campaign to emasculate laws allowing debtors relief from loans they cannot repay. As far back as 1978, he helped negotiate a deal rolling back bankruptcy protections for graduates with federal student loans, and in 1984 worked to do the same for borrowers with loans for vocational schools. Even when the ostensible objective lay elsewhere, such as drug-related crime, Biden did not forget his banker friends. Thus the 1990 Crime Control Act, with Biden as chief sponsor, further limited debtors' ability to take advantage of bankruptcy protections.

These initiatives, however, were only precursors to the finance lobby's magnum opus: the 2005 Bankruptcy Abuse Prevention and Consumer Protection Act. This carefully crafted flail of the poor made it almost impossible for borrowers to get traditional "clean slate" Chapter 7 bankruptcy, under which debt forgiveness enables people to rebuild their lives and businesses. Instead, the law subjected them to the far harsher provisions of Chapter 13, effectively turning borrowers into indentured servants of institutions like the credit card companies headquartered in Delaware. It made its way onto the statute books after a lopsided 74–25 vote (bipartisanship!), with Biden, naturally, voting in favor.

It was, in fact, the second version of the bill. An earlier iteration had passed Congress in 2000 with Biden's support, but President Clinton refused to sign it at the urging of the first lady, who had been briefed on its iniquities by Elizabeth Warren. A Harvard Law School professor at the time, Warren witheringly summarized Biden's advocacy of the earlier bill in a 2002 paper: "His energetic work on behalf of the credit card companies has earned him the affection of the banking industry and protected him from any well-funded challengers for his Senate seat." Furthermore, she added tartly, "This important part of Senator Biden's legislative work also appears to be missing from his Web site and publicity releases." No doubt coincidentally, the credit card giant MBNA was Biden's largest contributor for much of his Senate career, while also employing his son Hunter as an executive and, later, as a well-remunerated consultant.

It should go without saying, then, that Biden was among the ninety senators on one of the fatal (to the rest of us) legislative gifts presented to Wall Street back in the Clinton era: the Gramm-Leach-Bliley Act of 1999. The act repealed the hallowed Depression-era Glass-Steagall legislation that severed investment banking from commercial banking, thereby permitting the combined operations to gamble with depositors' money, and ultimately ushering in the 2008 crash. "The worst vote I ever cast in my entire time in the United States Senate," admitted Biden in December 2016, as he prepared to leave office. Seventeen years too late, he explained that the act had "allowed banks with deposits to take on risky investments, putting the whole system at risk."

In the meantime, of course, he had been vice president of the United States for eight years, and thus in a position to address the consequences of his (and his fellow senators') actions by using his power to press for criminal investigations. His longtime faithful aide, Ted Kaufman, in fact, had taken over his Senate seat and was urging such probes. Yet there is not the slightest sign that Biden used his influence to encourage pursuit of the financial fraudsters. As he opined in a 2018 talk at the Brookings Institution, "I don't think five hundred billionaires are the reason we're in trouble. The folks at the top aren't bad guys." Characteristically, he described gross inequalities in wealth mainly as a threat to bipartisanship: "This gap is yawning, and it's having the effect of pulling us apart. You see the politics of it."

Biden's rightward bipartisan inclinations are not the only source of his alleged appeal. In an imitation of Hillary Clinton's tactics in the lead-up to the 2016 election, Biden has advertised himself as the candidate of "experience." Indeed, in his self-estimation he is the "most qualified person in the country to be president." It's a claim mainly rooted in foreign policy, a field where, theoretically, partisan politics are deposited at the water's edge and Biden's negotiating talents and expertise are seen to their best advantage.

He boasts the same potent acquaintances with world leaders that helped earn Clinton a similar "most qualified" label on her failed presidential job application and, like her, has been a reliable hawk, not least when occupying the high-profile chairmanship of the Senate Foreign Relations Committee. An ardent proponent of NATO expansion into Eastern Europe, an ill-conceived initiative that has served as an enduring provocation of Russian hostility toward the West, Biden voted enthusiastically to authorize Bush's 2003 invasion of Iraq, was a major proponent of Clinton's war in Kosovo, and pushed for military intervention in Sudan.

Presumably in deference to this record, Obama entrusted his vice president with a number of foreign policy tasks over the years, beginning with "quarterbacking," as Biden put it, US relations with Iraq. "Joe will do Iraq," the president told his foreign policy team a few weeks after being sworn in. "He knows it, he knows the players." It proved to be an unfortunate choice, at least for Iraqis. In 2006, the US ambassador to Iraq, Zalmay Khalilzad, had selected Nouri al-Maliki, a relatively obscure Shiite politician, to be the country's prime minister. "Are you serious?" exclaimed a startled Maliki when Khalilzad informed him of the decision. But Maliki proved to be a determinedly sectarian ruler, persecuting the Sunni tribes that had switched sides to aid US forces during the so-called surge of 2007–8. In addition, he sparked widespread allegations of corruption. According to the Iraqi Commission of Integrity set up after his departure, as much as $500 billion was siphoned off from government coffers during Maliki's eight years in power.

In the 2010 parliamentary elections, one of Maliki's rivals, boasting a nonsectarian base of support, won the most seats, though not a majority. According to present and former Iraqi officials, Biden's emissaries pressed hard to assemble a coalition that would reinstall Maliki as prime minister. "It was clear they were not interested in anyone else," one Iraqi diplomat told me. "Biden himself was very scrappy—he wouldn't listen to argument." The consequences were, in the official's words, "disastrous." In keeping with the general corruption of his regime, Maliki allowed the country's security forces to deteriorate. Command of an army division could be purchased for $2 million, whereupon the buyer might recoup his investment with exactions from the civilian population. Therefore, when Islamic State erupted out of Syria and moved against major Iraqi cities, there were no effective defenses. With Islamic State fighters an hour's drive from Baghdad, the United States belatedly rushed to push Maliki aside and install a more competent leader, the Shiite politician and former government minister Haider al-Abadi. (Biden's camp disputed the Iraqi official's assertion that the United States pressed for Maliki in 2010. "We had no brief for any individual," said Tony Blinken, who served as Biden's national security adviser at the time.)

Biden devotes considerable space to this episode in *Promise Me, Dad*, his political and personal memoir documenting the year in which his son Beau slowly succumbed to cancer. But although we learn much about Biden's relationship with Abadi, and the key role he played in getting vital help to the beleaguered Iraqi regime, there is little indication of his past with Maliki aside from a glancing reference to "stubbornly sectarian policies."

Promise Me, Dad also covers Biden's involvement in the other countries allotted to him by President Obama: Ukraine, El Salvador, Guatemala, and Honduras. Anyone seeking insight from the book into the recent history of these regions, or of actual US policy and actions there, should look elsewhere. He has little to say, for example, about the well-chronicled involvement of US officials in the overthrow of Ukraine's elected government in 2014, still less on whether he himself was involved. He records his strenuous efforts to funnel IMF loans to the country following anticorruption measures introduced by the government without noting that much of the IMF money was almost immediately stolen and spirited out of Ukraine by an oligarch close to the government. Nor, for that matter, do we learn anything about his son Hunter's involvement in that nation's business affairs via his position on the board of Burisma, a natural gas company owned by a former Ukrainian ecology minister accused by the UK government of stealing at least $23 million of Ukrainian taxpayers' money.

Biden's recollections of his involvement in Central American affairs are no more forthright, and no more insightful. There is no mention of the 2009 coup in Honduras, endorsed and supported by the United States, that displaced the elected president, Manuel Zelaya, nor of that country's subsequent descent into the rule of a corrupt oligarchy accused of ties to drug traffickers. He has nothing but warm words for Juan Orlando Hernández, the next president, who financed his 2013 election campaign with $90 million stolen from the Honduran health service and more recently defied his country's constitution by running for a second term. Instead, we read much about Biden's shepherding of the Hernández regime, along with its Central American neighbors El Salvador and Guatemala, into the Alliance for Prosperity, an agreement in which the signatories pledged to improve education, health care, women's rights, justice systems, etc., in exchange for hundreds of millions of dollars in US aid. In the words of Professor Dana Frank of UC Santa Cruz, the alliance "supports the very economic sectors that are actively destroying the Honduran economy and environment, like mega-dams, mining, tourism, and African palms," reducing most of the population to poverty and spurring them to seek something better north of the border. The net result has been a tide of refugees fleeing north, most famously exemplified by the "caravan" used by Donald Trump to galvanize support prior to November's congressional elections. Biden's claims of experience on the world stage, therefore, cannot be denied. True, the experience has been routinely disastrous for those on the receiving end, but on the other hand, that is a common fate for those subjected, under any administration, to the operations of our foreign policy apparat.

Given Biden's all too evident shortcomings in the fields of domestic and foreign policy, defenders inevitably retreat to the "electability" argument, which contends that he is the only Democrat on the horizon capable of beating Trump—a view that Biden, naturally, endorses. Specifically, this notion rests on the belief that Biden has unequaled appeal among the white working-class voters that many Democrats are eager to court.

To be fair, Biden has earned high ratings from the AFL-CIO thanks to his support for matters such as union organizing rights and a higher minimum wage. On the other hand, he also supported NAFTA in 1994 and permanent normal trade relations with China in 2000, two votes that sounded the death knell for America's manufacturing economy. Regardless of how justified his prolabor reputation may be, however, it's far from clear that the working class holds Biden in any special regard—his two presidential races imploded before any blue-collar workers had a chance to vote for him.

It is this fact that makes the electability argument so puzzling. Biden's initial bid for the prize in 1988 famously blew up when rivals unkindly publicized his plagiarism of a stump speech given by Neil Kinnock, a British Labour Party politician. (In Britain, Kinnock was known as "the Welsh Windbag," which may have encouraged the logorrheic Biden to feel a kinship.) Biden partisans pointed out that he had cited Kinnock on previous occasions, though he didn't always remember to do so. Either way, it was a bizarre snafu. It also emerged that Biden had been incorporating chunks of speeches from both Bobby and Jack Kennedy along with Hubert Humphrey in his remarks without attribution (although reportedly some of this was the work of speechwriter Pat Caddell).

Another gaffe helped upend Biden's second White House bid, in 2007, when he referred to Barack Obama in patronizing terms as "the first mainstream African American who is articulate and bright and clean and a nice-looking guy." The campaign cratered at the very first hurdle, the Iowa caucuses, where Biden came in fifth, with less than 1 percent of the vote. "It was humiliating," recalled the ex-staffer. (The "gaffes" seem to take physical form on occasion. "He has a bit of a Me Too problem," a leading female Democratic activist and fundraiser told me, referring to his overly tactile approach to interacting with women. "We never had a talk when he wasn't stroking my back." He has already faced heckling on the topic, and videos of this behavior during the course of public events and photo ops have been widely circulated.)

Further to the issue of Biden's assurances that he is the man to beat Trump is the awkward fact that, as the former staffer told me, "he lacks the discipline to build the nuts and bolts of a modern presidential campaign." Biden "hated having to take orders from [David] Axelrod and the other Obama people as a vice-presidential candidate in 2008. Campaign aides used to say to him, 'I've got three words for you: Air Force Two.'" My inform-ant stressed that Biden "sucks at fundraising. He never had to try very hard in Delaware. Staff would do it for him." Certainly, Biden's current campaign funds would appear to confirm this contention. His PAC, American Possibilities, had raised only $2.5

million by the end of 2018, a surprisingly insignificant amount for a veteran senator and two-term vice president. Furthermore, although the PAC's stated purpose is to "support candidates who believe in American possibilities," less than a quarter of the money had found its way to Democratic candidates in time for the November midterms, encouraging speculation that Biden is not really that serious about the essential brass tacks of a presidential campaign—which would include building a strong base of support among Democratic officeholders.

Other organizations in the Biden universe behave similarly, expending much of their income on staff salaries and little on their ostensible function. According to an exhaustive *New York Times* investigation, salaries accounted for 45 percent of spending by the Beau Biden Foundation for the Protection of Children in 2016 and 2017. Similarly, three-quarters of the money the Biden Cancer Initiative spent in 2017 went toward salaries and other compensation, including over half a million dollars for its president, Greg Simon, formerly the executive director of Biden's Cancer Moonshot Task Force during the Obama administration. Outside the inner circle of senior aides, there does not appear to be an extended Biden network among political professionals standing ready to raise money and perform other tasks necessary to a White House bid, in the way that Hillary Clinton had a network across the political world composed of people who had worked for her and her husband. "Biden doesn't have that," his former staffer told me, "because he's indifferent to staff." It's a sentiment that's been expressed to me by many in the election industry, including a veteran Democratic campaign strategist. "Everyone else is getting everything set up to go once the trigger is pulled," this individual told me recently. "I myself have firm offers from the [Kamala] Harris and [Cory] Booker campaigns. The Biden people talked to me, too, but they could only say, 'If we run, we'd love to bring you into the fold.'"

At the start of the new year, Biden must have been living in the best of all possible worlds. As he engaged in well-publicized ruminations on whether or not to run, he was enjoying a high profile, with commensurate benefits of sizable book sales and $100,000 speaking engagements. Even more importantly, Biden found himself relevant again. "You're either on the way up," he likes to say, "or you're on the way down," which is why the temptation to reject the lessons of his two hopelessly bungled White House campaigns has been so overwhelming. Regardless of the current election cycle's endgame, though, it's safe to assume that his undimmed ego will never permit any reflection on whether voters who have been eagerly voting for change will ever really settle for Uncle Joe, champion of yesterday's sordid compromises.

Harper's Magazine, March 2019

7

The Offstage Convention

Democrats in Chicago, 2024

As a demonstration that politics have been refashioned as show business, the Democratic National Convention was beyond compare. Delegates chanted the requisite slogans—"We're not going back," "Do something," "Thank you, Joe"—in exuberant unison; volunteers distributed and collected placards and signs—many simply displaying names, including DOUG—with faultless efficiency. With exceptions (Bill Clinton, Chuck Schumer, Joe Biden), most speeches were mercifully brief. Some had unintentionally entertaining lines, as with Hillary Clinton's assertion that Harris "sat in the situation room and stood for America's values." Rumors circulating in the venue—"Taylor Swift and George W. Bush are on their way!"—were diverting, too.

Commentators tut-tutted at the timing of Biden's late-evening opening-night appearance, at an hour when East Coast viewers had gone to bed and privileged attendees had moved across the street to the free drinks and food at the CNN–Politico Grill (sponsored in part by major corporations, including IBM, the giant private-equity firm Blackstone, and the politically potent Stand with Crypto lobbying group). But it wasn't hard to side with suspicions that Biden's delayed appearance was all part of the plan. The president's bellowing recitation of his accomplishments served as a vivid reminder of the bullet so recently deflected by Nancy Pelosi and her ruthless fellow Democratic Party panjandrums in hustling the would-be nominee into political oblivion. Nevertheless, I detected no signs of bitterness among the onstage performers. Michelle Obama and Jill Biden may hate each other, as Washington rumor has it, but for public consumption their friendship is glossy and bright. There is no denying the success of the event as a well-staged performance, particularly in promoting Harris as a fresh and boundlessly energetic figure, her lackluster years as vice president wiped from official memory.

Watching the spectacle, albeit mostly in conditions of extreme discomfort from the crowded topmost tier of Chicago's United Center, or while eating the vile hot dogs on offer in the stifling halls surrounding the arena, I felt a surge of nostalgia for the days when conventions were nakedly political, replete with debate and rancor, rather than merely an exercise in entertainment. On the second day of the 1924 Democratic National Convention, at Madison Square Garden, for example, partisan divide reached the point where sweltering delegates, according to the *New York Times*, were "screaming, jeering, and waving their fists at each other" as 13,000 spectators in the galleries above literally spat at them. No wonder gallery tickets were being scalped for $100 a seat (roughly $1,800 in today's money).

Memory of the 1968 Democratic National Convention, also in Chicago, loomed large this year, marred as it was by the unbridled violence inflicted by Mayor Richard J. Daley's police on citizens protesting the Vietnam War. Given the current ongoing catastrophe in Gaza, largely enabled by American arms, expectation ran high that history would repeat itself. Conditions were, after all, undeniably similar: America, now as then, is engaged in the mass slaughter of a civilian population, albeit this time by proxy via bombs, bullets, intelligence, and money delivered to Israel without stint. Now as then, the nominee is a vice president in an administration exhibiting not the faintest indication of remorse for its policy. Now as then, one of the candidates on the ticket is a Minnesota politician, Tim Walz, with a commendably progressive record on domestic policy who loyally supports a foreign war just as Hubert Humphrey, the Democrats' candidate in 1968, stood by Lyndon Johnson while he rained bombs on the Vietnamese. Like Harris, Humphrey had bypassed the need for victory in the primaries, securing the nomination with the help of party machine bosses such as Mayor Daley of Chicago. (Given that machine's recent record of imposing its preferred candidate, whatever the people may think—Clinton in 2016, Biden in 2020—it's doubtful that the rituals of primary debates and soft-soap media interviews would have forestalled Harris's nomination.)

For those who looked, there were signs and portents of core Democratic policies pushed offstage. Harris has declared her principled opposition to the death penalty, for example, but a pledge to end capital punishment, a routine feature of the party's election-year platform, quietly disappeared from the document this year. On the final day of the convention, I ran into a lobbyist searching amid the throng on the floor for a DNC official who could explain why a particular health-care pledge in the platform had also vanished. Most prominent of all the silenced issues, of course, was the war on Gaza.

Most of the disorder predicted for this year's convention was largely absent. As the *New York Times* happily reported: "It wasn't 1968. It wasn't even close." Antiwar organizers had worked to mobilize a peaceful protest, fortified by polls suggesting that no fewer than 77 percent of Democrats, according to a CBS poll conducted in early June, favor a cutoff of American arms to Israel. "Seventy percent of Democrats support a permanent ceasefire; 60 percent want an arms embargo," Hatem Abudayyeh, spokesman for the March on the DNC, assured me. The City of Chicago, or at least its law-enforcement bureaucracy, did its bit to amplify tensions by enjoining onerous restrictions on rally facilities, such as the use of loudspeakers and stages, though these were ultimately withdrawn with the encouragement of Chicago's progressive mayor, Brandon Johnson. A rally and march on the first day of the convention drew perhaps 11,000 people. Two days later, another rally, this time largely attended by families from a long-established Palestinian community on the southwest side of the city, attracted only 8,000. A final rally and march on the last day drew an even smaller crowd, "a cross section of the Chicago activist community," as a local journalist told me. A few fences on the arena's extensive outer security perimeter were torn down on opening day, but that was it.

Some delegates arriving for the first evening of the proceedings literally plugged their ears as activists on the security perimeter shouted grim statistics of Gaza's death toll. Later that night, while Biden was speaking, a group of antiwar delegates smuggled in and held up a STOP ARMING ISRAEL banner. Outraged Harris delegates attempted to block the offending banner with WE LOVE JOE signs before eventually tearing it from the hands of Liano Sharon, a Jewish delegate from Michigan, and ripping it up.

Many attendees expressed muted sympathy for the Palestinians' desperate plight. Early in the week, I stood with Code Pink founder Medea Benjamin, a veteran activist, as she lobbied delegates lining up at one of the ubiquitous security checkpoints insulating conventioneers from the world outside. "Do you know that 183 women give birth every day in Gaza without anesthetic?" she asked a pregnant woman. "I can't begin to imagine that. It's horrible," the woman replied quietly. "I'm getting a lot of reactions like that," Benjamin told me. Days later, I came across Benjamin and her Code Pink co-founder, Jodie Evans, who reported cheerfully that they'd just interrupted Walz's address to the Democratic Women's Caucus, demanding an end to arms supplies to Israel. Overall, the random delegates I queried as to whether Gaza should be discussed at the convention tended to reply nervously, fearful of breaking a taboo and disturbing the harmony of the hive. One, from Washington State, told me that such discussion might be appropriate, "but not here this week, because that would affect the unity of the convention." "It's complicated," said another, from Oklahoma. Even so, by the end of the week, at least 300 Harris delegates had signed a petition for a ceasefire and weapons embargo.

In a hard-to-find windowless room allocated them by the DNC, deep in the maze of the tightly guarded McCormick Place, a secondary convention venue, uncommitted delegates made their case in the company of six doctors in hospital scrubs, who sequentially described the horrific conditions they had experienced firsthand in Gaza. "We cannot unsee what we witnessed. It gives us nightmares. Having worked in many other horrific conditions, I can personally testify and say I have never seen anything so horrific, so egregious, so inhumane," said Dr. Tanya

Haj-Hassan, an intensive-care pediatrician. "Entire families exterminated, humanitarian workers and health-care workers and journalists killed in record numbers, children with their extremities amputated ... All the records are being broken in the most horrific possible ways." As colleagues detailed their experiences in traumatizing detail, Haj-Hassan began quietly weeping. Soon, her colleagues, along with the uncommitted delegates, were crying too, passing tissues down the line.

Before the DNC began, the uncommitted group requested that Haj-Hassan be allowed to address the convention, but officials turned them down. They then asked that Ruwa Romman, a Palestinian-American state representative from Georgia, be allowed to take the stage, even offering organizers the opportunity to review and approve her speech. After several days of stalling, the DNC turned down that request also. As a result, the only focused discussion of the war in Gaza permitted in the United Center came in a moving address and call for ceasefire from the parents of Hersh Goldberg-Polin, an Israeli-American whose remains, along with those of five other hostages taken on October 7, would be recovered by Israeli troops from a tunnel in southern Gaza roughly a week after the convention ended, stoking demonstrations in Israel this week in favor of a ceasefire.

Regardless of whether the uncommitted group genuinely expected to be allowed a public platform, the idea that the Democratic machine would have made such a concession is inconceivable. After all, AIPAC, Israel's much-feared lobbying machine, and other pro-Israel groups had just spent $25 million to crush two congressional critics of Israel, Jamaal Bowman and Cori Bush, in their primary races—a financial overkill clearly designed to intimidate the country's critics. ("I'll be back," Bowman said, tugging me close for a selfie as he headed into the arena.) Unvarnished sentiments prevailing in the Israel lobby are well represented by the billionaire Haim Saban, who has said that he is "a one-issue guy and my issue is Israel." Saban contributed $7 million to build the Democrats' Washington, DC, headquarters, and in the current cycle he and his wife, Cheryl, have so far delivered almost $2 million to a Democratic PAC, and a further $1 million to AIPAC's election PAC. Biden's partial blockage of some heavy-weapons shipments to Israel earlier this year swiftly evoked a reprimand from the billionaire: "Bad ... decision, on all levels," wrote Saban to Biden aides. "Pls reconsider."

Leading lights of the party, including Schumer, Cory Booker, and Steny Hoyer, ignored or brushed aside questions from the reporter Max Blumenthal, of *The Grayzone*, who had penetrated a basement passage leading to a VIP area, about the influence of AIPAC money on their silence over the Gaza slaughter. Convention rhetoric itself was replete with tributes to the administration's allegedly "tireless" efforts to broker a ceasefire, repeated so frequently as to become the liberals' equivalent to Republicans' standard "thoughts and prayers" response to school shootings and other gun massacres. In her own carefully crafted speech climaxing the celebrations, Harris implausibly asserted that she and Biden were "working around the clock" for a ceasefire and hostage release. After predictably pledging enduring support for Israel in all its works, she segued into language that echoed in form the heartfelt pleas that I had been hearing all week from the doctors: "So many innocent lives lost. Desperate, hungry people fleeing for safety, over and over again. The scale of suffering is heartbreaking," she intoned. Once the hostages are released and the war is over, she claimed, "the Palestinian people can realize their right to dignity, security, freedom, and self-determination." While it was an abbreviated mention, it seemed to me, from the crowd, that her reference to Palestine drew a louder cheer than her pledge of fealty to Israel.

Somewhat depressed at the lower-than-predicted volume of outrage over Gaza, I left the convention bubble behind me to go look for Bill Ayers—militant opponent of the Vietnam War, prominent in the far-left organization Student for a Democratic Society, founder of the militant group Weather Underground, and survivor of years on the run from the FBI. I found him, entirely brisk and alert at nearly eighty, on a park bench on the city's South Side. Ruminating on the events of the week, he acknowledged the diminished protest turnout, which he attributed to the removal of "Genocide Joe" from the ballot and the substitution of an energetic candidate unburdened by his record.

Nevertheless, he bade me be of good cheer. "I'm hopeful because I thought the antiwar movement made a tremendous impact all week at the convention," he said. "I think we walk toward fundamental change on two legs. One leg is established politics, and the other leg is mobilization, organization, and education of masses of people. It took two years to mobilize people on Vietnam. I was first arrested in October of 1965, opposing the war. But it never really had the impact that it needed to have until 1967. And so it took us a couple of years. In ten months, the narrative has changed about Israel-Palestine."

As an alternative to the much-worked-over allusions to 1968, Ayers raised an earlier precedent: the 1964 Democratic National Convention, in Atlantic City. There, President Johnson, like Harris and her fellow speakers, spoke of "freedom" and "opportunities" in his speech accepting the nomination, determined not to alienate a key component of his coalition: the Southern Democratic bosses whose party faction had long been a bastion of white supremacy, leading to Blacks' being rigorously excluded from Southern delegations. Fannie Lou Hamer, a Mississippi sharecropper who had become a powerful voice for civil rights, led demands that delegates from the Mississippi Democratic Freedom Party, which she had co-founded, be allowed to sit at the convention. When she spoke to the credentials committee, Johnson held a press conference just to keep her off live TV, and the DNC determinedly rejected her request to seat the integrated delegation. "The Democratic establishment failed to acknowledge what was really going on in the world, in 1964 and in 1968," Ayers told me. "Had they acknowledged it, they would have animated a base that might have changed the outcome. But it wasn't the fault of the left that Hubert Humphrey didn't get elected. That wasn't their fault. They were raising a moral issue. And it was up to the political class to respond in kind to the raising of that issue. And they didn't. Didn't yet again this week, which is a damn shame."

This, to me, was the most important message of the convention. The event's producers had achieved their purpose by delivering exciting entertainment to uplift Democrats' spirits. But Ayers was surely correct: despite efforts to avoid the issue, the relevant powers could not entirely silence those who stood for Gaza any more than an earlier generation of bosses could appease the racist wing of the party. My interest was piqued by his reference to Fannie Lou Hamer, and I searched for a video of her speech demanding admission to the 1964 convention. I found it on Instagram, posted by the account of Win with Black Women, a group headed by the powerful Silicon Valley PR executive Jotaka Eaddy. The page juxtaposed Hamer's raw, powerful voice—"If the Freedom Democratic Party is not seated now, I question America … [where] we want to live as decent human beings"—with a clip from Harris's polished speech, delivered sixty years later to the day, in which she accepted the nomination on behalf of "everyone whose story could only be written in the greatest nation on earth." The connection was clear; the irony, doubtless unintentional. Ruwa Romman, the uncommitted delegate from Georgia, had also thought of the resonances between Mississippi sixty years ago and Gaza today. In the speech she was not allowed to deliver on the DNC stage, she was prepared to declare: "They'll say: this is how it's always been, that nothing can change. But remember Fannie Lou Hamer—shunned for her courage, yet she paved the way for an integrated Democratic Party … It's her example we follow."

Harper's Magazine (online), September 5, 2024

Postscript. Fifteen million Americans who voted for Biden in 2020 did not vote in 2024. A YouGov poll commissioned by the Institute for Middle East Understanding Policy Project, released in January 2025, found that 29 percent of those Americans who voted for Biden in 2020 and didn't vote for Harris in 2024 cited "ending Israel's violence in Gaza" as their principal (though not the only) reason for withholding their vote. Even in the swing states fatally ceded to Trump, 20 percent of those nonvoters cited Gaza as their main reason for sitting out the election.

8

The Pentagon's Silicon Valley Problem

How Big Tech Is Losing the Wars of the Future

Three months before Hamas attacked Israel, Ronen Bar, the director of Shin Bet, Israel's internal security service, announced that his agency had developed its own generative artificial intelligence platform—similar to ChatGPT—and that the technology had been incorporated quite naturally into the agency's "interdiction machine," assisting in decision-making "like a partner at the table, a co-pilot." As the Israeli news site *Tech12* explained in a preview of his speech:

> The system knows everything about [the terrorist]: where he went, who his friends are, who his family is, what keeps him busy, what he said and what he published. Using artificial intelligence, the system analyzes behavior, predicts risks, raises alerts.

Nevertheless, Hamas's devastating attack on October 7 caught Shin Bet and the rest of Israel's multibillion-dollar defense system entirely by surprise. The intelligence disaster was even more striking considering that Hamas carried out much of its preparations in plain sight, including practice assaults on mock-ups of the border fence and Israeli settlements—activities that were openly reported. Hamas-led militant groups even posted videos of their training online. Israelis living close to the border observed and publicized these exercises with mounting alarm, but were ignored in favor of intelligence bureaucracies' analyses and, by extension, the software that had informed them. Israeli conscripts, mostly young women, monitoring developments through the ubiquitous surveillance cameras along the Gaza border, composed and presented a detailed report on Hamas's preparations to breach the fence and take hostages, only to have their findings dismissed as "an imaginary scenario." The Israeli intelligence apparatus had for more than a year been in possession of a Hamas document that detailed the group's plan for an attack.

Well aware of Israel's intelligence methods, Hamas members fed their enemy the data that they wanted to hear, using informants they knew would report to the Israelis. They signaled that the ruling group inside Gaza was concentrating on improving the local economy by gaining access to the Israeli job market, and that Hamas had been deterred from action by Israel's overwhelming military might. Such reports confirmed that Israel's intelligence system had rigid assumptions of Hamas behavior, overlaid with a racial arrogance that considered Palestinians incapable of such a large-scale operation. AI, it turned out, knew everything about the terrorist except what he was thinking.

Such misplaced confidence was evidently not confined to Israeli intelligence. The November/December issue of *Foreign Affairs* not only carried a risibly ill-timed boast by national security adviser Jake Sullivan that "we have de-escalated crises in Gaza," but also a paean to AI by Michèle Flournoy. Flournoy is a seasoned denizen of the military-industrial complex. The undersecretary of defense for policy under Barack Obama, she transitioned to, among other engagements, a lucrative founding leadership position with the defense consultancy WestExec Advisors. "Building bridges between Silicon Valley and the US government is really, really important," she told the *American Prospect* in 2020. Headlined AI IS ALREADY AT WAR, Flournoy's *Foreign Affairs* article invoked the intelligence analysts who made "better judgments" thanks to AI's help in analyzing information. "In the future, Americans can expect AI to change how the United States and its adversaries fight on the battlefield," she wrote. "In short, AI has sparked a security revolution—one that is just starting to unfold." This wondrous new technology, she asserted, would enable America not only to detect enemy threats, but also to maintain complex weapons systems and help estimate the cost of strategic decisions. Only a tortuous and hidebound Pentagon bureaucracy was holding it back.

Lamenting obstructive Pentagon bureaucrats is a trope of tech pitches, one that plays well in the media. TECH START-UPS TRY TO SELL A CAUTIOUS PENTAGON ON AI ran a headline in the *New York Times* last November over a glowing report on Shield AI, a money-losing drone company for which Flournoy has been an adviser. Along with a review of the company's drone, the story cites: "The many hurdles that the new generation of military contractors face as they compete for Pentagon funding against the far bigger and more entrenched weapons makers that have been supplying the military for decades."

But the notion that the Pentagon is resistant to new technologies is hardly fair—it reportedly funds at least 686 AI projects, including up to $9 billion for a Joint Warfighting Cloud Capability contract awarded in 2022 to a slew of major tech companies destined to, per one Pentagon official, "turbocharge" AI solutions. Another AI project, Gamechanger, is designed to enable Pentagon employees to discover what their giant department actually does, including where its money goes. A press release from the Joint Artificial Intelligence Center from early 2022 that celebrates Gamechanger's inauguration noted "28 Authoriative [*sic*] Sources" and quoted a senior Pentagon accountant's excitement about "applying Gamechanger to gain better visibility and understanding across our various budget exhibits." Even so, the Pentagon failed to pass a financial audit in 2023, for the sixth year in a row.

Artificial intelligence may indeed affect the way our military operates. But the notion that bright-eyed visionaries from the tech industry are revolutionizing our military machine promotes a myth that this relationship is not only new, but will fundamentally improve our defense system—one notorious for its insatiable appetite for money, poorly performing weapons, and lost wars. In reality, the change flows in the other direction, as new recruits enter the warm embrace of the imperishable military-industrial complex, eager to learn its ways.

ॐ

The belief that software can solve problems of human conflict has a long history in US war-making. Beginning in the late 1960s, the Air Force deployed a vast array of sensors across the jungles of Southeast Asia, marking the Ho Chi Minh trail along which North Vietnam supplied its forces in the south. Devised by scientists advising the Pentagon, the operation, code-named Igloo White and designed to detect human activity by the sounds of marching feet, the smell of ammonia from urine, or the electronic sparks of engine ignitions, relayed information to giant IBM computers housed in a secret base in Thailand. The machines were the most powerful then in existence; they processed the signals to pinpoint enemy supply columns otherwise invisible under the jungle canopy. The scheme, in operation from 1967 to 1972 at a cost of at least hundreds of millions a year, was a total failure. The Vietnamese swiftly devised means to counter it; just as Hamas would short-circuit Shin Bet algorithms by feeding the system false information, the Vietnamese also faked data, with buckets of urine hung in trees off the trail, or herds of livestock steered down unused byways, which were then dutifully processed by the humming computers as enemy movements. Meanwhile, North Vietnamese forces in the south were well supplied. In 1972, they launched a powerful offensive using hundreds of tanks that went entirely undetected by Igloo White. The operation was abandoned shortly thereafter.

The IBM System 360 computers at the center of Igloo White were a prominent icon of the industry we now call Silicon Valley. Born of the electronics industry that helped secure victory in World War II, this sector flourished under Pentagon patronage during the Cold War. The development of integrated circuits, key to modern computers and first produced by Texas Instruments in 1958, was powered by an avalanche of defense dollars, and initially deployed in the guidance system for the Minuteman II intercontinental nuclear missile. Beginning with personal calculators, the microchip revolution eventually found a commercial market severed from the umbilical cord of government contracts, generating an industrial culture, eventually both physically and spiritually centered south of San Francisco—far removed from the Pentagon parent that had spawned it.

As America's manufacturing economy gradually declined from the 1980s on, its Rust Belt heartland increasingly studded with decaying industrial cities, the digital economy grew at an exponential rate. Less than a month after its stock market debut in December 1980, Apple Computer was worth more than Ford. It was an industry happy to be independent of the irksome constraints of government contracting. Apple's Macintosh personal computer, the young company imagined, would free citizens from the Orwellian world of government control "by giving individuals the kind of computer power once reserved for corporations." But even though the original freewheeling iconoclasts of the tech industry saw themselves as "cowboys," "rebels," and "revolutionaries," in the words of historian Margaret O'Mara, the divorce from defense was never absolute. The internet, hailed as a liberating technology, grew out of ARPANET, which had been developed by the Pentagon's Advanced Research Projects Agency. According to Yasha Levine in *Surveillance Valley*, the proto-internet was deployed almost immediately to collect information on the antiwar movement. Google founders Larry Page and Sergey Brin's early work at Stanford was funded in part by the same Pentagon agency, which by now had added "Defense" to its name to become DARPA. And Google Earth started as Keyhole EarthViewer, a mapping system partly funded by the CIA's venture capital offshoot In-Q-Tel, which was eventually acquired by Google.

Meanwhile, the Pentagon never lost sight of the unfulfilled dream of Igloo White: that computing power could make it possible to control the battlefield. Following the American retreat from Vietnam, vast sums were poured into Assault Breaker, in which powerful airborne radar would peer deep behind Soviet lines in Eastern Europe. It, too, abjectly failed its tests—the system could not distinguish tanks from cars, or from trees blowing in the wind—and the project was canceled the following decade. Yet military optimism was undimmed; senior commanders broadcast the notion of "netcentric warfare," and their aspirations found fruit in such projects as the Future Combat Systems program, which linked sensors and weapons via high-powered processors to strike targets so effortlessly, or so its proponents claimed, that it would no longer be necessary to install defensive armor on tanks. But after consuming almost $20 billion of taxpayer dollars, it came to nothing. Same with the Department of Homeland Security's Secure Border Initiative Network, marketed as a "virtual fence" equipped with computer-linked radar, cameras, and other surveillance sensors to detect intruders, which was canceled in 2011. Boeing had been a prime contractor on both of these baroque endeavors, a sclerotic contrast to the fast-paced dynamism of Silicon Valley. Surely the flourishing entrepreneurial culture of the West Coast could succeed where the old guard had failed.

Peter Thiel certainly thought so. A former securities lawyer, he had garnered his initial fortune as a co-founder of PayPal and grew vastly richer due to an early investment in Facebook. A professedly conservative libertarian contemptuous of "hippies" who had "[taken] over the country," he was determined, in the words of his biographer Max Chafkin, "to bring the military-industrial complex back to Silicon Valley, with his own companies at its very center." Founded in 2003 and based on technology developed for fraud detection at PayPal, Thiel's software company Palantir used data to detect and communicate patterns in simple visual displays. Despite proclaiming that "it's essential to preserve fundamental principles of privacy and civil liberties while using data," the CIA, via In-Q-Tel, was an early investor, and many of Palantir's initial contracts came from the intelligence community. As proof of its worth to such customers, it was claimed that Palantir had a major role in detecting not only the Chinese espionage network GhostNet in 2009, but the secret lair of Osama bin Laden in 2011. There is no evidence that these boasts were justified, but the claims entranced the media and attracted corporate customers. In the face of high-level military reluctance, Palantir marketed the wonders of its technology to mid-level Army officers and engaged cooperative lawmakers in Congress to lobby on its behalf.

Proponents of the Silicon Valley approach found friendly reception elsewhere in the upper tiers of the Pentagon—especially among acolytes of Andrew Marshall, the venerated former director of the Office of Net Assessment, an internal Pentagon think-tank. One of them, embedded in Washington's defense archipelago, was a former Marine named Robert O. Work. Appointed under Obama as undersecretary of the navy in 2009 and rapidly promoted, Work was an ardent advocate of the notion that the United States was losing its technological lead, previously assured by its superiority in nuclear weapons, and then by its precision-guided weapons. Now the Chinese and Russians, he warned darkly, had caught up, endangering America's military dominance. This threat, he believed, was rendered more urgent by caps on defense spending promised in the Budget Control Act of 2011. The danger could only be warded off by adopting, among other things, aerial and naval unmanned systems and AI-enabled battle networks. These were to be found in Silicon Valley.

In 2014, Secretary of Defense Chuck Hagel unveiled the Defense Innovation Initiative, overseen by Work, which, Hagel said, would "actively seek proposals ... from those firms and academic institutions outside DoD's traditional orbit." Hagel's successor, Ash Carter, made repeated pilgrimages to tech enclaves, shedding his tie and delivering boosterish homilies on the rewards of the collaboration. "They're inventing new technology, creating prosperity, connectivity, and freedom," he told a reporter following an early visit. "They feel they too are public servants, and they'd like to have somebody in Washington they can connect to." In 2015, Carter launched the Defense Innovation Unit Experimental ("Experimental" would later be dropped), with an office in Mountain View, near the headquarters of Google and Apple. The Department of Homeland Security had the same idea, setting up a satellite office nearby to "cultivate relationships with Silicon Valley technology companies, particularly non-traditional performers to help them understand DHS's challenges." In 2016, Carter gave the budding relationship potent bureaucratic heft, convening a Defense Innovation Advisory Board populated with heavyweights from the tech and military worlds tasked with making recommendations directly to the secretary of defense. Heading the board was Eric Schmidt, former executive chairman and CEO of Google. Schmidt's role soon grew larger, to head of the National Security Commission on Artificial Intelligence, with Work as his deputy. They were charged with advancing "the development of artificial intelligence, machine learning, and associated technologies to comprehensively address the national security and defense needs of the United States."

Among the aims of Work's AI initiative was a means to distill the vast amounts of information sucked up by satellites, phone intercepts, emails, and drones sitting in intelligence and military data banks into something accessible. In 2017, Google secured a contract for Project Maven, instituted by Work, aimed at accelerating "DoD's integration of big data and machine learning." Project Maven's initial goal was to develop processing tools for the unceasing torrent of drone footage in order to identify targets. The contract, according to internal emails leaked to *Gizmodo*, specified that Google's involvement was not to be revealed without the company's permission. "Avoid at ALL COSTS any mention or implication of AI," Fei-Fei Li, chief scientist for AI at Google Cloud, emailed colleagues. "Weaponized AI is probably one of the most sensitized topics of AI—if not THE most. This is red meat to the media to find all ways to damage Google." She was right. When news broke of the contract, uproar ensued. "Don't be evil" had once been Google's motto, but by the time of Project Maven it had been replaced by a more herbivorous pledge to "Do the right thing." Nevertheless, many of the company's more than 80,000 workers were shocked that Google was involved in the military's lethal drone assassination program. Around 4,000 of them signed a petition demanding "a clear policy stating that neither Google nor its contractors will ever build warfare technology." A handful resigned.

Amid the furor, no one appears to have noticed that Project Maven fit into the grand tradition of many other high-tech weapons projects: ecstatic claims of prowess coupled with a disregard for real-world experience. The "full motion video" to be processed through Google's technology was to be provided by Gorgon Stare, a system of pods arrayed with cameras mounted on Reaper drones. "We can see everything," the *Washington Post* had announced breathlessly in a report on the system's alleged capabilities back when it was first unveiled. But, as the Air Force discovered, that was not true. A testing unit at Eglin Air Force Base revealed in a 2011 report that, among numerous other deficiencies, the cameras could not "readily find and identify targets," and its transmission rate was too slow. The testers concluded that it was "not operationally effective" and should not be deployed in Afghanistan; the Air Force sent it anyway. "A lot of money has gone into it, and I'm telling you right now the fielded stuff still can't do it," a former fighter pilot and longtime Pentagon analyst familiar with the ongoing program informed me in 2023. After years of expensive effort, the "ATR [automatic target recognition] just doesn't work. Even driverless cars," he emphasized "are relatively easy problems to solve compared to ATR." Another combat veteran, now with a Pentagon agency working on these issues, told me that the AI developers he works with didn't seem to understand some of the requirements for the technology's military application. "I don't know if AI, or the sensors that feed it for that matter, will ever be capable of spontaneity or recognizing spontaneity," he said. He cited a DARPA experiment in which a squad of Marines defeated an AI-governed robot that had been trained to detect them simply by altering their physical profiles. Two walked inside a large cardboard box. Others somersaulted. One wore the branches of a fir tree. All were able to approach over open ground and touch the robot without detection.

Despite the moral objections of Google employees, Project Maven did not die. Following the company's withdrawal, subcontracts were picked up by Microsoft, Amazon, and Palantir, among others. There was no public announcement, but the new deals were unearthed by a Google employee who had quit in revulsion. Jack Poulson, a former Stanford professor who specializes in advanced supercomputers, had left academic life in 2016 "to go where the actual experts were, which clearly was Google at the time," as he put it to me. Once installed as a senior research scientist, he found that he disliked the corporate culture, despite the informality of the office, where some of his colleagues worked barefoot. It was their "sense of righteousness" that grated him. "Google culture was defined by an exceptionalism that they are the uniquely ethical company," he told me, but he found they were prepared to "look the other way" when the company did "terrible things." Poulson's final decision to quit was spurred by the information that, while eagerly pursuing Pentagon business, Google was simultaneously working with the Chinese government to build Dragonfly, a version of its search engine that would blacklist certain search terms, such as "human rights" and "student protest."

The following year, Poulson was invited to a meeting at a well-known conservative think-tank, alongside tech CEOs, high-ranking military officers, and intelligence officials. They were intrigued, he remembers, by what they regarded as Poulson's eccentric attitude toward defense work. One and all, they were eager to promote tech involvement in defense. "It was very shocking to me, the degree to which very senior US military officials were desperate to work in the tech industry," he recalls. "At one point, a high-ranking general was saying that one of the goals was to have at least a hundred flag officers in executive positions by the end of the next year."

Conscious that few outside, or even inside, the business understood the extent of tech's role in the military-industrial complex, Poulson, along with other dissidents, launched a website called Tech Inquiry. "There was so little coverage," Poulson told me. "I started looking into some of these organizations and the contracts with the Defense Innovation Unit—it just seemed like such a zoo of companies." Many of the details were obscure, buried in contracts accessible only through the relentless pursuit of Freedom of Information requests.

Google's retreat on the Maven contract sparked outrage in the burgeoning defense-tech complex. Thiel called Google's stance "treasonous," while Schmidt said he "disagreed" with the decision. *The Atlantic* ran a story headlined THE DIVIDE BETWEEN SILICON VALLEY AND WASHINGTON IS A NATIONAL SECURITY THREAT. Amazon overlord Jeff Bezos, during a live event with *Wired*, huffed that "if big tech companies are going to turn their back on the US Department of Defense, this country is going to be in trouble."

Bezos had a personal interest in the issue. Amazon had accelerated tech's intrusion into the defense complex back in 2013, winning a $600 million ten-year contract from the CIA for use of the Amazon Web Services cloud originally built to host commercial–customer transactions. Cloud computing was becoming the new profit frontier for corporations such as Amazon, Microsoft, Oracle, and Google, which had sloughed off the moral qualms of the Maven episode to bid for a slice of the $9 billion Joint Warfighting Cloud Capability contract. Though they still reaped vast profits from commercial services, corporate eyes were turning to the government as a stable source of bountiful revenue. If indeed there ever had been a tech–Pentagon divide, it was disappearing fast.

Much has been made of the impact of drones on the war in Ukraine, the implications being that they represent a revolutionary advance in weapons technology. But the most common and effective drones used by both sides have been simple, cheap devices whose parts are available to any consumer with an Amazon account, and jerry-rigged to carry small bombs or shells. They resemble the homemade IEDs deployed with deadly effect by insurgents in Iraq or Afghanistan more than high-tech DARPA products.

Nevertheless, the tech industry has been eager to show that it can do better. This past December, Anduril, another tech enterprise financially godfathered by Thiel to pursue the national security market, announced that it had developed Roadrunner, a small jet-powered drone purportedly capable of autonomous detection and destruction of jet-powered threats, including drones, before returning to its base, costing "in the low hundreds of thousands," according to *Newsweek*. The announcement included a slick video of a Roadrunner flawlessly completing a test. As is customary, the media applauded "America's latest game-changing weapon." Veteran Pentagon analyst Franklin "Chuck" Spinney had a less starry-eyed reaction. "Marketing drivel," he told me, expressing curiosity about how the drone was depicted landing tail-first in the desert with its exhausts hardly kicking up a plume of dust. (Anduril has not given any explanation for the apparent discrepancy.) Meanwhile, the Pentagon insider who alerted me to the cardboard box maneuver, and who has had the opportunity to review Anduril's products, described them as "the F-35 of that world ... complicated to operate and too pricey." Undeterred, the

Special Operations Command awarded Anduril a billion-dollar contract for a counter-drone system in January 2022.

Anduril, named, like Palantir, in a whimsical reference to *The Lord of the Rings*, is the brainchild of Palmer Luckey. As a teenager, Luckey developed Oculus, a virtual-reality headset company that he sold to Facebook for $3 billion. He then focused on defense work, lamenting that people with the relevant tech skills to build the weapons of the future were "largely refusing to work with the defense sector." After selling a border-surveillance system, Luckey turned his attention to drones and other weapons systems, all while harboring more ambitious visions for the future of warfare. Speaking to a sympathetic CNN interviewer in 2018, he revealed that Anduril was working on an "AI-powered sensor fusion platform" to "build a perfect 3D model of everything that's going on in a large area." Soldiers in the future, he predicted confidently, would be "superheroes" with "the power of perfect omniscience over their area of operations, where they know where every single enemy is, where every friend is, where every asset is."

However fanciful the idea might seem, Army leadership was sufficiently seduced by the prospect of perfectly omniscient soldiers to award Microsoft a $21.9 billion deal in 2021 for an Integrated Visual Augmentation System (IVAS) based on the HoloLens headset. Unfortunately, a report from the Pentagon's director of operational test and evaluation released in 2023 revealed that the majority of soldiers testing the system "reported at least one symptom of physical impairment to include disorientation, dizziness, eyestrain, headaches, motion sickness and nausea, neck strain and tunnel vision." They also complained of the system's "poor low-light performance, display quality, cumbersomeness, poor reliability, inability to distinguish friend from foe, difficulty shooting, physical impairments and limited peripheral vision." Congress withheld most of the procurement funding, but the Army promptly handed Microsoft another $125 million to tweak the system, with the price tag climbing to just under $23 billion. (The Army claims that "soldier feedback was positive" in its in-house tests on the tweaked system.)

The rewards of IVAS, at an estimated $60,000 per soldier, are no doubt welcome to Microsoft, given that the market for the HoloLens has been faring badly, but the giant corporation has a far more glittering prize in sight since the ecstatic reaction to OpenAI's unveiling of ChatGPT. Not everyone has been impressed. Commenting on the alleged threat of superintelligent machines, Meta's chief AI scientist Yann LeCun suggested that such alarms were "very premature until we have a design for a system that can even rival a cat in terms of learning capabilities, which we don't have at the moment." Nate Koppikar, who has made hundreds of millions of dollars betting against tech as co-founder of the investment firm Orso Partners, is another skeptic. "What's been going on in tech since 2016 has just been, for lack of a better term, a bunch of bullshit," he told me. He pointed out that the sector has been losing money and cutting staff following a bubble that finally burst in late 2021, losing industry investors roughly $7.4 trillion. "And then all of a sudden we're sold this promise of AI as the next big thing." He believes that the fears over evil AI robots "like Arnold Schwarzenegger's Terminator" are part of a marketing campaign to convince us of the awesome power of the technology which, as he pointed out, suffers from inherent defects, including a propensity to make things up, a seemingly intractable tendency known in the industry as "hallucinations." He pointed to Palantir, which, he said, had been losing money prior to going public in late 2020. (The stock went from a high of $45 in January 2021 to just under $8 two years later.) "So they've completely flipped the script," he said. "This year they turned themselves into an AI company."

I was curious about Palantir, whose stock indeed soared amid the 2023 AI frenzy. I had been told that the Israeli security sector's AI systems might rely on Palantir's technology. Furthermore, Shin Bet's humiliating failure to predict the Hamas assault had not blunted the Israeli Defense Force's appetite for the technology; the unceasing rain of bombs on densely packed Gaza neighborhoods, according to a well-sourced report by Israeli reporter Yuval Abraham in +972 *Magazine*, was in fact partly controlled by an AI target-creation platform called The Gospel. The Gospel produces automatic recommendations for strike targets based on what the technology identifies as being connected with Hamas, such as the private home of a suspected rank-and-file member of the organization. It also calculates how many civilians, including women and children, would die in the process—which, as of this writing, amounted to at least 22,000 people, some 70 percent of them women and children. One of Abraham's intelligence sources termed the technology a "mass assassination factory." Despite the high-tech gloss on the massacre, the result has been no different than the slaughter inflicted, with comparatively more primitive means, against Dresden and Tokyo during World War II.

To determine whether Palantir, which CEO Alex Karp has proudly proclaimed "stands with Israel," was playing a role in the mass killing, I contacted the company, but received no response. So I turned to AI. I first asked OpenAI's ChatGPT, which told me that it had no information because its training had ended in January 2022. I then asked Google's AI platform, Bard, which confirmed that there was indeed such an arrangement. "In 2019, Palantir announced a new partnership with the IDF to develop AI-powered tools for the IDF," it replied. "These tools are designed to help the IDF to identify and track potential threats, and to make better decisions about how to allocate resources." When I asked for the original announcement, it sent me a professional-looking press release, complete with supportive quotes from Karp and the IDF's chief of staff—exactly the information I sought. But there was a problem: it was a hallucination. (It was mistaken about the IDF chief of staff.) No such press release had ever been issued.

Harper's Magazine, March 2024

Postscript. The press release was a hallucination, but Palantir has certainly been a close collaborator in Israel's operations in Gaza. It was not alone. In January 2025, +972 reported that "dozens of units in the Israeli army have purchased services from Microsoft's cloud computing platform, Azure, in recent months—including units in the air, ground, and naval forces, as well as the elite intelligence squad, Unit 8200. Microsoft has also provided the military with extensive access to OpenAI's

GPT-4 language model, the engine behind ChatGPT, thanks to the close partnership between the two companies." Meanwhile in December 2024, it was reported that tech companies including Palantir, Anduril, SpaceX, and OpenAI were planning to form a consortium to bid on Pentagon contracts.

9

"Defensive Not Aggressive"

The Cuban Missile Crisis

In the vast and growing body of literature on the Cuban Missile Crisis of 1962, when the installation of Soviet warheads on the island elicited fears of nuclear war, there is barely a mention of the influence that US domestic politics may have had on the course of events. Theodore Voorhees's study, *Silent Guns of Two Octobers: Kennedy and Khrushchev Play the Double Game*, is different. He highlights the all-important fact that in October 1962 John F. Kennedy was about to face congressional midterm elections. The results would determine the fate of his presidency, as well as his prospects for re-election in 1964. Kennedy's New Frontier domestic agenda—which promised a huge house-building program, an increase in the minimum wage, affirmative action for federal jobs and equal employment rights for women—was hopelessly stalled in Congress. His poll numbers were sinking. It didn't help that in 1960 he had run on a militantly hawkish platform, and since taking office had lavished money on the military on the spurious premise that Eisenhower had allowed the Soviets to gain superiority, the infamous "missile gap." So he was especially vulnerable to Republican charges of weakness over the supposed danger of Cuba, a Soviet ally just ninety miles from Florida.

Kennedy was perfectly aware that nuclear missiles in Cuba posed no real threat to national security, even if they slightly narrowed America's enormous lead in weapons capable of reaching the other's homeland. The chairman of the Joint Chiefs of Staff had told him that a US nuclear attack would obliterate Soviet society but the inevitable retaliation might still kill as many as 15 million Americans. War with the USSR was therefore out of the question. "What difference does it make?" Kennedy said on October 16, 1962, the day he was presented with photographic evidence of the Cuban rockets. "They've got enough to blow us up anyway." But the presence of an enemy nuclear base in America's backyard nonetheless threatened him with political disaster. He dealt with the problem by making a deal with Khrushchev, behind the backs of most of his senior advisers, to withdraw US missiles from Turkey in return for a similar Soviet withdrawal from Cuba. The deal remained buried in secrecy long after Kennedy was dead.

For years, the accepted history of the crisis held that the young president faced down the Soviets' reckless gamble with calm and unyielding resolve. As Secretary of State Dean Rusk, who knew better, summarized it: "The other guy blinked." This version stood unchallenged not least because it was sanctioned by Kennedy himself in mendacious leaks to favored journalists and then set in stone in his younger brother's dramatic narrative, *Thirteen Days*. Bobby Kennedy's posthumously published account, which made much of his own role as a voice of reason, was buttressed by hagiographers of the Kennedy court, notably Arthur Schlesinger, the president's special aide, and Ted Sorensen, his main speechwriter. Graham Allison's 1972 study of the affair, *Essence of Decision*, largely sourced from those accounts, attained the status of holy writ in international relations courses, raising a generation of political scientists on the "bureaucratic model" of foreign policy decision-making.

Unfortunately for these confident narratives, Kennedy had secretly installed a taping system in various White House offices and covertly recorded the meetings of the National Security Council's executive committee throughout the crisis. With the probable exception of Bobby Kennedy, then attorney general, none of the members, including the secretaries of state and defense, knew they were being recorded. Fully declassified, accurately transcribed and finally released in the late 1990s, this indisputable record revealed that all previous insider accounts were both wrong and self-serving. Far from being the voice of reason, Bobby Kennedy had been belligerent to an almost hysterical degree, urging not only attacks on the offending missile sites but a full-scale invasion of Cuba—even though, as his own diaries show, he knew that the crisis was already on the way to being resolved through accommodation with the Soviets. Sorensen chose to suppress the story of the missile swap, as he later confessed, when he edited *Thirteen Days* following Bobby Kennedy's assassination in 1968, lest it expose the lies of so many of the participants, including Sorensen himself.

In reality, Kennedy was making the key decisions well away from the recorded meetings and communicating directly with Moscow outside the official US diplomatic apparatus. Had he been less ignorant of history, Donald Trump, harassed for much of his term by Democratic accusations of collusion with Vladimir Putin, might have made hay with the fact that Kennedy had been on close enough terms with a Soviet intelligence agent to employ him as a secret go-between. Georgi Bolshakov was a colonel in Soviet military intelligence working in Washington under cover as a journalist. Friendly enough with Bobby Kennedy to spend time at his home outside Washington playing with his children, Bolshakov was an emissary in discussions between the leaders on the ways in which Khrushchev might adjust Soviet policy to help Kennedy in the November elections. At the end of July 1962, with his poll numbers worsening, Kennedy met Bolshakov in the Oval Office and agreed to Khrushchev's offer to relax tensions over the Cold War flashpoint of West Berlin. In exchange, Kennedy pledged to end aerial reconnaissance of Soviet ships en route to Cuba, ships which were almost certainly carrying military supplies.

The proposed deal shows how understanding the leaders of opposing superpowers can be when it comes to each other's political priorities. Voorhees cites an instructive precedent from World War II. At a meeting in Tehran in 1943, Roosevelt openly appealed to Stalin to allow the people of Poland, soon to fall under Soviet control, to decide their own future. This moralistic appeal cut no ice with Stalin. But then Roosevelt came clean, explaining in private that in his campaign for re-election the following year he "did not want to lose the vote" of the millions of

Americans of Polish extraction. Stalin sympathized and agreed to keep his plans for Poland under wraps for the time being. Historians have tended to mention this exchange only in passing, despite the confirmation it provides that issues of foreign policy when divorced from domestic power had little relevance for such supremely professional politicians.

This kind of realpolitik requires a high level of trust. Here again, the relationship with Bolshakov is telling. According to Aleksei Adzhubei, Khrushchev's son-in-law and adviser, Kennedy ejected his press secretary and the official state department interpreter from a meeting in the Oval Office in January 1962, relying on Bolshakov to translate. While the Americans were still in the room the president was speaking "with a completely different tongue" and was "visibly more tense." Kennedy was conscious that everyone in Washington, inside and outside his administration, had their own agendas, including officials he had personally selected. As US reconnaissance detected signs of the accelerating Soviet military build-up in Cuba, Kennedy ordered that the intelligence be ever more tightly restricted, blaming "those CIA bastards" for leaks to his Republican enemies: "I'm going to get them if it's the last thing I ever do."

Kennedy believed that the Soviet presence in Cuba was a manageable political problem, because Khrushchev's emissaries had assured him that the armament was purely defensive. "Defensive" is of course a subjective term: when Khrushchev had earlier complained about American nuclear bases close to the USSR's borders, he too was told they were "defensive, not aggressive." The ominous political implications of the reconnaissance photographs of Cuba appear to have caused Kennedy briefly to consider a direct attack on the missile sites. But the mood soon passed. Within a few days he settled on the more pacific course of a naval blockade to stop further Soviet military supplies reaching Cuba—the minimum action he could get away with politically. The following day Bobby, via Bolshakov, suggested the idea of the missile exchange to the Soviet government.

Kennedy didn't lose sight of his own political priorities, as demonstrated by campaign trips to support his party's candidates in the mid-terms even as the situation grew more intense.

Orthodox historians of the crisis tend to describe such excursions as the president "keeping up appearances" in order not to excite public alarm. But this misses the point: for Kennedy, the crisis was entirely about politics. His targeted states included Indiana, where a Republican senator, Homer Capehart, had based his re-election campaign on the demand to "crack down on Cuba." Kennedy denounced Capehart and his allies as "self-appointed generals and admirals who want to send someone else's sons to war." He must have been encouraged by polls indicating that, by a slim margin, Americans believed that an attack on Cuba would lead to World War III.

Like Kennedy, Khrushchev sought to exit the crisis as quickly and peacefully as possible. He had apparently assumed that Kennedy would accept the presence of the "defensive" missiles, which he planned to unveil after the US elections, as a fait accompli, just as he himself had accepted the American missiles on the borders of the USSR. But when the president went public about his discovery of the missiles and his retaliatory blockade, Khrushchev knew he had badly miscalculated. He moved to cut his losses with an offer, conveyed through yet another unofficial go-between, to withdraw his missiles in return for a US pledge not to invade Cuba. Both leaders were equally anxious to make the crisis go away and each mooted more generous concessions than the other side was demanding.

Kennedy had prior experience in privately negotiating his way out of a crisis with Khrushchev. In October 1961 Khrushchev had threatened to upset the postwar agreements on Berlin, which was divided between Western and Soviet control. Pentagon officials responded with plans for military confrontation, up to and including a "limited" nuclear strike, but started by deploying tanks at the East–West crossing point in the city. They were quickly matched by Soviet tanks a short distance away on the other side. Kennedy issued the requisite trenchant public statements and authorized the Pentagon to publicize America's enormous numerical superiority in nuclear armaments. Meanwhile he deployed his brother to send a message to Khrushchev via the dependable Bolshakov offering to satisfy the Soviets' most basic demand—that US civilian officials not travel into

East Berlin—so long as the Russian tanks retreated first. Events proceeded as suggested and the tanks moved away, a denouement still usually characterized as "Khrushchev backed down." As Voorhees puts it, "The president needed to come out looking like the winner," whatever the reality.

A year on, Kennedy sought a similar outcome, but this time faced more formidable political obstacles. Left to himself, as he admits in a private conversation with his brother recorded on the secret tapes, he would have preferred to take no action over the missiles beyond diplomatic protests. But that was politically impossible—"They would have moved to impeach me"—so he ordered the blockade. In the same conversation the brothers made elliptical reference to the covert communication launched that day with Bolshakov about the proposed missile swap. Security officials had refused to take the idea seriously and were instead formulating increasingly aggressive plans. On October 19, the military service chiefs confronted Kennedy with demands for an immediate attack on Cuba by land, sea, and air.

The most hawkish among them, Air Force Chief of Staff Curtis LeMay, who had made his name incinerating hundreds of thousands of Japanese civilians during the war, openly taunted Kennedy with a reference to his father's record of appeasement at the time of the Munich Agreement. The Pentagon's eagerness for war was echoed by Democratic congressional leaders, including the chairman of the Senate Armed Services Committee and leader of the Southern segregationist bloc, Richard Russell, to whom Vice President Lyndon Johnson was leaking news from National Security Council meetings. The defense secretary, Robert McNamara, who had initially advocated a moderate course, soon swung in line behind his uniformed colleagues, and gave the moronic authorization for a nuclear-armed Soviet submarine to be bombarded with "practice" depth charges.

But Kennedy stayed the course. While continuing publicly to endorse a massive military build-up he was secretly finalizing the missile swap agreement. Khrushchev accepted his promise of US missile withdrawal from Turkey. Kennedy went further, too, withdrawing missiles from Italy, even though this was something the Soviets had never asked for. Khrushchev agreed to abide by

Kennedy's demand, vitally important to him politically, that the missile exchange would remain secret and never committed to writing. Kennedy was duly rewarded in the elections the following month, the Democrats adding four seats to their Senate majority, including the one formerly held by Homer Capehart.

Voorhees argues convincingly that there was never any real danger of war, since Kennedy and Khrushchev were equally determined to avoid one, and both were so dominant domestically that they could ensure it didn't happen. This conclusion is unlikely to disturb the consensus among historians that the world was on the brink of nuclear war. Serhii Plokhy certainly subscribes to the view that Armageddon was avoided by the narrowest of flukes. In *Nuclear Folly: A New History of the Cuban Missile Crisis*, he describes the dangerous delegation of launch authority for tactical nuclear weapons to Soviet commanders in the field. In hair-raising fashion he also embellishes the familiar story of how a Soviet submarine came close to launching a 10-kiloton nuclear torpedo at an American destroyer, desisting only because an officer happened to notice a placatory signal from the US ship. More seriously, he seems to believe that Kennedy was set on military action for much of the time, a conclusion clearly belied by the record. He also suggests that McNamara was a voice of sage and moderate counsel throughout. But a more accurate account is provided by Sheldon Stern, a former historian at the Kennedy Library who knows the tapes better than anyone. His wicked little book from 2012, *The Cuban Missile Crisis in American Memory*, pitilessly tracks the defense secretary's emotional lurches between moderation and belligerence.

Plokhy does recount many novel and arresting details of what it was actually like for the unfortunate Soviet soldiers and sailors charged with getting themselves and their deadly armory into position in Cuba. Their success in maneuvering 60-foot missiles down farm tracks and village lanes was a triumph in itself, not to mention the surreptitious transport into Cuba of more than 40,000 troops, sweltering below decks in overcrowded ships, without detection by the CIA, who believed that only a fraction of that number were in place. But Plokhy has little to say about the underlying politics of the affair. Indifference to domestic context among foreign affairs commentators is especially common when authoritarian regimes are concerned. Yet diligent inquiry suggests that foreign policy is just as much an instrument of domestic politics when the whims of an electorate aren't a leader's concern. As Richard Anderson, a former CIA officer who works on Soviet and post-Soviet politics at UCLA, once said to me: "To exercise power, you have to have supporters, whether they vote or not. Foreign policy is a way of buying support."

There are some clues as to why Khrushchev felt his huge and expensive Cuban military initiative was necessary for his own survival. He had sought to assuage the disquiet of the Soviet military over cuts in army numbers by promising to develop a new intercontinental nuclear missile force, production of which was entrusted to his favored supporter, Leonid Brezhnev. But Brezhnev failed to deliver. Only a very few of the huge new rockets—rife with technical problems—were built and deployed. Brezhnev was duly removed from his position as head of the Soviet defense apparatus in May 1960 and assigned a ceremonial post. Khrushchev's Cuban gambit to adjust the nuclear balance, however marginally, with a few medium-range missiles capable of striking the American homeland therefore made sense in terms of reasserting control over the powerful defense sector. "Politics stops at the water's edge," Senator Arthur Vandenberg said when urging bipartisan support for the creation of NATO, as if when it came to foreign policy domestic concerns were beside the point. But they're exactly the point.

London Review of Books, September 9, 2021

10

Why Didn't You Tell Me?

Long before Bush and Blair invaded Iraq, Iraqis suspected that foreign intelligence services were manipulating their country's domestic affairs. Since the 1920s—when Gertrude Bell maneuvered behind the scenes in the early days of the Iraqi state under the British mandate—otherwise inexplicable events were often attributed to the workings of "Abu Naji," a quasi-mythical figure used as shorthand to refer to the meddling British, and later the Americans. As Steve Coll makes clear in *The Achilles Trap: Saddam Hussein, the United States and the Middle East, 1979–2003*, Saddam Hussein was even more suspicious than most. Reviewing Saddam's diligently recorded private discussions with intimates, Coll notes that he "regularly steered the conversation around to the subject of conspiracies," crediting both the British intelligence services and the CIA with a clear understanding of Iraq's internal affairs. In Coll's view, the credit was undeserved. The Americans continually misread Saddam, notably failing to anticipate his invasion of Kuwait in August 1990 or to notice his secret disposal of his entire stock of weapons of mass destruction the following year—failures that ultimately contributed to the disaster of the invasion and occupation.

Coll's book is replete with arresting details about Saddam's years as dictator of Iraq. From 1979, when he assumed the presidency, his authority rested primarily on the brutal repression of minorities such as the Kurds, combined with the generous disbursement of the country's oil wealth to the rest of his subjects (before the 1991 Gulf War, the major problem facing Iraqi pediatricians was childhood obesity). Coll's trawling of the documentary archive reveals much about Saddam's dealings with his lethally fractious family. His eldest son, Uday, was a particular thorn in his side: in 1988 Uday beat his father's valet to death; seven years later he shot and severely wounded his uncle Watban.

Saddam was, according to his cousin Ali Hassan al-Majid, "so cruel you could not imagine." Given that al-Majid—aka Chemical Ali—was himself a mass murderer, this was saying something. Yet Coll also shows that Saddam was more than just a tyrannical thug. He could be self-deprecatingly humorous, and was deeply read in Arab and foreign literature (Hemingway was a favorite). Once, catching a TV presenter in a grammatical error, he phoned the minister of culture to complain, decreeing a six-month suspension for the offender. His own literary efforts occupied an inordinate amount of his time—*The Complete Writings of Saddam Hussein* (2001) filled eighteen volumes. As his regime came under growing pressure in the 1990s, he increasingly immersed himself in fiction, writing four allegorical novels of enormous length, typically about a humble ruler beset by hostile powers. Even as US tanks approached Baghdad in April 2003, he was overseeing the publication, with a 40,000 copy print run, of his last novel, *Get Out, Damned One!*, whose plot hinged on fearless resistance to foreign occupation. His first novel, *Zabiba and the King*, gave a telling clue to his approach to government: at one point, the heroine urges an Iraqi leader "to arrest all" who had known about an assassination plot, "as well as all those who *may* have taken part." A semi-autobiographical work, *Men and the City*, evoked the grim world of his rural upbringing in Tikrit, calling it "worse than the life of dogs."

Still, he made it to high school and then law school in Baghdad, before being recruited at the age of twenty as an assassin in the service of the Baath Party, which espoused a secular ideology of woolly socialism combined with fierce Arab nationalism. In 1963, when Saddam was twenty-five, the party overthrew the leftist regime of Abdul-Karim Qasim. The coup doubtless confirmed his sensitivity to foreign-influenced conspiracies. Coll leaves an open verdict on the widely rumored role of the CIA in removing Qasim, who had governed with the backing of the then powerful Iraqi Communist Party, since the agency's documents on the episode are still classified. However, Jim Critchfield, head of the CIA's Near East Division in 1963, told me late in life that "we had every t crossed and every i dotted on that one. We regarded it as our best coup." After a rocky start, the Baath Party consolidated power, and Saddam rose rapidly through its ranks, displacing his cousin, Ahmed Hassan al-Bakr, as president in 1979. He immediately cemented his control with a bloody purge of Baathists deemed insufficiently loyal to his rule.

The following year, Saddam attacked Iran, sparking an eight-year war that killed at least half a million people. Ayatollah Khomeini's recently installed theocratic government had inspired similarly militant aspirations in Iraq's own Shi'ite religious hierarchy, clearly a threat to Saddam. He seemed to believe that Tehran's forces, distracted by revolutionary chaos, would offer no serious resistance. But after initial setbacks the Iranians rallied and by 1982 were putting the Iraqi military under severe pressure. This generated serious concern in Washington, where the ayatollah's regime was then, as now, considered the ultimate bête noire.

As Coll chronicles, the US, while professing neutrality in the war, began supplying Saddam with vital intelligence, especially satellite maps, through CIA and Defense Intelligence Agency officials posted to Baghdad. Coll is silent on the US's role in fomenting this horrifyingly bloody conflict. The war turned out to have momentous consequences for Iraq, even leaving aside the mass slaughter: it effectively bankrupted the state, impelling Saddam to invade Kuwait in the hope of restoring his battered finances, thus setting off a chain of events that in the end destroyed not only his regime but Iraqi society itself.

It is therefore of interest whether Saddam received any endorsement from Washington before launching the war on Iran. There have long been rumors of American encouragement, but the absence of hard evidence has led at least one academic researcher, Hal Brands, to conclude that "the green light thesis has more basis in myth than in reality." Chas Freeman, a distinguished US diplomat, recently provided me with a clue as to what might really have happened. In January 1981, as the Carter administration was preparing to leave office, Freeman, who was at the time director for Chinese affairs at the State Department, was tasked with reviewing National Security Council files relating to China. Among the papers, he remembers coming across a "memcon" summarizing a meeting in late June 1980—three months before the war began—between Carter's national security adviser, Zbigniew Brzezinski, and a senior Iraqi diplomat. In the meeting Brzezinski clearly stated that America would be content with an Iraqi attack on Iran—a green light if ever there was one. Such a document would normally have been filed with papers relating to Middle Eastern affairs, but it had been misfiled with the China material (perhaps deliberately, Freeman suggested to me), and he handed the memcon over to a White House official. It was never seen again. "Probably shredded," Freeman said.

So anxious was Washington to assist Saddam in the war the US had encouraged that CIA emissaries posted to Iraq were authorized to deliver invaluable intelligence material without asking for any favors in return. High-level visitors from the US included Donald Rumsfeld, appointed special envoy to the Middle East in 1983. Rumsfeld's visits to the region were not generally popular (the US ambassador in Damascus would invariably leave town whenever Rumsfeld came to stay, locking the drinks cabinet and taking the key with him). But Saddam's coterie actually liked Rumsfeld "as a person," a US diplomat recorded, deeming him "a good listener" who made it clear that Saddam's use of poison gas to repel the Iranians wouldn't get in the way of harmonious relations with Washington. The budding friendship even survived the revelation in 1986 of Reagan's covert arms shipments to Iran and passing on of military intelligence (in a bloody battle on the al-Faw peninsula in early 1986, both sides worked off satellite maps provided by the Americans). Exposure of these dealings will have reminded Saddam that the Americans were not to be trusted. But Washington came through when it counted, furnishing diplomatic cover for his heavy deployment of chemical weapons. In 1988, when Iran-backed Kurdish groups occupied the city of Halabja in Iraqi Kurdistan, Saddam responded by showering the city with poison gas, killing as many as 5,000 civilians.

Coll suggests that the US response to the massacre was even-handed: the administration, he claims, "embraced flawed intelligence reports ... that both Iraq and Iran had resorted to gas." But in fact Washington made it perfectly clear whose side it was on. As Joost Hiltermann details in *A Poisonous Affair: America, Iraq and the Gassing of Halabja* (2007), within days of the attack, US diplomats around the world began publicizing the lie that Halabjans had died from Iranian chemical weapons, thereby eliciting a Security Council resolution which didn't explicitly condemn Iraq, but merely urged both sides to refrain from the use of chemical weapons. Encouraged by the absence of international opposition, Saddam proceeded to quell Kurdish rebellion with further gassing of the civilian population.

Once Iran had thrown in the towel in 1988, Saddam began laying plans to take over Kuwait, to which he owed billions of dollars in war loans. By this stage, Washington's interest in the Middle East had waned, as decision-makers focused on the accelerating decline of the Soviet Union. Yet signs of Saddam's aggressive intentions did attract the attention of some US envoys in the region. Freeman, who was now ambassador to Saudi Arabia, recalls attempting to alert Washington, but he was largely ignored. The ambassador in Baghdad, April Glaspie, vainly sought guidance on official policy regarding Saddam's designs on his oil-rich neighbor, but was given none.

Saddam apparently took this lack of interest as a sign of US acquiescence. Years later, as Coll records, he complained to an American official: "If you didn't want me to go in, why didn't you tell me?" When, following his conquest of Kuwait, it dawned on Washington that he was now in a position to help dictate the global price of oil, rapid action ensued with Operation Desert Storm. By March 1991, Saddam's army had been soundly defeated and driven from Kuwait. The US then ordained an indefinite siege of the Iraqi economy, securing UN endorsement of comprehensive sanctions that were formally justified by the belated discovery of Saddam's efforts to develop a nuclear weapon.

George H. W. Bush had refrained from advancing into Iraq to put pressure on the regime, but two months after the ceasefire he signed a secret "finding" enjoining the CIA to work for Saddam's removal. Frank Anderson, head of the agency's Near East and South Asia Division, accepted the directive with reluctance, scribbling "I don't like this" across the memo. He knew that there was little or no chance of subverting Saddam's well-entrenched government, and that Bush's order was little more than a pro forma gesture. As he reflected to me some years later, quoting the former CIA director Richard Helms, "covert action is frequently a substitute for a policy." Nevertheless, he set to work corralling opposition figures, especially the fraudster-banker Ahmed Chalabi. Chalabi was selected by the CIA because, as Anderson frankly admitted to me, "he was weak," with no useful connections inside Iraq, making him easier to control.

At the same time, sanctions were proving to be a lethal weapon against the Iraqi population at large. By the summer of 1991, the middle classes, impoverished by rocketing inflation, were selling off their possessions to buy food, while plutocrats, including Uday Hussein, grew vastly rich from black market profiteering. Coll touches only briefly on the misery inflicted by the sanctioneers, though he pays attention to Saddam's rake-offs from the Oil for Food program instituted later in the 1990s, which permitted Iraq to export some oil. But as Denis Halliday, UN supervisor of aid distribution under Oil for Food, remarked on resigning his post in 1998 in protest at the ongoing sanctions, the blockade was destroying the underpinnings of Iraqi society as young people lost hope and sought relief through emigration or immersion in religious fundamentalism.

The sanctions were always publicly justified as a means to get Saddam to relinquish any and all nuclear, chemical, and biological weapons. In fact, he had destroyed his entire arsenal of WMDs in 1991, but had done so in secret, keeping no record of their disposal. The secrecy was supremely ill-judged, making it difficult later to prove that he had no such weapons. A UN inspection force, UNSCOM, led by the Swedish diplomat Rolf Ekéus and partly manned by CIA undercover agents (with his acquiescence), combed the country for years in search of the nonexistent WMD stockpiles. By the first few months of 1997, Ekéus had concluded there was nothing more to be found: "Iraq had completed the disarmament phase of the ceasefire agreement," he wrote in *Foreign Affairs* in 2012. The way should have been clear for lifting the sanctions. But, as Ekéus went on to say,

The United States took a different view. In the spring of 1997, former US secretary of state Madeleine Albright gave a speech at Georgetown University in which she stated that even if the weapons provisions under the ceasefire resolution were completed, the United States would not agree to lifting sanctions unless Saddam had been removed from power. With regime change now a stated US objective and the easing of economic sanctions off the table, Saddam lost his appetite for co-operation.

After subjecting the inspectors to increasing harassment, Saddam finally kicked them out. This, Ekéus suggested to me, was exactly what the administration hoped to achieve with Albright's provocative statement. Finding an excuse not to lift sanctions protected Bill Clinton from Republican accusations that he was being soft on Saddam. "The Unscom inspectors," Clinton stated without a blush in February 1998, "believe that Iraq still has stockpiles of chemical and biological munitions … and the capacity to restart quickly its production program and build many, many more weapons." Later that year, Clinton signed the Iraq Liberation Act, written by a congressional Republican staffer, Stephen Rademaker, with input from Ahmed Chalabi, who had by then fallen out with the CIA but had found new allies among neocons eager for an aggressive military policy in the Middle East. Passed by Congress with overwhelming bipartisan majorities, the law called for the US "to support efforts to remove the regime headed by Saddam Hussein from power in Iraq," citing among other justifications Saddam's expulsion of the weapons inspectors.

America's path to war was already clearly marked by the time George W. Bush became president. The 9/11 attacks accelerated the pace. The Pentagon was still burning when, according to an aide's notes, Rumsfeld, now defense secretary, instructed the acting chairman of the Joint Chiefs of Staff, General Richard Myers, to find the "best info fast. Judge whether good enough [to] hit S.H.[Saddam Hussein] @same time … not only U.B.L.[Osama bin Laden] Hard to get good case. Need to move swiftly—Near term target needs—Go massive—sweep it all up. Things related and not. Need to do so to get anything useful." From then until

March 2003, Bush led his government and his obedient ally Blair inexorably toward war. Just as the White House had disregarded warnings that bin Laden was planning an attack in the United States, it now disregarded or suppressed all evidence that Saddam did not possess weapons of mass destruction. The CIA obligingly confirmed that the desired conclusions were correct. For his part, Saddam believed that the CIA knew full well his weapons store was empty—which meant he was the subject of yet another conspiracy. Experience had taught him that was usually the case, and he was right.

London Review of Books, July 4, 2024

11

Big Six v. Little Boy

The official justification for the bombing of Hiroshima and Nagasaki was set out by Henry Stimson, the former US secretary of war, in the February 1947 issue of *Harper's*. There had been "no other choice," he said. Had the bombs not been dropped, a bloody invasion of Japan would have been inevitable, and might have "cost over a million casualties to the American forces alone." But in the atomic bomb the US possessed "a weapon of such a revolutionary character that its use against the enemy might well be expected to produce exactly the kind of shock on the Japanese ruling oligarchy which we desired, strengthening the position of those who wished peace, and weakening that of the military party."

The article was written in urgent response to a growing public feeling, unwelcome to those who had presided over the development and use of the atomic bomb, that the nuclear attacks had been unnecessary to Japan's defeat and had brought horrific suffering to a vast number of civilians. In July 1946 the US Strategic Bombing Survey had concluded that—thanks to the destruction of its economy by conventional bombing and a comprehensive blockade—"in all probability prior to November 1, 1945, Japan would have surrendered even if the atomic bombs had not been dropped." Eminent scientists, including Einstein, had issued statements deploring the use of the bomb, while the August 31, 1946, issue of the *New Yorker* had been entirely devoted to John Hersey's unsparing account of what the nuclear attack had meant for civilians in Hiroshima. Stimson's 7,300-word testimonial— which was in fact written by McGeorge Bundy, later national security adviser to Kennedy and Johnson, with input and edits from a number of senior officials intimately involved with the Manhattan Project—was an authoritative counterattack, and it was entirely successful. The message that the bomb had saved a million American lives, in the words of the historian Paul Ham, "put the American mind at ease, [and] slipped into folklore." When, in 1994, the Smithsonian Institution announced plans to exhibit *Enola Gay*, the B-29 bomber which had destroyed Hiroshima, along with contextual commentary casting doubt on the necessity and morality of the mission, there was a storm of outraged protest and the exhibition was canceled. Even today, conversations on the topic with otherwise well-informed Americans tend to elicit reminiscences of how fathers and other relatives, veterans of the Pacific and European wars, had nurtured mordant expectations that they wouldn't survive the prospective invasion of the Japanese home islands. They had been saved by the atomic bombs that had brought about Japan's surrender.

But Stimson, or his ghostwriter, had been highly selective in the evidence presented. There was no mention of the debate in the summer of 1945 among senior US officials over whether to modify the demand for unconditional Japanese surrender, which US intelligence had reported was the principal reason the enemy were refusing to throw in the towel. Military estimates of potential US casualties from an invasion had been far lower than a million. Nor did the article make reference to the argument among officials about whether to give the Japanese warning of the impending nuclear attack, or to stage a demonstration of the bomb's power, rather than killing hundreds of thousands of people. Stimson's claim that the bombs had "destroyed active working parts of the Japanese war effort" was not true: they had deliberately been aimed at people's homes.

The *Harper's* article was so successful in instilling the notion of a million lives saved that dissenting statements, even from eminent military authorities, failed to gain traction. "The use of this barbarous weapon at Hiroshima and Nagasaki was of no material assistance in our war against Japan," Admiral William Leahy, wartime chairman of the Joint Chiefs of Staff, wrote in his 1950 memoir. "The Japanese were already defeated and ready to surrender." Eisenhower later said it had been his belief at the time "that Japan was already defeated and that dropping the bomb was completely unnecessary." At one time or another almost all the senior American commanders in the Pacific war voiced similar sentiments. Among them was Carter Clarke, a former brigadier general who declared to an interviewer in 1959 that "when we didn't need to do it, and we knew we didn't need to do it ... we used [Hiroshima and Nagasaki] as an experiment for two atomic bombs." Clarke spoke with particular authority. During the war, he had headed the Special Branch of the Military Intelligence Service, set up in the wake of the attack on Pearl Harbor. This secret group had the sole responsibility for analyzing intercepted enemy communications, including high-level Japanese discussions indicating growing despair in the last months of the war. As Clarke once put it to me, "They were having kittens with bonnets on!"

But next door to the closely guarded Special Branch office in the Pentagon was another office, equally well guarded: that of the Manhattan Project. Neither group knew of the other's existence. So when the news broke, via an announcement by Truman, of the bombing of Hiroshima, complete with promises of more to come, the reaction among Clarke's supremely well-informed intelligence officers was shock and outrage. When I talked to them forty years later, veterans of the organization recalled the shouts of "Why?" and "How could they do that?" echoing round the office.

By the time I interviewed them, in the 1980s, the official story had already come under attack from scholars. The historian Gar Alperovitz had launched a powerful opening salvo in 1965 with the publication of *Atomic Diplomacy: Hiroshima and Potsdam*, in which he argued, drawing on Stimson's posthumously released diaries, that the true objective of the bombings had been to intimidate the Soviet Union and render Stalin more amenable to American demands regarding Eastern Europe. Alperovitz pursued the story relentlessly over subsequent decades. His book *The Decision to Use the Atomic Bomb and the Architecture of an American Myth* finally appeared in 1995, setting out the case that the bombings had been pointless when it came to the defeat of Japan but had marked the starting point of the Cold War.

Evan Thomas, author of several respectful works on various pillars of the Washington establishment, will have none of that. Summarizing a selection of critiques of the bombing, he declares in *Road to Surrender: Three Men and the Countdown to the End of World War Two* that "the facts are otherwise." His consideration of the Soviet Union's entry into the war is limited to remarks made almost in passing, yet he forthrightly concludes that "the atomic bombs not only saved many thousands and possibly millions of Japanese lives, they saved the lives of even more Asians beyond Japan." In short, Thomas closely follows Stimson, whose verdict was published three-quarters of a century ago. His story is centered on sympathetic portraits of three individuals: Stimson himself, Carl "Tooey" Spaatz, the Air Force general in command of the nuclear bombing force, and Shigenori Togo, Japan's foreign minister.

The two Americans were, to judge from their letters and diaries at the time, subject to fits of doubt and conscience about the slaughter their bombers inflicted on civilian populations in Germany and Japan, even before the advent of nuclear weapons. Both had clung to the supposition, central to American doctrine, that "precision bombing" of military targets was not only desirable but feasible. But years spent pursuing this objective in Europe had demonstrated that it didn't work, since the bombs, wherever they were aimed, still tended to fall far from their targets and on the surrounding population. The British, by contrast, had abandoned the pretense of precision early on and taken to targeting cities with the objective, euphemistically termed, of "dehousing" the population at large. Eventually the US bombing force in Europe, commanded by Spaatz until he was reassigned to the Pacific after Germany's defeat, followed the British lead, sharing in the destruction of Dresden in February 1945, igniting a firestorm that killed nearly 25,000 people. The atrocity apparently haunted Spaatz, though when he arrived in the Pacific he found his massive bomber fleet routinely burning down Japanese cities. The strategy had been adopted by his subordinate commander, Curtis LeMay, after earlier attempts to precision-bomb military targets from a high altitude, for which the B-29 bomber had been developed at enormous cost (more than the Manhattan

Project), had utterly failed. In March 1945 a fire raid on Tokyo by B-29s—flying so low that their crews could smell burning flesh—destroyed much of the city and killed upwards of 100,000 people. With no interference from Spaatz, LeMay progressively laid waste to one Japanese city after another, more than sixty of them by early August 1945.

Stimson, who had half-heartedly pressed for an investigation of the American role in the Dresden atrocity, was meanwhile enthusiastically supervising the development and plans for use of the atomic bomb, though permitting himself some private agonizing over the prospect of "the terrible," "the awful," "the diabolical." As a recipient of Clarke's intelligence reports, he was cognizant of Japanese peace moves, and understood that the major obstacle was Emperor Hirohito, who felt implicitly threatened by the Allies' demand for unconditional surrender. An intercepted message to Tokyo's ambassador in Moscow on July 12, 1945, stated: 'His Majesty the Emperor ... desires from his heart that [the war] may be quickly terminated, but so long as England and the United States insist upon unconditional sur- render, the Japanese Empire has no alternative but to fight on." In response, Stimson supported an initiative to let the Japanese know that the emperor would be left unmolested on his throne. This was to be conveyed in an official message from the Allied leaders at a summit in Potsdam scheduled for mid-July.

But Stimson and other powerful figures who favored this approach were outmaneuvered by James Byrnes, a wily politician from South Carolina whom Truman had appointed secretary of state. As a senator, Byrnes had shepherded Roosevelt's New Deal legislation through Congress, and as head of the Office of War Mobilization controlled much of the country's industrial economy. A master bureaucratic infighter, he had no truck with half-measures on the bomb's use, such as prior warning or a demonstration. Any failure to deploy a potentially war-winning weapon, he asserted, would spark public outrage and lead to furious investigations in Congress regarding the $2 billion it had cost to develop. As is usually the case, domestic political considerations were the dominant factor in determining foreign policy. "The president would be crucified," Byrnes declared, if he settled for anything less than unconditional surrender. He steered an Interim Committee on bomb policy, established by Stimson, to decide that the weapon would be used as soon as it was available, without warning, on a war plant surrounded by workers' homes. Stimson was mollified by the suggestion that the target would principally be military, and took pride in removing the shrine-city of Kyoto from the target list.

Accompanying Truman to the Potsdam meeting with Stalin and Churchill, Byrnes edited a proposed declaration setting out terms for a Japanese surrender. Stimson and colleagues had drafted a passage indicating compromise on the issue of the emperor, but Byrnes struck it out. Accordingly, the Potsdam Declaration offered no specific mention of the bomb, threatening only "prompt and utter destruction" if the demands for unconditional surrender weren't met. The terms did include a promise that occupying forces would be withdrawn once Japan had secured a peaceful and democratic government "in accordance with the freely expressed will of the people."

Thomas's insistence that the bomb was necessary to bring about Japan's surrender is largely contradicted by his own evidence. In the most interesting and vivid part of his book, he takes us into the hot, humid, mosquito-ridden bunkers at the heart of the devastated Japanese capital, suffused with the ashes of 100,000 inhabitants incinerated in LeMay's fire raids, where a sweating, tiny ruling circle, the so-called Big Six, argued and intrigued. They all knew Japan had lost the war. Food was running out; the economy, with supplies of raw materials shut off by a comprehensive blockade, was almost at a standstill. The navy was at the bottom of the sea, while the air force was resorting to decrepit wooden machines often fueled with oil extracted from pine roots. Most threatening of all to this elite group was the possibility that the Japanese people, driven beyond endurance by their ongoing misery, might revolt. As early as February 1945, Hirohito's influential adviser Prince Konoe had advocated peace for fear that the population might turn to communism.

But there were dissenters. Both the war minister, Korechika Anami, and the army chief of staff, Yoshijiro Umezu, were adamant that they should deal a bloody nose to an American invasion by mobilizing 20 million Japanese for a suicidal "final battle" in order to extract more generous peace terms. They successfully insisted that the Potsdam Declaration be treated with "silent contempt." Among other incentives for maintaining a hard line was a realistic fear of lethal protest from fanatical junior officers. Emperor Hirohito, by hallowed custom presiding in silence over the meetings, was maneuvering with close advisers to bring the war to a close so long as his own position remained secure. For all sides, the most urgent question was the attitude of the Soviet Union, which had so far been neutral in the Pacific war. The emperor's advisers hoped to enlist Stalin as mediator in peace talks with the Western Allies in return for major territorial concessions. The hardliners also hoped Stalin would remain neutral, knowing that a Soviet attack would doom any possibility of success in confronting an American invasion.

"Little Boy" exploded over Hiroshima at 8.15 a.m. on August 6, 1945, wiping most of the city off the face of the earth and killing 80,000 people instantly. But the "shock" to the leadership in Tokyo envisaged by Stimson and assumed by Thomas failed to materialize. Togo, Hirohito's foreign minister, relayed Truman's announcement of the event and his threats of more to come, but the Big Six's reaction amounted to little more than a decision to register a strong protest with the International Red Cross. Anami was skeptical as to whether it really was an atomic bomb that had been used and demanded further investigation. After all, the Americans had already destroyed more than sixty cities, and one more didn't make a great deal of difference. True, Hirohito reportedly observed that "now this has happened, we must bow to the inevitable. No matter what happens to my safety, we should lose no time in ending this war so as not to have another tragedy like this." But as the Japanese historian Tsuyoshi Hasegawa has found, the statement is sourced to a postwar report by Hirohito's senior courtier, Marquis Kido, who would have had every reason to portray the monarch as exhibiting a tender regard for his people, an emotion previously unexpressed while they burned and starved. At a meeting with Togo the next day, Hirohito was allegedly "petrified" at the prospect of another bomb, one aimed at him. Thomas claims that they considered accepting the Potsdam terms, but there was no change in policy, which was still to rely on the Soviets to mediate an acceptable peace. The Nagasaki bomb was treated with even greater insouciance, the news barely causing an interruption when it arrived during a meeting. Far from accepting defeat, Anami blustered that "a hundred atomic bombs" would not make Japan cave in.

Reaction to the sudden Soviet attack in Manchuria, hours before the Nagasaki bomb, was another matter, and casts the story of the surrender in a very different light. The military high command was shocked. (Japanese military intelligence had correctly divined the attack but was ignored.) There was now no hope that Stalin, who had been stringing the Japanese along while he readied his forces, would help them in their hour of need. As the Red Army crashed through the once mighty Japanese Kwantung Army, overrunning an area the size of Western Europe and racing to claim territory ever nearer the homeland, it fanned fears that communism might be imposed in Japan itself. Togo, his strategy of reliance on peaceful Soviet intervention in tatters, now urged acceptance of the Potsdam terms. While the military hardliners still argued for fighting on, Hirohito defied custom and finally made a proactive intervention, agreeing with Togo on the grounds that there was no hope of victory and it was now time "to bear the unbearable." But the message accepting the Potsdam terms, dispatched on August 10, contained the proviso that it would not "comprise any demand which prejudices the prerogatives of His Majesty as a Sovereign Ruler."

Though US headlines delightedly declared "War Is Over," and crowds danced in the streets of American cities, the Truman administration was divided. Stimson and Leahy were all for accepting the Japanese proviso as inconsequential. Stimson argued the urgent need "to get the homeland into our hands before the Russians could put in any substantial claim to occupy and rule it." Byrnes, firm in his insistence that American voters would not forgive any concessions after years of Hirohito's vilification, finally came up with an acceptable formula: the emperor could stay on his throne, but "subject to the authority of the Supreme Commander of the Allied Powers." It was an artful compromise, bellicose in tone but conceding on what had long been the major impediment to surrender. The concession might not have been politically possible if Truman hadn't first dropped the bombs. Even so, Japan's diehard military faction held out, saying they could never accept this degree of foreign control and that they would fight on for better terms. An intercepted message from headquarters to military attachés in Europe pledged determination to fight to the bitter end, though admitting that the Soviet attack posed a major threat. There was no mention of the atomic bombs.

But inside the ruling circle, the realists were gaining ground. The navy minister, Admiral Mitsumasa Yonai, said he was now in favor of accepting the American peace terms, "not because I am afraid ... of the atomic bombs or Soviet participation in the war. The most important reason is my concern over the domestic situation." Finally, on August 13, a week after Hiroshima, Hirohito told a sobbing cabinet it was "impossible for us to continue the war any longer," and offered to make a public announcement of surrender over the radio. Enraged, a faction of fanatical army officers began the long-feared coup, but it petered out within hours when senior generals, including Anami, refused to support it. The recording of Hirohito's surrender speech was smuggled out of the palace, evading the coup plotters' attempts to intercept it. Hirohito's stated explanation for the decision stressed his desire to relieve his people's suffering, and did refer to the atomic attacks: "The enemy has begun to employ a new and most cruel bomb, the power of which to damage is, indeed, incalculable, taking the toll of many innocent lives." But a second speech, broadcast to the Japanese armed forces two days later and unmentioned by Thomas, omitted any mention of the bomb: "Now that the Soviet Union has entered the war against us, to continue the war under the present internal and external conditions would be only to increase the ravages of war." The Japanese people, whom leaders both in Tokyo and Washington had assumed would fight to the death, made no protest over the surrender. The Japanese literary scholar Masao Miyoshi had been an air force cadet in 1945, training to be a kamikaze pilot. Years later, asked by an interviewer whether he had been shocked when the emperor surrendered, he said that "all the cadets were thrilled not to have to fight. They threw their hats in the air and cheered."

The folklore endures. Among the exhibits at the US Air Force's enormous museum in Dayton, Ohio, is *Bockscar*, the B-29 that dropped the Nagasaki bomb. It is proudly identified as "the aircraft that ended World War Two."

London Review of Books, November 16, 2023

12

How the US Military Got Rich from the Afghan War

The departure of American troops from Afghanistan is being lamented (or hailed—see the Chinese press, passim) as a defeat. But this is a shortsighted attitude, at least from the point of view of the US military and the multitude of interested parties who feed at its trough. For them, the whole adventure has been a thumping success, as measured in the trillions of taxpayer dollars that have flowed through their budgets and profits over the two decades in which they successfully maintained the operation.

The truth of this was forcefully brought home to me once by a friend of mine who, as a mid-level staffer, attended a conclave of senior generals discussing Donald Trump's Afghan mini-surge back in 2018. As he related the conversation, they were unanimous that the move would make absolutely no difference to the war, "but," they happily agreed, "it will do us good at budget time."

Years before, Col. John Boyd, the former Air Force fighter pilot who famously conceived and expounded a comprehensive theory of human conflict, had pointed out that there was no contradiction between the military's professed mission and its seeming indifference to combat success. "People say the Pentagon does not have a strategy," he said. "They are wrong. The Pentagon does have a strategy. It is: 'Don't interrupt the money flow, add to it.'"

I was reminded of this eternal truth by an announcement buried amid the blizzard of Afghan withdrawal news in July: as part of our ongoing largesse to the Afghan people, it said, we were sending the Afghan air force thirty-seven UH-60 helicopters. Few readers, not including the reporters copying out the

Pentagon press release, would have appreciated the rich irony of the news, a reminder of the war's real, squalid history, so tragic for so many Afghans, so profitable for some Americans.

A new UH-60 costs some $12 million, so this parting gift amounts to around $450 million, a not inconsiderable addition to the $3.3 billion already budgeted for support of Afghan security forces over the next year, though a mere drop in the bucket compared to the overall $2.26 trillion tab for our two-decade campaign. It was without doubt entirely welcome to the Lockheed Martin Corporation, owners of the helicopters' manufacturer, Sikorsky. The aircraft will join fifty-three UH-60s already dispatched to the Hindu Kush in recent years. Few of these can still fly, because Afghan mechanics were known to be entirely incapable of maintaining the complex machines, the job being left to highly paid (by us) American contractors. On the other hand, the Afghans had been well able to look after the helicopters they had previously flown—the Russian MI-17, a simple, rugged machine on which local pilots and mechanics had decades of experience. It also had the benefit of being able to operate in the higher parts of the mountainous country, which the UH-60, deficient in altitude capability, is quite unable to do. For some years, the US Army had sensibly purchased overhauled Russian helicopters at a cost of (at most) $4.5 million apiece to pass on to the Afghans, but the deal went awry when the Army colonel running the program, Norbert Vergez, entered into corrupt dealings with sinister elements in Russia to jack up the price. Vergez pleaded guilty to a "conflict of interest" and received a light sentence, and the Army seized the opportunity to transfer the contract to Sikorsky/Lockheed. The Afghans were consequently forced to exchange a useful weapon for one that has proved effectively useless. (It should never be said, however, that US forces, even as they stole away in the middle of the night from their huge base at Bagram, casually abandoned costly equipment to whoever might need it. Although they indeed left hundreds of trucks behind, they were careful to take the keys with them.)

The little-publicized helicopter scandal was one of many investigated by John Sopko, who, as the Special Inspector General for Afghan Reconstruction, has served as the Cassandra of the

Afghan war. Since Congress created his office in 2012 he has been diligently relating details of the colossal waste associated with the war in handsome full-color annual reports, but with little effect. "It was a disaster ready to happen, and it happened," he told me a few years into the job. "We wasted a lot of money. It wasn't that people were stupid, and it wasn't that people didn't care; it's just the system almost guarantees failure." As example he pointed to a plastic model of a twin-engined transport plane, an Italian G-222, sitting on his windowsill. Twenty of these had been bought for the Afghans at a cost of $500 million. "They were the wrong plane for the country, the altitude, the weather. The Afghans couldn't be trained on them." Unable to fly, they had been abandoned as soon as they arrived. Sopko had come across them on the edge of Kabul airport, "rusting, with trees growing through them." No one, he said, had been fired or even disciplined for this initiative, or for any of the similarly blatant examples of squandered money. "I doubt that anyone missed a promotion, or even a bonus. Welcome to my world."

Few people realize that much of the time, the war itself was paid for by a bonus, an add-on to the main Pentagon budget in the form of a special fund for "Overseas Contingency Operations" —money duly appropriated to the military for actually fighting this and other ongoing wars, rather like a police department charging extra for catching criminals. As the years passed, the Pentagon began quietly diverting its so-called "war budget" to more urgent priorities, such as funding new weapons programs. By 2020 the diversion had become official—the budget request for that year brazenly acknowledged that $98 billion of the OCO money is for routine "base requirements," rather than fighting abroad.

This year Congress has finally been shamed into abolishing the war budget, so ongoing combat deployments, such as the "Stryker Combat Team" from the 4th Infantry Division dispatched to Syria even as other units crept away from Bagram, will now have to be paid for out of the actual Pentagon budget. At $715 billion, this is being decried as inadequate by both Republicans and Democrats, who cite, among other examples of woeful want, the burgeoning costs of the nuclear force modernization program bequeathed to us by Barack Obama. Even for hardened scrutineers of US defense-spending excesses, the exploding price tags of the Obama nuclear bequest are eye-watering. The first of twelve new Columbia-class ballistic missile submarines, for example, is now slated to cost just over $15 billion, an increase of $637 million in the last year alone. Among other things, this constitutes a historic achievement on the part of the submariners, marking the first time a submarine has cost more than a 100,000-ton aircraft carrier, the newest variant of which, the Ford class, currently clocks in at $13 billion, itself a record for carriers. (There is no guarantee, however, that later Ford models will not strive successfully to close the gap.)

Long ago, A. Ernest Fitzgerald, an Air Force cost management official fired in 1969 on the direct orders of President Richard Nixon for revealing a multibillion cost overrun on an Air Force contract, explained that the basic business of the US defense industry was not selling weapons, but "selling costs." Since their profits were guaranteed as a percentage of the cost, the more the programs for which they were contracted went up in price, the greater their profit. In essence, despite much touted "acquisition reforms," little has changed, except that the sums involved have gotten larger and the corruption more egregious.

A 2018 investigation by Mandy Smithberger of the Washington watchdog group Project on Government Oversight, for example, found that from 2008 to 2018 at least 380 high-ranking department officials and military officers became lobbyists, board members, executives, or consultants for defense contractors within two years of taking off their uniforms. James Mattis, to take one prominent example, retired as a four-star Marine general, ascended to the board of leading defense contractor General Dynamics, where he served for three years, taking home $900,000 in compensation, then spent two years as Trump's defense secretary, after which he returned to the General Dynamics board. Lloyd Austin, the current secretary of defense, garnered as much as $1.7 million worth of stock as a director of Raytheon, the nation's second-largest defense contractor, in the four years between retiring from the Army and assuming his current august post, along with other lucrative positions in the defense business.

Every time the US military withdraws from the field of martial combat, commentators opine that the occasion might be marked by a respite from gargantuan defense budgets. A glance at the historical record confirms that such hopes are misplaced. From Korea onwards, falloffs in spending have lasted little longer than the parades for returning troops. Even when the core justification for America's entire defense effort, the Soviet Union, utterly collapsed in 1991, the budget faltered only briefly before resuming its upward climb. A sophisticated examination of US defense-spending statistics since the end of the Korean War by former Pentagon analyst Franklin Spinney has revealed an intriguing pattern: overall, the budget has grown at a steady rate of 5 percent a year. Every time the number has sunk below that trend, a fearsome "threat" has appeared right on cue to justify remedial action.

It should come as no surprise therefore that, just as American forces exit Afghanistan, leaving those decaying helicopters and undrivable trucks as memorials, calls from the defense lobby for a prompt boost of, yes, 5 percent in defense spending are growing louder. Although the Russian bear, albeit undeniably mangy compared with the departed ever-reliably threatening USSR, is still pressed into service for old times' sake, the People's Republic of China has now stepped forward in a starring role as a foe guaranteed to endure for many budget cycles to come. As a foretaste, the US Navy has sold the Pacific Deterrence Initiative, reminiscent in some ways of the recently departed Overseas Contingency Operations boondoggle, a package of demands for extra spending to thwart the Middle Kingdom's designs in the Pacific Ocean amounting to at least $27 billion over the next five years.

Testifying in support of the initiative this last March, Adm. John C. Aquilino, commander of the Indo-Pacific Command, spoke ominously of a potential Chinese invasion of Taiwan in the near future, and the commensurate need to spare no effort, and of course no money, in standing firm against their aggressive designs. His spotless uniform was resplendent with rows of brightly colored ribbons, awards for an illustrious career. I noticed that among them was the green, red, black, and white of the Afghanistan Campaign Medal, signifying his service during the epic conflict in that landlocked nation.

It was a relief to see that lessons acquired at such cost will not be forgotten.

Spectator, July 19, 2021

13

Narco-in-Chief

Washington's Longtime Drug Trafficking Friend in Honduras

In January 2021, thousands of Hondurans gathered in the city of San Pedro Sula and began walking toward the Guatemalan border, the first barrier in their journey north to the United States. They were a long way off, but our frontier defenders were already on full alert. "Do not waste your time and money, and do not risk your safety and health," the acting head of US Customs and Border Protection had announced a week earlier. "Migrant caravan groups will not be allowed to make their way north in violation of the sovereignty, standing public-health orders, and immigration laws of the respective nations throughout the region." The presumptive secretary of state, Antony Blinken, echoed the sentiment, saying simply: "Do not come." Soon after the migrants crossed into Guatemala, that message was reinforced with the clubs and tear gas of the US-financed Guatemalan police, forcing the crowds back into the country they had fled.

The men, women, and children in the caravan had hardly been risking their own "safety and health" by setting out on the hazardous journey, precisely because they had so little of either to begin with. Even before two back-to-back hurricanes tore a path of destruction across the country last November, the population was in desperate straits. Sixty percent lived in extreme poverty, almost 40 percent were unemployed, and predatory corruption by the ruling elite reigned supreme. The pandemic had added its own agonies—not only did COVID-19 sicken hundreds of thousands of people, but government insiders stole almost the entire budget intended for emergency medical treatment, and the police and military imposed a near-total countrywide lockdown, arresting thousands for curfew violations.

For the people making this exodus, braving the perils of the journey was evidently a safer bet than staying put. For example, a young man who would give only his first name, Francisco, told the journalist Sandra Cuffe that the hurricanes had put an end to his $8-a-day bricklaying job and that a mining company was ravaging the area where he lived, hiring thugs (often connected to the military) to terrorize him and other locals opposed to the environmental devastation. Elsewhere in the crowd, a twenty-eight-year-old mother named Olga Ramírez carried the youngest of her four children in her arms while two of the others rode in a decrepit stroller pushed by her husband. She tearfully explained to a reporter that they had lost their precarious living selling food in the municipal bus terminal in Danlí, a provincial town east of the capital, Tegucigalpa, after the local mayor privatized the terminal and summarily ejected Ramírez and her fellow vendors. "They threw us out like we were dogs, like garbage, as if we were worthless," she said as she trudged along.

"I think the whole country would leave if they could," Jean Stokan, a justice coordinator for the Catholic group Sisters of Mercy of the Americas, told me. Stokan has spent decades witnessing the plight of Central Americans. "Honduras today is like El Salvador in the eighties, death squads and all," she said, recalling the bloody US-supported counterinsurgency. She talked of corrupt police officers enjoying impunity; community leaders, human rights activists, and labor organizers being threatened, abducted, and jailed; and a wave of femicides—"women's bodies chopped up and discarded in plastic garbage bags." It thus came as no surprise to Stokan that Hondurans were fleeing their country by the tens of thousands. "You know the phrase 'a person doesn't leave their home unless it is in the mouth of a shark?'" she asked. "That's Honduras."

In recent years, Washington has expressed its fair share of laments over the little country's desperate condition, and has poured a lot of money into projects aimed at eliminating the so-called push factors driving people to flee. USAID spent $90 million in 2020 alone promoting "good governance," fostering "competitive, resilient, and inclusive market systems," and creating "economic opportunities that incorporate women."

Our partner in these worthy efforts has been Juan Orlando Hernández, often referred to as JOH, the stocky, frequently charming president of Honduras. Since he took office in 2014, Washington has relied on Hernández to implement US-devised programs for alleviating his country's ills: unemployment, violence, corruption, and most importantly, the cocaine trade. But despite insistent protests locally and abroad that Hernández oversees a repressive and corrupt regime, the United States has continued to treat him as an indispensable partner.

Any lingering pretense that Hernández has been on America's side in the drug war, however, was ripped away this January by federal prosecutors in New York. The occasion was a filing in the case of a major Honduran drug trafficker, Geovanny Fuentes Ramírez, who was arrested at Miami International Airport last year while trying to flee the country. Fuentes Ramírez's crimes, as alleged in the motion, included cocaine smuggling, bribery, and murder. According to court documents, Fuentes Ramírez had worked with a number of CCs, or co-conspirators—in particular, one referred to as CC-4. In the filing, the prosecutors included the report of an informant who had much to say about Fuentes Ramírez's dealings with this obviously powerful co-conspirator:

> In approximately 2013 and 2014, CC-4 promised to protect the defendant from arrest and extradition; promised to help the defendant transport cocaine with the assistance of Honduras's armed forces; said he wanted to use the defendant's laboratory because of its proximity to a key shipping port; directed the defendant to work with Tony Hernández (CC-4's brother) with respect to drug-trafficking activities; and stated that he was going to "shove the drugs right up the noses of the gringos."

The reference to CC-4's brother made it absolutely clear who the prosecutors were talking about: the president.

Prosecutors made the accusation explicit at Fuentes Ramírez's trial in March, but in Honduras there was never any doubt about the co-conspirator's identity. Protesters, including many who had been part of the caravan, flourished signs reading CC-4 = JOH. Among those who knew the truth was Bertha Oliva, a Nobel Prize–nominated activist who has been fighting for human rights in Honduras since her husband was disappeared by a military death squad in 1981. When I asked her whether she was surprised by the prosecutors' revelations, she made clear that she has no patience for those who claim prior ignorance of Hernández's criminal behavior. "Let's leave the surprises to children, to those who have no memory, or who can't think clearly," she answered.

The suggestion that Hernández might be associated with the narcotics trade was not new in the United States, either. His brother Tony had already been tried and convicted as a major trafficker in New York in 2019. Testimony in his trial was replete with references to the Honduran leader. Still, the president's crude gangster talk about shoving drugs up people's noses was a slap in the face to all the high-level US officials who had professed esteem for him over the years.

Joe Biden, for instance, recalls the warm relationships he built as vice president with certain Central American leaders in his book *Promise Me, Dad*, citing Hernández as one of his "friends," and a "confidant." General John Kelly, who commanded Southcom—the Pentagon's Central and South American division—from 2012 to 2016, was another powerful supporter (he would later become Donald Trump's chief of staff). Concluding a visit to Tegucigalpa in June 2014, the four-star general commended the "incredible and impressive" fight against drug trafficking and organized crime being waged by Hernández and his government. The following year, he declared to Congress that the Honduran government was "working hard to combat the drug trade … and take meaningful action to protect human rights." In 2018, the Florida senator Marco Rubio tweeted, "Met with President @JuanOrlandoH and Foreign Minister Lara of #Honduras to thank them for their support of #Israel and US at the @UN and his partnership targeting drug traffickers." Year in, year out, it seemed that no official US encounter with the Honduran narco boss was complete without a tribute to his prowess as an antidrug crusader.

The United States has long been involved in Honduras, from its days as an effective colony of the United Fruit Company, down through the era when it served as a base for America's illegal war in Nicaragua. That was in the eighties, when Battalion 3-16, a Honduran death squad, kidnapped, tortured, and murdered at will with the protection of the US Embassy. Many say things are even worse now. "The situation has been deteriorating for forty years," the émigré scientist Salvador Moncada told me. One of the world's preeminent medical researchers, knighted by Queen Elizabeth in 2010, he described his anguish over his country's descent: "There's a total state of corruption. Now it is almost a failed state, and the United States is not innocent!"

If Washington could ever claim innocence, that right was surely lost in the summer of 2009, when members of the Honduran military hauled the democratically elected president, Manuel Zelaya, out of the presidential palace at five-thirty in the morning, bundled him onto a military plane, and flew him out of the country. Along the way, they stopped at the joint US-Honduran military base at Soto Cano to change planes, then deposited Zelaya on a Costa Rican runway, still in his pajamas. US officials were careful to avoid publicly labeling it a military coup. (Hugo Llorens, the US ambassador at the time, unequivocally called Zelaya's removal an "illegal coup" in a classified cable released later by WikiLeaks.)

The plotters' threadbare excuse was Zelaya's support for a constitutional amendment that would allow a president to run for a second term, even though he was not planning on running again. Though a scion of the local oligarchy that had traditionally held power, Zelaya had made powerful enemies at home by enacting a series of modest social-democratic reforms. Perhaps more importantly, he had received warnings from Washington regarding his affable relationship with its bête noire, Venezuela's leftist president Hugo Chávez. Later, a detailed investigation by Jake Johnston for *The Intercept* revealed that US military officers operating out of the Center for Hemispheric Defense Studies, in concert with both senior State Department officials and powerful Republican senators such as Jim DeMint of South Carolina, were deeply involved in facilitating widespread acceptance of the takeover in Washington. The United States maneuvered to block efforts to reinstate Zelaya until subsequent elections could bestow a veneer of legitimacy on the coup. Hillary Clinton, who was then serving as secretary of state, wrote in her 2014 memoir *Hard Choices* that her strategy was to get Honduras to hold elections quickly, "which would render the question of Zelaya moot"—an imprudent admission that she deleted from the paperback edition.

The November 2009 elections, closely controlled by the army and largely boycotted by Zelaya's supporters, took place in a climate of intimidation and violence. Crowds protesting the coup were met with tear gas and clubs. One leftist presidential candidate was forced to withdraw after being severely beaten by the police. Nevertheless, the US government quickly moved to recognize Porfirio "Pepe" Lobo of the National Party as the victor. The State Department praised the Honduran people for "peacefully exercising their democratic rights to select their leaders."

Shortly after Lobo's purported victory, the Honduran Congress also chose a new leader for itself: Juan Orlando Hernández. A graduate of SUNY Albany, Hernández was first elected to the National Congress in 2001, when he was thirty-two. Early on, he displayed a willingness to work with the United States, allowing US officials the use of his office in 2003 to lobby for support for the Iraq invasion. After he became president of the Congress in 2010, he engineered the dismissal of four Supreme Court justices, a move that gave him effective control of the government, including the police and the military. In her book *The Long Honduran Night*, the historian Dana Frank quotes a local oligarch observing that in fifty years of Honduran politics he'd "never known a more Machiavellian, dangerous figure than Juan Orlando Hernández."

By 2013, he was ready to move on to the top office, running for president as the National Party's candidate after Lobo obligingly stepped aside. It would not be a walkover—the coup and the militarized repression that followed had inspired a surge of opposition. But Hernández could draw on many sources of support, including security forces flush with US aid money (which had soared since the coup) and plundered public funds. Amid a welter of fraud and intimidation reported by international observers, Hernández claimed 36 percent of the vote while his leading opponent—Zelaya's wife—drew 27 percent. Again, State Department officials congratulated the Honduran government for "ensuring that the election process was generally transparent, peaceful, and reflected the will of the Honduran people."

Hernández had run on a law-and-order platform, promising to crack down on escalating gang violence with a *mano dura* by putting "a soldier on every corner." The bedrock of his support, however, was among bigger, more violent gangsters, chief among them his brother Tony. Already a rising narco power in western Honduras, Tony proudly stamped his bales of cocaine with TH, a trademark inspired by the Tommy Hilfiger logo. By the time he was arrested, he had moved 200 tons of cocaine into the United States. As early as 2010, according to court testimony, Tony confided to an associate that his brother would be the next National Party presidential candidate, promising rich dividends for the TH brand if he won.

Others in the business also appreciated the possibilities of a Hernández presidency. According to assistant US attorney Jason A. Richman's opening statement at Tony's trial, $1 million from "El Chapo" Guzmán, the infamous cartel leader, made its way to Hernández's campaign. As a trafficker named Alexander Ardon (who admitted to fifty-six murders and "some torture") would testify, the fearsome drug lord had packed the cash in plastic bags, which Ardon handed to Tony himself. "We counted it in the car."

Once in power, Hernández actively liaised with his brother and other associates on matters necessary to the smooth function of business, such as securing police and military protection for cocaine shipments, while simultaneously earning plaudits in Washington by extraditing traffickers he deemed expendable for trial and conviction in the United States. It is unclear whether he knew, or cared, that not everyone in the US government took his crime-fighting credentials at face value. In 2013, the Drug Enforcement Administration opened an investigation into the

Hernández family. Five years later, Tony was arrested on multiple cocaine-trafficking charges after agreeing to meet with agents in Miami. (His misplaced confidence may have been due to the fact that he had coolly talked his way out of trouble in an earlier meeting.)

The investigation presumably had high-level approval, at least within the Justice Department, which has a representative on the DEA's Sensitive Activity Review Committee, the body that evaluates politically thorny cases. The State Department, however, does not have a seat on the committee, which may explain the answer I got from a DEA agent when I asked whether anyone had objected to the Hernández investigation. "Only the State Department," he replied with a laugh. When I queried James Nealon, who served as US ambassador to Honduras from 2014 to 2017, about whether he had known that US law enforcement had the president of Honduras in its sights, he chose his words carefully. "During my time as ambassador to Honduras," he said, "I was never informed by DEA or the Department of Justice that they were investigating President Hernández, and I asked repeatedly."

As the DEA investigation edged closer to the Casa Presidencial, conditions in Honduras were steadily deteriorating. With Washington's hearty approval, international financial organizations had begun enforcing free-market orthodoxy. In 2014, the International Monetary Fund agreed to provide Honduras with a three-year, $189 million loan, and in return demanded the privatization of key economic sectors such as the phone and electric companies. At a time when the unemployment rate was already over 50 percent, the IMF agreement alone cost 10,000 workers their jobs within two months. The privatization of the Danlí bus terminal that destroyed Olga Ramírez's livelihood and led her to try to flee the country was the fruit of a public-private partnership promoted and funded by the World Bank. Ramírez and her fellow stallholders could not afford the higher rent demanded for space in the refurbished building, which thus remained empty.

Along with this job squeeze and tax hikes that fell disproportionately on the poor came injunctions to open the country to foreign investment. At its most extreme, this has taken the form of Zones for Economic Development and Employment.

Apparently inspired by the crackpot doctrines of Ayn Rand and her free-market disciples, ZEDEs are corporate-owned enclaves that operate outside Honduran sovereignty, free to make their own laws and set their own taxes. Hernández liked the idea so much that he made sure his overhauled Supreme Court nullified a previous decision and legalized the zones. The first such libertarian paradise, a tourist development featuring homes for wealthy foreigners on the Honduran island of Roatán, is currently under construction. The presiding authority, Próspera, a Washington-based corporation, will control everything down to who is allowed to live there.

Elsewhere, US companies stepped in to take advantage of relaxed investment laws, lower wages, and union repression. A 2016 *BuzzFeed News* investigation found that factory workers in a tax-free zone outside the city of Choloma were sewing shirts for meager wages in 100-degree heat on a subcontract for a clothing line owned by Donald Trump. Foreign investors have also taken to exploiting the land itself. The iron-oxide mining operation that drove Francisco to join the January caravan was partly backed by Nucor, the largest US steel manufacturer. Huge areas of countryside farmed by small cooperatives—consisting largely of indigenous peoples—were taken over by magnates (who were often narcos themselves) and turned into environmentally destructive palm oil plantations.

Equally ruinous for Hondurans have been the ubiquitous hydroelectric projects, most notoriously the Agua Zarca dam on the Gualcarque River. The project became famous largely because of Berta Cáceres, the daughter of a local midwife who led the Lenca people in protests against the dam and was murdered in 2016. Thanks to her efforts, prospective international investors, including the World Bank, eventually backed out. But DESA, a power company led by former US-trained military intelligence officers, pressed on. Two of the hit men who eventually broke into Cáceres's home and killed her were former DESA employees. So many campaigners were murdered in struggles against land grabs that the nonprofit Global Witness labeled Honduras "the deadliest country in the world to be an environmental activist."

∾

The Cáceres murder sparked international outrage, particularly on Capitol Hill. The state of human rights in Honduras had already become an issue during the violent repression that followed the 2009 coup. Now the fury among prominent human rights defenders reached a crescendo. The Vermont senator Patrick Leahy told the State Department that he would block aid until the Honduran government fully investigated the killing. In the House, progressives put forward a petition calling for the United States to pressure the Honduran government to block the dam and protect activists. Soon after, Hank Johnson of Georgia introduced the Berta Cáceres Human Rights in Honduras Act, which called for the immediate suspension of all aid to the Honduran police and military pending effective reforms, including removing the military from domestic policing operations. The bill got a swift response, not only from a wide range of activist groups, but also from Hernández, who flew to Washington to lobby against it. He found an attentive audience among centrists, and Johnson's bill never made it to the floor.

In 2017, Hernández ran for reelection. The constitution barred second presidential terms; Zelaya's cautious initiative regarding a change had been used as the pretext for his overthrow. But Hernández's handpicked Supreme Court, in a decision greenlit by the United States, simply repealed the rule, deeming it a "human rights" issue. With control of the electoral machinery and campaign coffers flush with cocaine cash, Hernández's prospects looked promising.

The opposition, meanwhile, had united behind Salvador Nasralla, a popular TV personality. On election night, with 57 percent of the votes counted, Nasralla was several points ahead, whereupon the count was abruptly halted. After it resumed, Hernández emerged as the victor by a narrow margin. Furious Hondurans took to the streets, and the military police responded with rifle fire, killing twenty-two people. But the most important reaction to the almost certainly fraudulent result came from Washington, where a senior State Department official told reporters that they had "not seen anything that alters the final result."

Now insulated against domestic challengers, Hernández gambled on the idea that Washington would continue to accept his fraudulent battle against corruption and the drug trade, thereby ensuring that US aid to the police and military continued to flow. (The total amount is artfully concealed in Pentagon accounting.) Given previous US support, it was a reasonable bet. Progressives in Congress still pressed for an aid cutoff, but centrists in both parties maintained their resistance. Hernández was even invited by the California representative Norma Torres to defend his record before members of Congress. The president's connections in the drug trade, however, were becoming harder to ignore. In January 2015, two brothers leading the rich and powerful Cachiros, a rival trafficking clan, made a deal with the DEA, turned themselves in, and offered chapter and verse on the trafficking activities of the Hernández brothers and their inner circle, leading eventually to Tony's arrest.

Not even the scandalous revelations from Tony's trial, however, have been enough to undo the two countries' special relationship. Two days before Tony's verdict, a tweet from the US Embassy in Honduras affirmed that "our governments cooperate on a wide range of issues including migration, security, the fight against narcotics, and economic development." Hernández's official Twitter account featured a photo of himself in jocular conversation at a military parade with the US chargé d'affaires, Colleen Hoey. A State Department official even declared Hernández "a reliable partner." Within weeks of the trial's revelations, the US military made it clear that nothing had fundamentally changed: Admiral Craig Faller, the commander of Southcom, flew to Tegucigalpa to present the country's top general, René Ponce Fonseca, who would feature in Fuentes Ramírez's trial as CC-13, with the Legion of Merit for his work on "the capability to interdict illicit flows."

As the caravan retreated from Guatemala this January, the newly sworn-in Joe Biden promised $4 billion in aid to Central America. Expressing commendable sentiments about immigrants with "little more than the clothes on their backs and hope in their hearts," Biden signed an executive order repealing many of Trump's more baleful antimigrant measures. He also called for a Root Causes Strategy that would discern and address the incentives leading to migration and proposed an international anticorruption commission that would aid Central American prosecutors in pursuing crooked officials.

This was familiar territory for Biden. As vice president, he had encouraged the creation of the Organization of American States's Mission to Support the Fight Against Corruption and Impunity in Honduras (MACCIH). More importantly, Biden had fostered the Alliance for Prosperity in the Northern Triangle (official parlance for Honduras, El Salvador, and Guatemala that neatly excludes migrant-free Nicaragua). The program, which launched in 2014 as border crossings exploded into a political crisis for the Obama administration, was funded by the United States to the tune of at least $750 million. It was billed as a way to foster economic development and the rule of law, empower women, hire police officers and teachers, and crack down on narcotics cartels, among other worthy commitments.

In his 2020 campaign, Biden touted the Alliance for Prosperity as a triumphant success, recounting how the "strategy [had] engaged the leaders of the region to take responsibility for improving economic prosperity through poverty reduction and regional integration programs, deepened security cooperation to reduce gang violence and combat transnational criminal organizations," and promised that he would follow a similar path as president. This was well received in the region by, among others, Hernández, who congratulated Biden on his inauguration: "We acknowledge your commitment with the Alliance for Prosperity and welcome your renewed support for the region." Alluding to the disastrous effects of the hurricanes and the pandemic, he added, "We can address this and other challenges effectively working together as we did in the past; for example our fight against drug dealing."

Hernández's enthusiasm was unsurprising, given that Biden's previous efforts had not changed much in Honduras. Desperate migrants continued to journey north—the total increased by 171 percent the year that the Alliance for Prosperity was launched—and MACCIH steered clear of anyone in or close to the Hernández regime. (After Trump abandoned even a rhetorical interest in fighting corruption, MACCIH was shut down in 2020.)

Juan Gonzalez, Biden's senior adviser on Latin America, declared sternly in a January interview with a Salvadoran paper that "a leader who won't attack corruption won't be a US ally." In that case, Hernández is surely disqualified. But in Honduras, people are getting impatient. The day before Gonzalez's remarks were published, forty human rights organizations signed a letter to Biden denouncing the support Hernández had received from the Obama and Trump administrations and "respectfully demanding the suspension of all military aid to Honduras." One of the principal authors was Oliva, the activist. I asked her whether a suspension of aid would stop people from fleeing the country. "People have left in caravans toward the land of those who created the problem and sustained it," she answered. "They left because they had lost hope that things would change and because many smelled death approaching. They ran out of time to wait for Washington to sort out the mess it created down here." If Hondurans were allowed to dismantle that regime without interference, she said, "of course it would make a difference."

Honduran human rights organizations may have little sway in Washington, but US senators from the majority party are a different matter. The Honduras Human Rights and Anti-Corruption Act, introduced on February 24 by the Oregon senator Jeff Merkley, demands that the United States designate Hernández as a narcotics trafficker, cut off all aid and arms sales to the Honduran military and police, and cooperate with the United Nations in monitoring human rights.

Merkley considers the security aid cutoff essential. "If we don't apply such pressure, then we're just facilitating and strengthening the force that is part of the problem," he told me the day after introducing the bill. "If we're going to be partners with them, to be part of the solution, they have to be a very different force." I asked whether Hernández, who had already responded to the bill by threatening to stop cooperating on antitrafficking efforts, was beyond redemption. "Just the fact that he would say 'I'll give the drug traffickers free rein if you try to have my security forces be part of the solution,'" Merkley replied, "tells you a lot about the type of person we're dealing with." I took that as a yes.

Despite the unwelcome attention, Hernández may be hoping that the United States will let him serve out the remaining year of his term in peace, or even run again. He would do well, however, to reflect on the fate of Manuel Noriega, Panama's dictator in the eighties. Heavily involved in the drug trade, Noriega was a cherished US partner until the day the military picked him up and consigned him to a prison cell for the rest of his life. I asked Colonel Keith Nightingale, a Special Forces veteran who participated in the strongman's capture, what had prompted Noriega's old friends to turn against him. "He had," Nightingale said, "become too obvious."

Harper's Magazine, May 2021

Postscript. Unfortunately for Hernandez, he too had become "too obvious." Due to term limits, he did not run again in the 2021 presidential election. Shortly after leaving office, he was extradited to the US, charged with multiple counts of drug trafficking and ultimately sentenced to forty-five years in jail after a New York trial in 2024. However, in November 2025, Trump pardoned Hernandez and freed him from prison.

14

The A-10 Saved My Ass

On January 24, US Central Command, which oversees military operations across the Middle East and West Asia, issued a press release reporting that the USS *Gravely*, an Arleigh Burke–class destroyer, had shot down two missiles fired by Yemeni Houthis at a US-owned container ship, the MV *Maersk Detroit*, in the Gulf of Aden. A third Houthi missile had landed in the sea. There was no damage to the ship. The *Gravely* was part of Operation Protective Guardian, deployed to safeguard commercial shipping through the Houthi blockade of the Bab-el-Mandeb strait and the Red Sea. The Americans and their allies claimed to have the measure of the situation. For the previous two weeks the US, assisted by the RAF, had been targeting Houthi missile bases with cruise missiles and precision-guided bombs. The *Gravely* was commissioned in 2010 and built at a cost of around $2 billion, with a sophisticated weapons system designed to intercept enemy missiles. The missiles fired by the Houthis are thought to have been AS-5 "Kelts," first deployed by the Soviet navy almost sixty years ago, and were targeted by very basic means, relying on the merchant ships' own tracking beacons, the Automatic Identification System (AIS) used by all commercial ships to broadcast their location. Despite the technological imbalance, the US Navy lost the battle, as revealed in a detail omitted from CentCom's five-line press release. After the incident, to avoid further missile attack, the *Maersk Detroit* and another Maersk vessel abandoned their attempt to run the blockade and headed to safer waters in the Arabian Sea, followed by a costly diversion around the African continent. Using comparatively primitive technology, the Houthis have disrupted a significant component of the global economy.

The word "disruptive" crops up a lot in Andrew Krepinevich's exhaustive treatise on military innovation, *The Origins of Victory: How Disruptive Military Innovation Determines the Fates of Great Powers*. His contention is that the adoption of innovative military technology ahead of rivals leads to victory. In support of his argument he delves into areas usually frequented only by specialists. Among them are the Fisher Revolution, which involved an initiative to build up-to-date warships for the Royal Navy in the years preceding the First World War; the evolution of Blitzkrieg in the German army between the world wars; and the development of aircraft carrier tactics by the US Navy, beginning in the 1920s. In each case he cites the advent of new or improved technology, such as long-range torpedoes in the British example, or fast Panzer units adopted by the Germans before World War II. He finds room to highlight the role played by leaders, such as the dynamic Admiral Jackie Fisher, sponsor of the "dreadnought revolution"; Generals Hans von Seeckt and Heinz Guderian in the creation of Hitler's Wehrmacht; and assorted interwar US naval leaders. But it is his evident belief that technology proved the decisive factor.

These historical precedents are merely a prelude to Krepinevich's cherished core example: the "precision warfare revolution," technologies pioneered by the US Air Force in the late twentieth century to guide bombs and missiles to their targets with unprecedented accuracy. His celebration of this long-sought achievement, dramatically demonstrated to the wider world in the 1991 war against Iraq in Operation Desert Storm, when TV audiences could watch videos beamed directly from the bombs as they destroyed Iraqi targets, comes with a cautionary warning. Putative enemies, the Russians and Chinese, have now introduced precision in their own forces, obviating the US advantage. This prompts Krepinevich, a defense policy analyst, to invoke the exciting possibilities of nascent technologies, such as the incorporation of AI, autonomous drones, cyberwar, space war, and other emerging "domains."

The book's argument should come as no surprise, given Krepinevich's relationship with the late Andrew Marshall, who directed the Pentagon's Office of Net Assessment for more than forty years. Krepinevich praises Marshall as "one of our country's greatest and most underappreciated strategists of the post–World War Two era" and "my principal intellectual mentor." The notion that Marshall has been underappreciated, especially in the higher reaches of the US defense complex, is hard to accept, since his prescriptions rarely if ever cut against the grain of the military's wishes, especially in the matter of spending; indeed, they were eagerly implemented by decision-makers, including successive secretaries of defense and military chiefs.

Most pertinently, Marshall promoted the proposition that advances in precision targeting had brought about a "revolution in military affairs" that had changed the nature of warfare. The triumph of 1991 served as a vindication of his high-tech approach. Krepinevich reports that, "armed with only a handful of stealthy aircraft and a small stockpile of precision-guided munitions … the coalition, led by the US Air Force, quickly suppressed Iraq's air defenses," whereupon the targeting switched to Iraqi ground forces so effectively that when coalition troops attacked Kuwait, "the Iraqi army simply collapsed." Unsurprisingly, this association of sweeping victory with the revolutionary technologies of stealth and precision targeting was accepted without challenge by the military and its industrial partners.

With Marshall's encouragement, Krepinevich wrote a celebratory report in 1992 titled "The Military-Technical Revolution: A Preliminary Assessment," which laid out the thesis of the "origins of victory," with reference to the historical examples of dreadnoughts, Blitzkrieg, and aircraft carriers. The stage was set for what became the standard US approach to warfare: aerial precision strikes against air defenses and "high-value" targets, as deployed in the Kosovo war of 1999, the Afghan and Iraq invasions at the beginning of the twenty-first century, and subsequent conflicts up to and including current engagements in Iraq, Syria, and Yemen.

All these operations have relied on the presumed ability of aerial bombardment not only to disable an enemy's defenses but also, in Krepinevich's words, "to identify a relatively small number of targets that, when successfully engaged (or engaged on a recurring basis), lead to the crippling of an enemy's military effectiveness or capacity to resist." The US Air Force was in fact devoted to this doctrine even before it achieved its independence from the Army in 1947. The idea was conceived in the 1930s at the Air Corps Tactical School and was deemed practicable thanks to the purported potential of the Norden bombsight, which measured an aircraft's direction and speed in order to predict the trajectory of the bombs it released. This was a military-technical revolution that clearly failed, as the bomber generals implicitly conceded when they switched to indiscriminate fire-bombing of Japanese cities late in World War II. In Vietnam, Air Force planners thought they had identified Hanoi's oil fuel storage tanks as a "critical node" essential to the enemy's war effort and duly destroyed them, only to find that the Vietnamese had anticipated the attack and stored their fuel in hidden sites elsewhere. A further attempt to eliminate Vietnamese supply lines down the Ho Chi Minh Trail by means of ingeniously designed sensors designed to detect enemy movements similarly failed, thanks to simple countermeasures deployed by the Vietnamese.

In this light it is worth examining the earlier military-technical revolutions Krepinevich invokes to buttress his arguments. They tell a story somewhat at variance with his conclusions. Admiral Fisher, one of Krepinevich's heroes, believed that the answer to the advancing technology of submarines and long-range torpedoes, which had called into question Britain's traditional strategy of closely blockading enemy ports, lay in fast ships armed with massive guns that could outrange enemy forces. He constructed a fleet of heavily gunned battleships and cruisers that shed some defensive armor in order to provide more speed and firepower. But in the only full-scale naval battle of World War I, at Jutland in 1916, the comparatively thinly armored British cruisers fell victim to accurate German fire, while British shells—thanks to deficient fuses—often failed to penetrate their well-armored German adversaries. Even so, superior British numbers might have brought about a significant victory (the battle was largely deemed a draw) were it not for a failing that had little to do with technology.

As Andrew Gordon explained in *The Rules of the Game* (1996), his brilliant dissection of the Royal Navy that fought at

Jutland, the service had become progressively encrusted over the previous century with a rigid mindset exacerbated by an ever more elaborate system of command and control exercised largely through signaling flags, which made it impossible for subordinate commanders to exercise initiative. Krepinevich considers Jutland a strategic victory for Britain, because it deterred the German surface fleet from further attempts to break out of the North Sea and attack Britain's Atlantic supply lines. But the German submarine fleet suffered no such inhibitions, wreaking havoc on unescorted merchant ships and bringing Britain to the brink of starvation and defeat. An honest review of the record casts the British naval leadership in a very poor light. As David Lloyd George explained in his memoirs, "before the War, the Board of Admiralty had concentrated so much on big and still bigger ships that they neglected essential weapons like mines, armor-piercing shells and torpedoes—all of which were inferior to those manufactured by the Germans." When he and other politicians pressed for the adoption of merchant ship convoys protected against submarines by naval escorts, they were met with what Lloyd George described as "implacable and prolonged resistance" from Fisher's protégés at the Admiralty. Only when sailors were forced to accept convoys did the tide turn.

When considering the German army that brought most of Europe under Hitler's control in the early years of World War II, Krepinevich pays due tribute to the military leaders who foresaw that the static and bloody attrition of the previous world war could be avoided by focusing on mobility and maneuver. Accordingly, they invested in fast-moving tank formations as well as an air force primarily dedicated to working in conjunction with ground troops. Though acknowledging the conceptual insights of generals like von Seeckt and Guderian, Krepinevich is happiest when dwelling on the technology they utilized, especially relatively speedy mechanized forces. But the real secret of German success lay in the encouragement and facilitation of initiative by lower-level commanders on the front line, who were free to devise the best means of accomplishing their mission without the interference of superiors. Aided by Guderian's insistence on putting a radio in every tank, they were able to adapt to and exploit changing circumstances on the battlefield faster than equally well armed but rigidly controlled opponents could respond. Hermann Balck, one of the most successful Panzer generals, later observed that "the German higher commander rarely or never reproached their subordinates unless they made a terrible blunder. They were fostering the individual's initiative." In other words, the system was geared to operate on the basis of an implicit understanding of what needed to be done, rather than relying on explicit instructions on the execution of the high command's plans.

Krepinevich devotes a section to the development by far-sighted exponents of American aircraft carrier tactics that culminated in their crushing victory over the Japanese navy at the Battle of Midway in June 1942. He once again identifies the seminal role of a few visionary leaders, such as Admiral Joseph Reeves, who pioneered a policy of operating carrier forces independently of battleship-heavy fleets. Krepinevich has little to say about similar trends in the Japanese navy, which would have led to the destruction of America's Pacific carrier force had the carriers not been fortuitously absent from Pearl Harbor on the day of Japan's surprise attack. The Japanese defeat at Midway six months later was in large part due to the success of US naval codebreakers in decrypting Japanese messages and the willingness of Admiral Chester Nimitz to concentrate his forces at Midway in defiance of orders from Washington. The readiness of lower-ranking officers to rapidly adapt fighter tactics and firefighting techniques thanks to lessons learned in the preceding Battle of the Coral Sea gave them a significant advantage over the more rigidly controlled enemy.

Fortified by his reading of historical examples from earlier in the twentieth century, Krepinevich turns his attention to the Gulf War triumph of 1991, and celebrates another 'leading visionary', US Air Force General Wilbur Creech. Krepinevich's glowing assessment of the 1991 success is unencumbered by any doubts as to the veracity of official accounts. Fortunately, we have an independent study by the General Accounting Office, carried out over several years with full access to detailed records (obtained in the face of strenuous official resistance), which paints a rather different picture. The F-117 "stealth" bomber, for example, purportedly invisible to radar, had often required the company of a host of escorting planes to jam enemy detection systems that supposedly could not see the bomber anyway. Far from "one target one bomb," as claimed by exultant laser-guided bomb manufacturers, the F-117 used an average of four, and sometimes ten, of the most accurate weapons to destroy a target. Overall, the investigators concluded, "many of [the Pentagon's] and manufacturers' postwar claims about weapon system performance … were overstated, misleading, inconsistent with the best available data, or unverifiable."

It can't be denied that the destruction of power plants, oil refineries, communications centers and other "high-value" targets identified by the planners as key to the functioning of Saddam Hussein's war machine did reduce Iraq to a preindustrial state. But the US offensive didn't induce the collapse of the Iraqi army, or the regime. Saddam evaded strenuous attempts to locate and kill him by avoiding his known headquarters, traveling unescorted in a Baghdad taxi. The elimination of the Iraqi army in Kuwait was largely accomplished not only by the evident unwillingness of Iraqi troops to fight, but by the US decision to abandon its initial plan for a frontal assault in favor of a "left hook" round the Iraqi flank, and by the heavy use of a weapon developed and operated on very different principles from the complex systems touted by Krepinevich. The A-10 close support plane, which a reluctant Air Force deployed to Saudi Arabia only on the direct order of the commanding US Army general, inflicted heavy damage on the Iraqi forces—so decisively that Chuck Horner, the local US air commander, cabled Washington in the immediate aftermath of the war to report that "the A-10 saved my ass." Armed with a quick-firing heavy-caliber cannon and designed to survive damage from antiaircraft fire, the plane enabled pilots to fly low, selecting targets on the basis of their own observation, without the fallible intervention of radar and other sensors.

This highly effective weapon had emerged from within an initiative that Krepinevich vehemently derides, the so-called military reform movement, which attracted significant attention and support in the press and Congress in the 1980s. This loosely constituted group, with a number of combat veterans at its core, including the legendary fighter pilot and theoretician of conflict Colonel John Boyd, argued that the complex and expensive weapons systems championed by the Pentagon and its industrial partners were inevitably unreliable and often ineffective in combat. Instead, they advocated cheaper, simpler, and thoroughly tested systems such as the A-10 and the lightweight F-16 fighter, programs trenchantly opposed by the Air Force high command.

Time has shown that the reformers were right. The course doggedly pursued by the Pentagon has ensured a force with shrinking numbers of basic weapons and personnel, despite ever more money being spent on defense. Money is lavished on advanced weapons systems whose effectiveness is questionable, and which are vastly expensive to maintain. The number of fighter and attack planes in the US Air Force, which stood at more than 4,000 forty years ago, has dwindled to just over 2,000 today. The complexity of the weapons that do get bought means that they are diminishingly available for training and combat. In the 1990s, military pilots spent an average of twenty hours a month in the air; today they fly for between five and ten hours a month. At any one time, 40 percent of the US Navy's attack submarines are out of commission for repairs.

None of these sobering details trouble Krepinevich, who prefers to dwell on the urgent necessity of developing increasingly fantastical programs: hypersonics, genetic engineering, quantum computing, and of course AI. Copious sums are indeed being lavished on such projects. In 2019 the Pentagon inaugurated an AI system called Gamechanger, in the hope of enabling it to discover where all its money goes—so far without success, as it has continued to fail an audit of its accounts.

The US military is heavily involved in ongoing conflicts—either by proxy, as in Ukraine, or directly, as in the Middle East. To date, the results have shed a poor light on the military-technological revolution. Successive "game-changing" systems dispatched to Ukraine, notably the High Mobility Artillery Rocket System (designed to hit targets with great precision at long range), have failed to produce victory while eliciting effective countermeasures on the part of the Russians. Artillery has dominated the battlefield, consuming massive quantities of shells which in the West are in short supply thanks to the prevailing preference for the production of more exotic weapons. Drones, it's true, have brought major changes to the battlefield, but the machines that have had the most striking impact are cheap ones originally designed for the consumer market and adapted in the field for lethal purposes by frontline troops—conceptually similar to the jerry-rigged explosive devices that caused havoc to Western armies in Iraq and Afghanistan. In the Middle East, the US still seeks out and strikes "high-value" targets, as it has done for the past three decades, picking off insurgent leaders who are then predictably replaced with equally or more determined commanders. All the wonders of precision targeting and comprehensive surveillance notwithstanding, the Houthi blockade of the Red Sea is as effectively disruptive as ever.

London Review of Books, March 21, 2024

15

The Worst Defense Program of All

When Vladimir Putin took over Crimea in 2014, the immediate reaction among defense lobbyists was "borderline euphoric," as one denizen of that world told me at the time. As might be expected, the invasion of Ukraine has brought a bountiful harvest for the military-industrial complex, as manifested in the $782.5 billion budget for 2023 recently waved through by congressional appropriators. In every respect, the proposed budget reflects the Pentagon's core strategy, which, in the words of the late Col. John Boyd, is "Don't interrupt the money flow, add to it." Thus it is that we continue to pour cash into notorious sinkholes such as the F-35 fighter, still unable to pass operational tests and for most of the time incapable of carrying out its combat missions.

But despite the F-35's regular reminders that our system of "defense" hardly deserves the name, there is another Air Force program, largely unknown in the wider world, that to my mind is the quintessence of everything that is rotten about the system; a perfect case study not only in straightforward financial malfeasance, but also in the unceasing and disastrous effort to substitute technology for human actions. I refer to the KC-46 aerial tanker.

Flying tankers, "gas stations in the sky," are the arteries of global US military operations, essential for deploying troops, supplies, and bombing missions around the globe. Since the 1950s, this vital service has been largely provided by the Boeing KC-135, which first flew in 1956, as well as a smaller number of McDonnell Douglas KC-10s, dating from the 1970s. These aircraft supply fuel via a retractable boom which is guided onto the recipient plane by an operator looking through a window at the back of the tanker. The system is simple, and has worked with minimal mishap for some seventy years.

In 2001 the Air Force requested bids for a new tanker to replace its aging fleet. Boeing won with a design based on its existing 767 airliner, securing a contract for 100 tankers. But rather than simply buying the planes in the normal fashion, the Air Force agreed to lease them from Boeing. This novel arrangement was burdensome to the taxpayer but vastly profitable to the corporation, adding at least $10 billion to the cost of the program. Subsequent investigation revealed that Darlene Druyon, the senior Air Force official negotiating the deal, known to her peers as "the Dragon Lady," had simultaneously negotiated a fat post-retirement contract for herself. Other senior Pentagon officials, including the secretary of the Air Force as well as the Pentagon's chief weapons-buyer, were also revealed to have worked hard on Boeing's behalf. Druyun ultimately went to jail, along with a senior Boeing executive. Asked in a Senate hearing whether in thirty-three years of government service he had "ever seen a deal as dirty as this one," the chief auditor of the Pentagon's Inspector General's office replied, "No, sir, I have not."

Following exposure of these squalid dealings, Boeing's contract was canceled. A new competition handed the prize to a consortium of the Northrop-Grumman Corporation and Europe's Airbus which offered a variant of the Airbus 330 airliner. Boeing fought back fiercely and succeeded in getting the Airbus deal canceled. A further competition, seemingly tilted in Boeing's favor, handed the contract back to the corporation in 2011. Development proceeded, with the plane, dubbed the KC-46 "Pegasus," projected to enter service in 2017. The inevitable schedule slippages and cost overruns ensued, and of course the KC-46 did not come into service on time. In early 2021, the US Air Force cleared the plane for only limited use, meaning that it could refuel some but not all of its planes and fly exclusively over the continental US, thus making the KC-46 useless for combat operations.

Amid a host of problems such as leaking fuel and "foreign objects" mislaid by careless construction workers inside the fuselage, one fundamental defect defies solution, despite hundreds of millions of dollars sluiced into efforts to solve it. As noted, existing refueling systems rely on a boom-operator using his own two eyes to guide the boom. It's simple, and it works. But the Air Force had a better idea, which it mandated be employed in any new tanker. Discarding the low-tech option of human eyesight, the KC-46 moves boom control up to the front of the plane, where a crewman sits in front of a video monitor featuring an image of the recipient plane and attempts to guide the boom via its Remote Vision System.

It doesn't work. As a Government Accountability Office report stated dryly in January this year, the system did not provide "visual clarity," meaning that a lot of the time boom operators can't properly see the plane they're trying to refuel, or connect with it properly when they do. "The lack of visual clarity also resulted in undetected contacts with some receiver aircraft and, in some cases, damage to the receiver aircraft's coating," meaning that receiving pilots risk having their fuselages dented or windshields cracked. Boeing is now working on a second iteration of this disastrous system, "RVS 2.0, which will feature high-definition 4k video cameras, infrared cameras, laser rangefinders, and "augmented reality," all in an effort to reproduce the visual clarity, especially depth perception, that comes with the traditional benefits of three-dimensional human eyesight.

No one, it seems, bothered to ask the people who would be on the receiving end of the wondrous new technology. A veteran combat pilot friend who has "tanked" hundreds of times from various tankers put it this way to me in a recent email: "The problem is that most systems we have tried to build to replace the human in the boom seem to be epic fails. Human eyes are still better at seeing things like closure rates / depth perception / and through high cloud ice crystals. I have had some wicked close calls that were saved by a human in the boom."

Under its 2011 contract, Boeing was supposed to shoulder any development costs exceeding the "fixed price" $4.9 billion contract, which might suggest stern resolve by the military to make the contractor pay for its failures. Of course, the defense business doesn't work like that. Uncle Sam, or at least General

Sam, always looks after his own. Thus the Air Force is pledged to continue buying twelve to fifteen planes a year, at around $180 million a pop, regardless of the fact that they are largely useless. Meanwhile, the promised RVS 2.0 will not be independently tested before 118 planes, altogether 60 percent of the production run of 179 KC-46s, have already been built. In other words, the Air Force has agreed to take Boeing at its word that the new system actually works. On the likely assumption that it won't, the taxpayer will have to bear the burden of further attempts to fix the system.

This is not only a particularly egregious case of defense corruption, but also an example of a deeper problem: the urge to displace direct perceptions of the real world in favor of costly and therefore profitable technological interfaces. At its most extreme, this has given us drone warfare, in which "pilots" in Nevada or some such remote location select human targets on the other side of the world. Reality does not need to be augmented.

Responsible Statecraft, March 26, 2022

16

The $850 Billion Chicken Comes Home to Roost

Watching a recent video of Ukrainian troops scrambling out of a US-supplied Bradley armored fighting vehicle just after it hit a mine, I remembered how hard the US Army bureaucrats and contractors who developed the weapon had fought to keep this vehicle a death trap for anyone riding inside.

As originally designed, the Bradley tanks promptly burst into flame when hit with anything much more powerful than a BB pellet, incinerating anyone riding inside. The armor bureaucrats were well aware of this defect, but pausing development for a redesign might have hurt their budget, so they delayed and cheated on tests to keep the program on track. Prior to one test, they covertly substituted water-tanks for the ammunition that would otherwise explode. Only when Jim Burton, a courageous Air Force lieutenant colonel from the Pentagon's testing office, enlisted Congress to mandate a proper live-fire test were the Army's malign subterfuges exposed and corrected. His principled stand cost him his career, but the Bradley was redesigned, rendering it less potentially lethal for passengers. Hence, forty years on, the survival of those lucky Ukrainians.

This largely forgotten episode serves as a vivid example of an essential truth about our military machine: It is not interested in war. How else to understand the lack of concern for the lives of troops, or producing a functioning weapon system? As Burton observed in his instructive 1993 memoir *Pentagon Wars*, the US defense system is "a corrupt business—ethically and morally corrupt from top to bottom."

Nothing has happened in the intervening years to contradict this assessment, with potentially grim consequences for men and women on the front line. Today, for example, the US Air Force is abandoning its traditional role of protecting and coordinating with troops on the ground, otherwise known as Close Air Support, or CAS. Given its time-honored record of bombing campaigns that had little or no effect on the course of wars, CAS has probably been the *only* useful function (grudgingly) performed by the service.

The Air Force has always resented the close support mission, accepting the role only because handing it to the Army would entail losing budget share. Thus, the A-10 "Warthog" aircraft, specifically dedicated to CAS, was developed by the Air Force only to ward off a threat from the Army to steal the mission with a new helicopter. As it turned out, the A-10, thanks to the dedicated genius of its creators, notably the late Pierre Sprey, was supremely suited to the mission. But its successful record cuts no ice with the Air Force, which has worked with might and main to get rid of the A-10 ever since the threat of an Army competitor in the eternal battle for budget share had been eliminated.

That campaign is now entering its final stages. The Air Force is not only getting rid of its remaining fleet of A-10s, it is also eliminating the capability to perform the close air support mission by phasing out the training for pilots and ground controllers essential for this highly specialized task. True, the service claims that the infamously deficient F-35 "fighter" can and will undertake the mission, but that is a laughable notion for many reasons, including the fact that the plane's 25 mm cannon cannot shoot straight.

The consequences for American troops on the ground in future wars will be dire, but their fate apparently carries little weight when set against the unquenchable urge of the Air Force to assert its independence from the messy realities of ground combat, where wars are won or lost. Thus, its hopes and budget plans are focused on costly systems of dubious relevance to warfare such as the new B-21 bomber, the new Sentinel ICBM, and the Next Generation Air Dominance fighter, none of which will fly for years to come, except in the form of cash out of our pockets.

Pentagon spending this year is projected to nudge $850 billion (the total national security bill is already way past a trillion, but that's another story). Yet, even when endowed with such a gigantic pile of cash, the system is apparently incapable of furnishing the wherewithal for even a limited war, such as the one currently underway in Ukraine. The conflict has been marked by successive announcements that progressively more potent weapon systems are being shipped to the Ukrainians—Javelin anti-tank missiles, 155 mm howitzers, HIMARS precision long-range missiles, Patriot air defense missiles, Abrams tanks, with F-16 fighters in the offing. A US military intelligence officer pointed out to me recently the actual basis on which these systems are selected: "when we run out of the last system we were sending."

Now Biden has generated global outrage by promising to send cluster bombs, known for their ability to kill and maim children fifty years after the relevant war has ended, as any Laotian farmer could tell you. The military rationale for their use is their supposed utility against "soft" targets such as dismounted infantry, radars, and wheeled vehicles. However, a former armor officer and veteran of the 1991 Gulf War recalled to me that "we disliked them intensely and pleaded with the artillery and Air Force not to employ them. They simply damaged support elements and wheels that followed us into action. After the war we treated numerous people wounded by them including our own soldiers, as well as civilians (children)."

Biden has admitted that these devices are being sent only because the US is running out of the artillery ammunition that the Ukrainians actually require. "This is a war relating to munitions. And they're running out of that ammunition, and we're low on it," he told a TV interviewer. So off go the cluster bombs, their passage lubricated by crocodile tears from administration officials: "I'm not going to stand up here and say it was easy … It's a decision that required a real hard look at the potential harm to civilians," National Security Adviser Jake Sullivan told reporters. (Back when it was reported that the Russians were using cluster bombs in Ukraine, then White House Press Secretary Jen Psaki denounced such action as "a war crime.")

Thus, the richest war machine in history, having scraped its cupboard bare, is now reduced to fielding a device of dubious military utility deemed illegal by over a hundred countries. That's what we get for our $850 billion.

As Russian forces steadily advance in the Kharkiv region, it is becoming ever more clear that the Ukraine war has been a disaster for the US defense machine, and not just because our aid has failed to save Ukraine from retreat and possible defeat. More importantly, the war has pitilessly exposed our defense system's deep, underlying faults.

Critics have long maintained that our obsession with technologically complex weapons inevitably yields unreliable systems produced in limited numbers because of their predictably high cost. They are furthermore likely to fail in combat because of the military's lack of interest in adequate testing (lest realistic tests reveal serious shortcomings and thereby threaten the budget). The unforgiving operational test provided by the Ukraine war has shown that the critics were absolutely right. Successive "game changing" systems—such as the Switchblade drone, the M-1 Abrams tank, Patriot air defense missiles, the M777 howitzer, the Excalibur guided 155 mm artillery round, the HIMARS precision missile, GPS-guided bombs, and Skydio drones endowed with artificial intelligence, were all dispatched to "the fight," as the military like to call it, with fanfare and high expectations. All were destined to fail for reasons rooted in the fundamental problems cited above. The $60,000 Switchblade drone, produced in limited numbers due to cost, proved useless against armored targets and was quickly discarded by Ukrainian troops in favor of $700 Chinese commercial models ordered online. The $10 million Abrams tank not only proved distressingly vulnerable to Russian attack drones but in any case broke down repeatedly and was soon withdrawn from combat, though not before the Russians put several out of action and captured at least one, which they took to Moscow and added to a display of Nato weaponry in a Moscow park that included an M777 howitzer and other items of NATO hardware. The M777 cannon, though touted for its accuracy, has proved too delicate for the rough conditions of sustained combat, with barrels regularly wearing out and requiring replacement in Poland far from the front lines. Notoriously, its 155 mm ammunition has been in short supply. Thanks to the consolidation of the US defense industry into a small number of monopolies, an ill-judged policy eagerly promoted since the Clinton administration, US domestic production of 155 mm shells is reliant on a single aging General Dynamics plant in Scranton, Pennsylvania, which is struggling to meet its targets. President Zelensky has been loudly demanding more Patriot launchers and missiles to defend Kharkiv, which is curious, given the apparent ease with which the Russians have targeted Patriots defending Kyiv, and the system's declining effectiveness against Russian ballistic missiles. HIMARS long-range missiles initially had deadly effect on high-value Russian targets, such as ammunition dumps, but the Russians adapted by dispersing and camouflaging such dumps and other likely targets.

Strikingly, many of the failures of US weapons in Ukraine have been due to their reliance on a highly vulnerable guidance system: GPS. The Russians, who have long devoted intense care and attention to electronic warfare, have proven increasingly adept at jamming GPS. This has been most witheringly expressed by Maria Berlinskaya, a pioneer in Ukraine's use of drones and head of the country's aerial reconnaissance support center, who recently stated that "most Western systems have proven to be [worthless]" thanks to Russian jamming. Her gloomy assessment was confirmed in April by none other than William LaPlante, undersecretary of defense for acquisition and sustainment, who told a CSIS conference how a company (Boeing, though he did not name it) had proposed adapting their small diameter GPS guided bomb as a warhead for the HIMARS. It had been accordingly rushed through development and into production, with little or no testing, and shipped off to Ukraine. "It just didn't work," admitted LaPlante, thanks to Russian GPS jammers that threw it off course and caused it to miss. The same sad fate seems to have befallen the Skydio drone, product of an eponymous Silicon Valley startup, whose AI features trumpeted by the company— "Skydio drones have the compute capacity to see, understand, and react in real time"—did not prevent it from being driven off course by Putin's jammers.

Needless to say, none of these assorted failures were anticipated by the US military high command, few of whom would be eager to denigrate the wares of contractors with lucrative post-retirement board seats on offer. We might hope that our senior civilian leadership would be aware of such biases and temper their expectations accordingly. Unfortunately, they drank the Kool Aid, as evidenced for their high expectations for the 2023 Ukrainian counteroffensive. Despite high hopes and lavish supplies of weapons, including tanks, ammunition, drones, intensive training on the territory of NATO allies, and a grounding in US command-and-control doctrine, the counteroffensive was an immediate and total failure. Planners were apparently caught by surprise by the depth of Russia's (easily visible) defensive fortifications, especially minefields and the effectiveness of its electronic jamming. Ever since then, Ukraine has been steadily retreating, losing in the process its reserves of military manpower.

Responsible Statecraft, July 18, 2023, and May 29, 2024

17

The Failure of Russian Sanctions

Summarizing British plans for economic warfare against Germany in World War I, Winston Churchill wrote that the objective of the blockade, as sanctions used to be called, was to "starve the whole population of Germany—men, women and children, old and young, wounded and sound—into submission."

Germany's defeat in 1918 convinced the victors that the strategy had succeeded and that sanctions of a similar nature could henceforth be deployed in bringing recalcitrant nations to heel at little or no cost to the sanctioneers. In fact, it is not at all clear that the blockade *had* indeed been the cause of German food shortages, which were equally likely brought about by the government's mismanagement of the German agricultural economy. Such quibbles did not trouble the economic warriors of the time, nor have they since.

Confidence in the efficacy of the weapon has been unaffected by a record of unbroken failure, as evidenced in the boasts a month into the war in Ukraine of Daleep Singh, then deputy NSC director for international economics, in a *60 Minutes* interview titled "Economic Shock and Awe." Polished and confident, Singh, billed as the author of the "sanctions doctrine," assured his unquestioning interviewer that "Russia is on a fast track to a 1980s-style living standard. It's looking into an economic abyss." His boss, President Joe Biden, echoed this theme, claiming that the ruble would soon be "rubble."

True to form, nothing of the kind has come to pass. The Russian currency is trading slightly higher than when Singh's prediction went on the air. Inflation is at almost the same level. Moscow shops continue to offer a full range of Western consumer goods, while e-commerce trade with the outside world has actually grown by 30 percent. The IMF is projecting that the Russian economy will actually grow this year and next. Despite baroque efforts to crimp Putin's oil export income, "Urals crude" continues to flow at levels—roughly 4 million barrels a day—unchanged from prewar levels, not least through Indian, Turkish, Chinese, and Senegalese refineries, whence it moves unimpeded into European gas tanks and power plants.

Such blatant circumvention of the sanctions regime is studiously ignored by the sanctioneers, since it is necessary to ward off catastrophic energy price inflation in western economies. Efforts to at least crimp the price at which Russia sells its oil via a "price cap" mechanism appear to have had little effect: Asian refiners are reportedly paying full price. (In a less publicized example of officially endorsed sanctions evasion, Russian exports of enriched uranium, originally mined in Kazakhstan, are duly labeled "Kazakh" and continue to power US reactors.)

The fundamental miscalculation underlying this apparently unforeseen failure of the economic weapon parallels the record of another instrument of coercion cherished by the US over the course of the last century. Strategic bombing targeted against "critical nodes" of an opponent's war-making apparatus has, like its economic counterpart, singularly failed to achieve its desired objectives, most recently in the "targeted killing" campaign against the Taliban's human infrastructure.

Both strategies rest on a mechanistic view of the targeted system in which components deemed essential to its functions can be identified and destroyed. Taliban and similar insurgent operations always adapted speedily to the loss of supposedly key individuals. Just as Hitler's Germany did to US bombing of "critical" ball bearing factories, so Putin's Russia has adapted to Singh's confident assault.

It has become clear that he or whoever planned the sanctions strategy didn't really understand the Russian economy very well, especially its place in the global system. Instead, US strategy appears to have proceeded on the assumption that Russia, in the words of the late John McCain, was merely "a gas station masquerading as a country" as opposed to an essential source for everything from oil to grain to metals such as nickel, well able to feed itself and maintain industrial output at a high level.

Furthermore, this mode of economic warfare inflicts penalties on the perpetrator of a kind escaped by the latter's military counterparts. Apart from the moral obloquy attendant on incinerating German and Japanese cities, or obliterating Afghan families with Hellfire missiles, the air-attack strategy incurs only the cost of a bloated arms budget and, most recently, defeat in the relevant war.

The economic war against Russia is likely to have more serious consequences for US power, since it accelerates the de-dollarization of the global economy—quite certainly accelerated by the ill-considered "shock and awe" initiative in seizing $300 billion of Russia's foreign exchange reserves lodged in Western banks. In response to this mammoth heist, China is overseeing a shift away from the dollar in energy trades, most significantly in paying for Saudi oil in renminbi, an ominous development for the US.

Putin has been derided for his misplaced assumption that his small invasion force could seize control of Kiev in a coup de main. Biden and his advisers thought that "shock and awe" would bring swift victory. That may have been an even more serious mistake. Meanwhile Daleep Singh himself has moved on to greener pastures as chief global economist and head of global macroeconomic research at PGIM Fixed Income, one of the world's largest fixed income asset managers with $890 billion under management. Thus situated at a commanding height of the global economy, he will be answering to more inquisitive observers than a credulous TV interviewer.

Responsible Statecraft, February 22, 2023

Postscript. Daleep Singh returned to the White House as deputy national security adviser in May 2024, his confidence in the sanctions weapon undimmed, despite its ongoing failure to bring

Russia to heel. At the very end of Biden's term he announced the imposition of yet more sanctions, declaring, "Sanctions have sapped the most essential sources of Russia's economic vitality" and were forcing Putin to face "hard choices." Needless to say, he was wrong, again.

18

Weed Whackers

Monsanto, Glyphosate, and the War on Invasive Species

On a Friday evening in January 2015, a thousand people at the annual California Native Plant Society conference in San Jose settled down to a banquet and a keynote speech delivered by an environmental historian named Jared Farmer. His chosen topic was the eucalyptus tree and its role in California's ecology and history. The address did not go well. Eucalyptus is not a native plant but a Victorian import from Australia. In the eyes of those gathered at the San Jose DoubleTree, it qualified as "invasive," "exotic," "alien"—all dirty words to this crowd, who were therefore convinced that the tree was dangerously combustible, unfriendly to birds, and excessively greedy in competing for water with honest native species.

In his speech, Farmer dutifully highlighted these ugly attributes, but also quoted a few more positive remarks made by others over the years. This was a reckless move. A reference to the tree as "indigenously Californian" elicited an abusive roar, as did an observation that without the aromatic import, the state would be like a "home without its mother." Thereafter, the mild-mannered speaker was continually interrupted by boos, groans, and exasperated gasps. Only when he mentioned the longhorn beetle, a species imported (illegally) from Australia during the 1990s with the specific aim of killing the eucalyptus, did he earn a resounding cheer. California native-plant partisans are a committed lot, and not only in their dislike of eucalyptus trees. Many of them are influential in local government, and they yearn to restore the

treeless "native" grassland that greeted the first European settlers of the Bay Area in 1769. (For centuries, Native Americans
had cleared the trees to facilitate hunting.) Thus the romantic
Monterey cypress is a frequent target for the chain saws of the
San Francisco Recreation and Parks Department—even though
two small stands in Monterey, just fifty miles south, are cherished
and protected as natives. The cypress is not the only item on the
nativist hit list. Over the next few years, more than 450,000
trees in Oakland, Berkeley, and neighboring areas are due to be
destroyed in the name of "wildfire-risk reduction."

Defining "native" and "invasive" in an ever-shifting natural
world poses some problems. The camel, after all, is native to
North America, though it went extinct there 8,000 years ago,
while the sacrosanct redwood tree is invasive, having snuck in at
some point in the past 65 million years. The National Invasive
Species Council defines the enemy as "an alien species whose
introduction does or is likely to cause economic or environmental
harm or harm to human health." But the late, great evolutionary
biologist Stephen Jay Gould dismissed such notions as "romantic drivel." Natives, he wrote, are simply "those organisms that
first happened to gain and keep a footing," and he ridiculed
the suggestion that early arrivals "learn to live in ecological
harmony with [their] surroundings, while later interlopers tend
to be exploiters."

Even so, anti-invasive ideology is prevalent across the country,
from university biology departments to wildlife bureaucracies
to garden clubs. In Virginia, where I spend part of my time, a
nice lady from the Virginia Native Plant Society told me that
her idea of a truly natural landscape was the one viewed by the
Jamestown settlers in 1607. To that end, she sternly urged me
to uproot my yellow-blossomed forsythia (of Balkan origin)
and replace it with a "good native shrub." In Texas, George W.
Bush used to devote much of his presidential vacation time to
destroying the tamarisk trees—reviled Eurasian imports—that
grew on his ranch. Many states maintain invasive-plant councils (and sometimes exotic-pest plant councils) to monitor and
eradicate alien invaders. Last year, the North Carolina Invasive
Plant Council gave its annual Certificate of Excellence to two

forest rangers who had detected a small patch of cogongrass—an invasive unwittingly imported from Asia in packing crates, which the Vietnamese call "American weed," because it spread on land defoliated by Agent Orange.

As it happens, an erstwhile supplier of Agent Orange, the Monsanto Company, also manufactures America's most popular remedy for cogongrass: glyphosate. The active ingredient in Monsanto's Roundup and many other weed killers, glyphosate is the weapon of choice for battling all sorts of invaders. A 2014 study by the California Invasive Plant Council found that more than 90 percent of the state's land managers used the compound, which is particularly recommended as a slayer of eucalyptus trees. Discussing *Phragmites australis*, the reed found in wetlands throughout the country, Massachusetts conservation officials similarly tout this "effective" weed killer. Pennsylvania urges glyphosate's deployment against purple loosestrife, while Illinois recommends it for Japanese knotweed. The Louisiana Department of Wildlife and Fisheries prescribes it for cogongrass but warns that "multiple applications for full control" may be required.

This anti-invasive mania is not merely a local phenomenon. It is the official position of the federal government, as expressed by the State Department, that "invasive alien species pose one of the most serious threats to our environment, affecting all regions of the United States and every nation in the world." In February, National Invasive Species Awareness Week was celebrated in Washington, complete with a reception on Capitol Hill. Last year, the federal government spent more than $2 billion to fight the alien invasion, up to half of which was budgeted for glyphosate and other poisons.

That's small change, nativists argue, when measured against the damage such interlopers inflict on the national economy. The Department of the Interior claims that the annual tab is $120 billion. But this number comes from a 2005 report by David Pimentel, an ecologist and scholar at Cornell, whose dislike of aliens apparently extends to the human variety, as evidenced by his public opposition to both legal and illegal immigration. Pimentel extrapolated at least some of his findings from such dubious assumptions as the dollar value of grain consumed by each rat in the United States. In an earlier paper, he concluded that cats were costing us $17 billion every year, after calculating that our furry (and, in his view, nonnative) friends kill an annual 568 million birds, and arbitrarily valuing each bird at $30.

On close examination, other examples of the damage said to be caused by exotic invaders look no less questionable. The supposedly supercombustible eucalyptus, for example, survives fires that consume surrounding plant life—and rather than unfairly appropriating water, the tree actually irrigates soil by absorbing moisture from the coastal fogs through its leaves and funneling it out through its roots. (Though still cited as the prime culprit in the devastating 1991 Oakland firestorm, the eucalyptus was in fact cleared of responsibility in a FEMA report.) Monarch butterflies belie its reputation for repelling wildlife, the eucalyptus being their favored wintering abode in California.

As for the tamarisk, it consumes no more water than the beloved cottonwood, native to the Southwest. Nor, contrary to rumor, is it inhospitable to other species, as certified by the endangered southwestern willow flycatcher, which delights in roosting amid the tamarisk's foliage. According to Matthew Chew, a historian of biology at Arizona State University, the tree's sorry reputation dates to a ploy during the 1940s by a local mining corporation, whose operations required enormous quantities of river water—which had already been allocated to local farmers and other businesses. The solution was to generate studies demonstrating the heinous quantities consumed by the thirsty tamarisk. The destruction of the trees would theoretically free up huge quantities of "new" water in the rivers, which could then be used by the selfsame mining corporation. Then there is the zebra mussel. This immigrant from the Caspian Sea is a perennial target of the nativists, thanks to its tendency to reproduce in vast numbers, encrust jetties, clog water-intake pipes, and crowd out God-fearing American mussels. But zebra mussels have successfully filtered pollution in the notoriously filthy Lake Erie and other waterways, thus promoting the revival of aquatic plants. The mussel also feeds a growing population of smallmouth bass and lake sturgeon.

It is the common reed, however, that has inspired one of the most determined and dubious campaigns of extermination. Phragmites is accused of robbing other plants, fish, and wildlife of essential nutrients and living space. Delaware has responded by spraying and respraying on an annual basis a 6,700-acre expanse of the Delaware River estuary with thousands of gallons of glyphosate-based weed killer. In 2013, locals in the Hudson River community of Piermont, New York, discovered a plan to destroy a 200-acre reed marsh fronting the town. Outraged, they fought back. "We love the marsh," an indignant Marthe Schulwolf, who is active in opposing the scheme, told me. "It's beautiful, a living environment, with lots of wildlife, and it protected us from the Hurricane Sandy storm surge." The townspeople were especially alarmed to learn that the state's "toolbox" for eradication included heavy spraying of herbicides—glyphosate being the customary choice—right next to two playgrounds.

As usual, the nativist dream of eradicating the interloper is intertwined with a fantasy of restoring the landscape to its "original" condition. The common reed has also covered vast stretches of the New Jersey Meadowlands, to the irritation of nativists who yearn for the return of the original cordgrass. Peter Del Tredici, formerly a senior research scientist at Harvard's Arnold Arboretum, points out that the New Jersey Turnpike bears much of the blame: by blocking tidal flows, inimical to phragmites, it has allowed the reed to flourish. Ripping out the highway would bring back the cordgrass soon enough. "Meanwhile," he adds, "there are over five hundred landfills in this area that are leaking nitrogen and phosphorus, and phragmites is actually cleaning the site up." In any case, he said, the very idea of "re-creating a lost landscape is an impossibility, because the conditions under which these landscapes evolved no longer exist. The world is a totally different place as a result of human activity. There's no going back in time."

Mark Davis, a professor of biology at Macalester College and a frequent critic of anti-invasive hysteria, put it more pungently. "It's the same perspective as ISIS wanting to re-create the seventh-century caliphate," he remarked. "It's ecological fundamentalism, the notion that the purity of the past has been polluted by outsiders." Far from crowding out native species, he argued, invasives tend to move into areas that have been ravaged, or at least disturbed, by human activity. They are, in other words, a symptom, not a cause. Cogongrass is one striking example, but the same pattern recurs with many vilified species. Ailanthus, a salt-friendly seaside tree from China, spread inland from the East Coast along the fringes of America's interstates, tracking the salt religiously spread by highway departments during winter snowstorms.

If the anti-invasive movement rests on such debatable foundations, why has it flourished in this country, winning endorsement from activists, local, state, and federal bureaucracies, and respected academics? It's not as though hostility to newly arrived plant species has been a great American tradition. In California, the eucalyptus was once universally cherished for its graceful and colorful appearance in a land often devoid of trees—indeed, during the 1870s, it was planted by the hundreds of thousands. A century ago, the tamarisk was promoted by the US Army Corps of Engineers as an ideal means to prevent soil erosion in the Southwest. Even kudzu was once hailed as the "Lord's indulgent gift to Georgians": government nurseries grew millions of seedlings and distributed them to farmers as a restorative for depleted soil.

Nowadays, the notion that plants and animals have a "natural" habitat, from which outsiders must be expelled, has taken firm hold in the United States—first among a cadre of biologists, then in the media, and ultimately at the highest levels of the federal government. What happened? David Theodoropoulos, a California naturalist and seed merchant and the author of *Invasion Biology: Critique of a Pseudoscience*, is blunt about what he sees as a deadly inversion of environmental priorities. "Thirty years ago," he told me, "the greatest threats to nature were chain saws, bulldozers, and poisons. Now the greatest threats are wild plants and animals. And what do we use to fight them? Chain saws, bulldozers, and poisons. Who does this serve?"

Retracing some recent history may help to answer his question. During the Reagan era, when environmentalists were still imbued with the spirit of Earth Day, nobody worried about invasive species. Instead, well-organized, militant groups were busy fighting chemical pollution, nuclear power, shale-oil drilling, logging devastation, and other corporate onslaughts. According to Jeffrey St. Clair, a historian of environmentalism, "People like [Reagan's interior secretary] James Watt definitely mobilized the movement, and so the corporations weren't really able to get all that they wanted."

By 1992, the movement had a self-appointed standard-bearer in the political arena: Senator Al Gore of Tennessee. That year he published his best-selling *Earth in the Balance*, in which he manfully vowed to bear the political costs of his environmental crusading:

> Every time I pause to consider whether I have gone too far out on a limb, I look at the new facts that continue to pour in from around the world and conclude that I have not gone far enough … The time has long since come to take more political risks—and endure more political criticism—by proposing tougher, more effective solutions and fighting hard for their enactments.

These uplifting sentiments were not always matched by actions. Critics noted Gore's championship while in Congress of the $8 billion Clinch River breeder-reactor project, riddled with fraud and bribery. They also pointed out his legislative maneuvers on behalf of the Tellico Dam, on the Little Tennessee River, a $100 million boondoggle denounced by David Brower, the founder of Friends of the Earth, as "the beginning of the end of the Endangered Species Act." Following the 1992 election, former Gore staffers moved into key environmental posts at the EPA and elsewhere. There they would benefit would-be polluters such as Disney (which had just been fined for dumping sewage in the Florida wetlands) and food processors (irked by a 1958 ban on carcinogens, soon to be repealed under the 1996 Food Quality Protection Act).

Nevertheless, as far as the public was concerned, nature had no more stalwart defender than Gore. So when Senator Bob Graham of Florida wrote to him in June 1997 about "the growing environmental threat posed by alien (non-indigenous) invasive species," he received an enthusiastic response. In fact, the issue was already on Gore's mind. A few weeks earlier, he had received a letter signed by a large group of biology professors, including the eminent scholar and ant expert E. O. Wilson, warning that "a rapidly spreading invasion of exotic plants and animals not only is destroying our nation's biological diversity but is costing the US economy hundreds of millions of dollars annually." Among the ominous examples cited were the zebra mussel and the invasion of San Francisco Bay by a new exotic species "on the average of once every twelve weeks."

Gore sprang into action. He reassured Graham that Clinton's circle of scientific advisers had already established a Biodiversity and Ecosystems Panel, which would "be considering the issue of invasive species and will report their recommendations at the end of the year." The panel's chair, he noted parenthetically, was Peter Raven.

The official White House biography of Peter Raven listed him as the director of the Missouri Botanical Garden, and noted that he held a professorship at Washington University in St. Louis. That description failed to convey the full reach of his power and prestige as America's leading botanist. Wade Davis, an ethnobotanist at the University of British Columbia, describes Raven as a "total force of nature. He took a staid Midwest botanical garden and put it on steroids, turning it into the greatest institution of its kind on earth." A former president of the American Association for the Advancement of Science, *Time* magazine Hero for the Planet, chairman of the National Geographic Society's Committee for Research and Exploration, Raven was (and is) a hugely influential figure, with a network that extends through academic, government, and corporate bureaucracies. He originally made his name in scientific circles with a 1964 paper, "Butterflies and Plants: A Study in Coevolution," written with Paul Ehrlich, a biologist later famous for the dire (and unfulfilled) predictions sketched out in his 1968 bestseller, *The Population Bomb*. Like Ehrlich, Raven tended to express a gloomy view of the planet's prospects. He regularly lamented the wholesale loss of our biodiversity, brought about by the accelerating extinction of plant and animal species. "We're over the mark anyway in preserving the world's sustainability," he told me in a recent conversation. "We've passed the point at which we can really do that effectively."

Raven's panel set to work and released its report, *Teaming with Life: Investing in Science to Understand and Use America's Living Capital*, in March 1998. The report took a bearish view of the ecological future, sounding an apocalyptic note on the first page:

> Collectively, all human beings, including Americans, are playing a crucial role in the sixth major extinction event to occur in the course of more than three billion years of life on Earth ... During the history of the United States, more than 500 of its known species have been eliminated (half of these since 1980) by various causes, including destruction of habitat by human activities or invasive species.

Although the document repeatedly stressed the virtues of bio-diversity, it showed little sympathy for "invasive species such as killer bees, zebra mussels, fire ants, and the Mediterranean fruit fly," which were supposedly devastating the natural environment and posing "threats to the health of our human population." The zebra mussel, receiving no thanks for its heroic pollution-control efforts, was singled out for obloquy, having "cost more than $5 billion just to clean out pipes clogged by extremely densely clustered populations." (A decade later, a careful study by a team of Cornell scientists assessed zebra-mussel damage at one twentieth of that amount over fifteen years.) Amid the gloom, however, the report identified a ray of hope: genetically modified organisms (GMOs). "It is anticipated that the US market for seeds of genetically modified crops will grow to $6.5 billion during the next ten years," it noted, "and the annual production value of the plants derived from those seeds will be many times that amount."

The Monsanto Company could not have put it better. This was not surprising, since Raven (who retired in 2010) and Monsanto were close, both geographically and financially. The Missouri Botanical Garden was located just a few miles from Monsanto headquarters in St. Louis, and it owed much of its explosive growth to the beneficence of the corporation, which was in the process of changing its public identity from a chemical manufacturer and purveyor of Agent Orange to a "life sciences company"—one heavily invested in GMOs. In April 1996, Monsanto CEO Robert Shapiro joined Raven to break ground for the Monsanto Center, a four-story structure designed to house the garden's unique collection of botanical books and dried plants. Monsanto had contributed $2 million toward the center's construction, and had also donated the land and $50 million for the Danforth Plant Science Center, another GMO-intensive research facility.

"Monsanto loved Raven," a former senior executive at the company told me. "They were always showing off the Missouri Botanical Garden, bringing important visitors down to meet him, having him give tours, talks. He was definitely our show-piece." For his part, Raven spoke publicly about the virtues of GMOs. The company's grand scheme was to genetically modify crops—particularly corn, soybeans, and cotton—to render them immune to the glyphosate in Roundup. This would allow farmers to spray weeds without killing the crops. *Teaming with Life* featured a Monsanto photograph of a flourishing bioengineered plant next to a pathetic nonengineered plant obviously about to expire. "Major companies will be, *are*, a major factor if we are going to win world sustainability," Raven told an interviewer in 1999. "There is *nothing* I'm condemning Monsanto for." (In his conversation with me, Raven defended his former patron even more stoutly, noting Monsanto's many civic philanthropies and absolving the company of any ill intent: "They obviously have no interest in poisoning everybody or doing something bad.")

I asked Raven whether his efforts to protect the natural world didn't clash in some way with his support for something very unnatural: GMO technology. "What's natural anymore?" he replied. "If we're going to play God, we might as well be good at it."

While Monsanto played God during the 1990s, the Clinton administration had its back—a policy consistent with its corporate-friendly approach to environmental issues. When, for example, the French balked at allowing GMO corn into their country, the president, the secretary of state, the national security adviser, and assorted US senators pleaded Monsanto's cause. (The French finally caved when Gore himself phoned the prime minister to lobby on the corporation's behalf.) In addition, Washington's revolving door whirled many Clinton administration officials onto the Monsanto payroll, while the president's committee of science and technology advisers included Virginia Weldon, the corporation's senior vice president for public policy.

The Raven panel's recommendation to join battle with invasives got rapid traction. "The invasion of noxious weeds has created a level of destruction to America's environment and economy that is matched only by the damage caused by floods, earthquakes, wildfire, hurricanes, and mudslides," cried Interior Secretary Bruce Babbitt when the report was released. Within a year, Clinton signed Executive Order 13112, creating the National Invasive Species Council "to prevent the introduction of invasive species and provide for their control and to minimize the economic, ecological, and human health impacts that invasive species cause." Among the founding members of the council's advisory committee was Nelroy E. Jackson, a product development manager and weed scientist for Monsanto who had helped to develop Roundup formulations specifically for "habitat-restoration markets"—that is, for eradicating invasives.

For all Monsanto's talk of "life sciences," the company's profits, especially in those days, rode on glyphosate. According to Tao Orion's book, *Beyond the War on Invasive Species*, the compound was originally invented to clean dishwashers and other appliances. Then someone noticed that it destroyed any plant it touched. By the late 1990s, Monsanto's Roundup revenues were growing at 20 percent a year, and the compound was duly revered inside the corporation. As the former company executive put it to me: "Roundup was God at Monsanto." Such divine status was assured by its symbiotic relationship with Monsanto's bioengineered corn and soybeans. The strategy worked. Farmers were planting GMO crops in ever-increasing amounts—from just over 4 million acres worldwide in 1996 to 430 million in 2013.

The results of this exotic intervention were not so positive, however, for Raven's treasured biodiversity. The larva of the monarch butterfly, for example, feeds exclusively on milkweed, a plant that glyphosate is tremendously effective at killing: unlike other herbicides, it attacks the milkweed's roots. As the rain of glyphosate increased, surpassing 141,000 tons on US crops in 2012, the butterfly's food supply dwindled to the vanishing point. In 1995, at the dawn of the Roundup Ready era, a billion monarchs fluttered over America's fields; by 2014, the number had fallen to 35 million, and there was talk of declaring the butterfly an endangered species.

Raven remains optimistic about the monarch, citing Monsanto's "very exciting" plan to foster milkweed growth in noncultivated areas. Such natural oases, however, are few and far between in the Corn Belt. Those that remain are likely to host other invasive plants, such as garlic mustard, denounced as a "serious invader from the east" by Iowa State University, which inevitably recommends "spot applications" of glyphosate as a remedy. Meanwhile, the growth curve in glyphosate use has steepened, thanks to a practice that began in 2004. Late in the season, many farmers are now spraying the compound on crops that are *not* bioengineered to resist it, in order to kill them off and produce artificially early harvests.

"You can imagine the residue levels on the damn wheat," said Charles Benbrook, an agricultural economist at Washington State University. "If you buy whole-wheat bread, the glyphosate will be ground up with the whole-wheat kernel and it will be part of the flour. It's a very high exposure. When they make white flour, the bran gets separated out and is used in the food supply in other places. That bran will have three or four times the concentration of glyphosate, because that's where the residues are lodged. It's insanity."

Over the years, there have been repeated allegations that glyphosate is dangerous for humans—charges vehemently denied by Monsanto and its friends in high places. "Table salt and baby shampoo are more toxic, or as toxic, as glyphosate," Rand Beers told *60 Minutes* in 2001. Beers, George W. Bush's assistant secretary of state for international narcotics, was defending the US-funded spraying of a glyphosate-based compound on millions of acres in Colombia as part of an effort to wipe out coca plantations. Despite Beers's dutiful denials, however, the mixture turned out to be a lot more dangerous than baby shampoo, afflicting the population with painful rashes and other ailments. It also did a fine job of wiping out the vegetables and poultry that made up the local food supply, while often failing to kill the coca plant, its intended target.

This disaster made no difference. Nor did a 1985 EPA study suggesting that glyphosate might give humans cancer, a finding that the EPA reversed in another study six years later. In 2013, a French report on the compound's carcinogenic effect on rats was withdrawn in the face of an intense lobbying effort by the company. Through thick and thin, Monsanto stuck, in the words of a company spokesperson, to its mantra: "All labeled uses of glyphosate are safe for human health and supported by one of the most extensive worldwide human health databases ever compiled on an agricultural product." Then came a massive speed bump. This past March, seventeen scientists met in Lyon, France, under the auspices of the International Agency for Research on Cancer, an arm of the World Health Organization, to assess the carcinogenic potential of several chemicals. The group was led by Aaron Blair, an internationally renowned epidemiologist and the author of more than 450 scientific papers, who spent thirty years at the National Cancer Institute. Among the chemicals they evaluated was glyphosate.

As Blair explained to me, the group reviewed three kinds of data: lab tests on animals, epidemiological studies on humans who had been repeatedly exposed to glyphosate, and "mechanistic" analyses of the ways in which the compound could cause cancer. The animal studies, Blair said, "found excesses of rare tumors." Absent glyphosate exposure, the tumors "are *really* rare. They almost never just occur." The studies on human beings, conducted in the United States, Canada, and Sweden, pointed to an equally grim conclusion. "They showed a link between people who used or were around glyphosate and an increased risk of non-Hodgkin's lymphoma. Different studies, in different places, suggested that they might go together."

According to Blair, there were good grounds to declare that glyphosate definitely causes cancer. This did not happen, he said, because "the epidemiologic data was a little noisy." In other words, while several studies suggested a link, another study, of farmers in Iowa and North Carolina, did not. Blair pointed out that there had been a similar inconsistency in human studies of benzene, now universally acknowledged as a carcinogen. In any case, this solitary glitch in the data caused the group to list glyphosate as a probable (instead of a definite) cause of cancer.

The reaction from Monsanto was predictably irate. GMO Answers, a PR website put together by the biotech-food industry, featured a host of derisive posts about the study. Sympathetic journalists went to bat on behalf of the lucrative toxin. Hugh Grant, Monsanto's chairman and CEO, was curtly dismissive: "It's unfortunate that junk science and this kind of mischief can create so much confusion for consumers."

As it had on previous occasions, the company demanded a retraction of the report. When we talked, it didn't sound as if Blair was likely to do any such thing. "Historically, the same thing happened with tobacco, the same thing happened with asbestos, the same thing happened with arsenic," he said. "It's *not* junk science." The French government agreed, promptly banning the sale of Roundup by garden stores in response to Blair's report. The Colombian authorities meanwhile halted the coca-spraying program, over US government protests. The program had not been a huge success, of course, given the target plant's remarkable ability to survive the spray.

But unintentional glyphosate resistance is not confined to coca. Although Monsanto scientists had deemed such a development nearly impossible for weeds targeted by the Roundup Ready system, species subjected to prolonged exposure began to adapt and survive even as farmers were harvesting their first bioengineered crops. "It's a disaster," said Benbrook. "As resistant weeds spread and become more of an economic issue for more farmers, the only way they know how to react—the only way that they feel they *can* react—is by spraying more." It has now become common for farmers to spray three times a season instead of once, and Benbrook estimates that the extra doses of herbicide will add up to 75,000 tons in 2015.

All of which brings us to horseweed, or mare's tail, a plant native to North America and once highly prized for its medicinal qualities. It has hairy stems, and grows about four feet tall. A nuisance in corn and soybean fields, it has naturally been a glyphosate target. But in recent years, farmers have been encountering a new kind of mare's tail: a superweed produced by years of glyphosate treatment. Not only does it refuse to die when drenched with four times the recommended dose, but it appears to gain strength from the experience, growing up to eight feet tall, with stems thick enough, according to one farmer, to "stop a combine in its tracks."

Harper's Magazine, September 2015

19

Spent Fuel

The Risky Resurgence of Nuclear Power

Last June, Bill Gates delivered a video address to a crowd of politicians and reporters assembled in Cheyenne, Wyoming. "Fifteen years ago I assembled a group of experts to solve the dual problems of global energy poverty and climate change," the sweater-clad multibillionaire declared. "It became clear that an essential tool to solving both is advanced nuclear power." But the technology, he continued, needed to become safer and less expensive. To this end, he had promised to invest $1 billion in TerraPower, a company he founded in 2008 to develop small modular reactors that can be churned out on an assembly line. He was now happy to announce the construction of a plant on the site of a defunct coal facility in Wyoming.

Gates and other backers extol the promise of TerraPower's Natrium reactors, which are cooled not by water, as commercial US nuclear reactors are, but by liquid sodium. This material has a high boiling point, some 1,600 degrees Fahrenheit, which in theory enables the reactor to run at extreme temperatures without the extraordinary pressures that, in turn, require huge, expensive structures. "It's smaller, cheaper, and inherently safe," Jeff Navin, the director of external affairs at TerraPower, told me.

As concern about climate change grows, nuclear power has gained new appeal, particularly on the left, for its promise as a supplement to wind and solar power in eliminating carbon dioxide emissions. What's more, the prospect of cheaper and "safer" technology may relieve nuclear energy of unsavory historical baggage, notably the disastrous accidents at Chernobyl in 1986 and Fukushima in 2011. Early in her first term, Representative Alexandria Ocasio-Cortez hailed the shutdown of the half-century-old Indian Point nuclear plant just north of New York City, but cautioned that "one plant built decades ago is not emblematic of the technology that we have today," adding that "the Green New Deal leaves the door open on nuclear." She reiterated this position a year later, calling nuclear power "a critical part of this conversation," even if "we have to make sure that the technology is vetted."

Saikat Chakrabarti, who helped draft the Green New Deal in 2019 as Ocasio-Cortez's chief of staff, was less equivocal. "We took a tech-agnostic position on nuclear in the original deal because nuclear is such a polarizing issue," he told me. But their internal analyses concluded that "there's a big baseload problem that cannot be solved with wind and solar," because they are intermittent. Acknowledging residual public fears, he insisted that "nuclear power is now extremely safe to operate, and the technology is improving all the time with these small modular reactors," such as TerraPower's design.

"It's generational," observed Navin. "If you were active in the environmental movement in the Seventies, if you went through Three Mile Island"—the plant near Harrisburg, Pennsylvania, that sparked panic in 1979 when it began melting down—"you're likely to be antinuclear today. But for young people concerned about the environment, anyone under thirty-five, it's not an issue. The polls barely registered a blip over Fukushima." The Sunrise Movement, a grassroots group founded in 2017 to recruit an "army of young people" to fight climate change, has at times backed the idea of a hybrid grid that combines renewables and nuclear power. Even groups long noted for opposing nuclear power, such as the Union of Concerned Scientists and the Sierra Club, seem quietly ready to temporize on practical matters, such as allowing existing plants to continue as transitional energy sources. The "sobering realities" of climate change, wrote the UCS's then president Ken Kimmell in 2018, "dictate that we keep an open mind about all the tools in the emissions reduction toolbox—even ones that are not our personal favorites." As

Navin put it, "the environmental movement has changed focus from local issues, such as protecting air and water, to climate change. That's the driving focus, a realization that we have to move from climbing a lot of hills to climbing one very tall hill in a very short time." He has no doubt that nuclear power, which he noted is currently generating half of all clean energy in the United States, will play a central role in the path to a carbon-free future.

The nuclear-power industry has long enjoyed establishment support. Navin was acting chief of staff at the Department of Energy under Barack Obama. The current energy secretary, Jennifer Granholm, says that the Biden administration plans to launch more nuclear energy projects across the country, and touts in particular Natrium's promise of "345 megawatts of clean and affordable and reliable baseload power." The White House climate czar, Gina McCarthy, stresses the need to keep existing plants in operation, as well as the prospects for "these small nuclear reactors, these modular reactors," in which "people are really investing significant resources." The State Department has launched an effort to foster similar small reactor programs abroad. Most significantly, even amid bitter fights over the administration's infrastructure and social-reform bills, the inclusion of $41 billion of industry subsidies in the legislation has received unquestioning bipartisan backing. "We've been getting quite a bit of attention from the administration and from Congress," Maria Korsnick, the president of the Nuclear Energy Institute, told me. "I'm happy that the broader conversation has brought it round to recognition of the positive value of nuclear [for] the environment." But the conversation needs to be a lot broader than that.

Dwight Eisenhower's "Atoms for Peace" program, unveiled in 1953, set the optimistic tone for nuclear power: "The United States knows that peaceful power from atomic energy is no dream of the future. The capability, already proved, is here today," and would "rapidly be transformed into universal, efficient, and economic usage." Four years later, Moorpark, a small town northwest of Los Angeles, became the first American community to draw its electricity from a nuclear reactor. Moorpark's power came from the Sodium Reactor Experiment, operated by the

Atomic Energy Commission at the Santa Susana Field Laboratory twenty miles away. The AEC—a precursor to today's Department of Energy—invited Edward R. Murrow to commemorate the event on his television show. "Enrico Fermi once looked at a reactor and said, 'Wouldn't it be wonderful if it could cure the common cold?'" intoned Murrow. "Here at Moorpark, a chain reaction that started with him washed the dishes and lit a book for a small boy to read." No such lyrical announcement marked the day in July 1959 when the plant's coolant system failed and its uranium oxide fuel rods began melting down. With the reactor running out of control and set to explode, desperate operators deliberately released huge amounts of radioactive material into the air for nearly two weeks, making it almost certainly the most dangerous nuclear accident in US history. The amount of iodine-131 alone spewed into the southern California atmosphere was 260 times that released at Three Mile Island, which is generally regarded as the worst ever US nuclear disaster. None of this was revealed to the public, who were told merely that a "technical" fault had occurred, one that was "not an indication of unsafe reactor conditions." As greater Los Angeles boomed in the following years, the area around the reactor site—originally chosen for its distance from population centers—was flooded with new residents. No one informed them of the astronomical levels of radioactive contaminants seeded deep in the soil.

Meanwhile, utilities were commissioning scores of nuclear plants across the country and promising electricity "too cheap to meter," incentivized by the 1957 Price-Anderson Act, which shifted financial liability in the event of a serious accident onto taxpayers. Rapid development throughout the sixties engendered hopeful predictions from the AEC that more than a thousand reactors would be operating in the United States by the turn of the century. But it was not to be. As the environmental movement gathered strength in the seventies, the dangers associated with nuclear power—from the routine disposal of radioactive waste to the risk of catastrophic meltdowns—galvanized a determined, informed, and organized opposition. Then, in 1979, one of two reactors at Three Mile Island had a partial meltdown. Officials from the president on down issued soothing reassurances, downplaying the health risks. Negative assessments were discouraged; when the Pennsylvania state health secretary, Gordon MacLeod, criticized the state's response, he was promptly fired by the governor. MacLeod later revealed that child-mortality rates had doubled within a ten-mile radius of the plant. Cost overruns in plant construction, sometimes two times above industry estimates, were a further deterrent to expansion. Ultimately, more than 120 projects were canceled, and construction ground to a halt. "The failure of the US nuclear power program ranks as the largest managerial disaster in business history, a disaster on a monumental scale," *Forbes* magazine commented in 1985, a year before Chernobyl. "Only the blind, or the biased, can now think that most of the money has been well spent."

Amid the gloom, a distant ray of light for the industry began to flicker. On a hot day in June 1988, the NASA scientist James Hansen told a packed Senate hearing, "with ninety-nine percent confidence," that the earth's temperature was at its warmest on record and that this was because of carbon dioxide emissions. By the following January, the *New York Times* was editorializing that THE GREENHOUSE EFFECT IS FOR REAL and calling for "a new generation of safer, cheaper nuclear power plants." Later that year, Hans Blix, the chairman of the International Atomic Energy Agency, told the United Nations that "the public should be aware that nuclear energy emits ... no carbon dioxide whatever." Given this assumption (which discounts the enormous quantities of carbon dioxide generated during plant construction), nuclear power's high cost could be offset by rewarding its low emissions. One way to limit pollution is to put a price on it, a point not lost on at least one farsighted industry executive. In 1992, John Rowe, then CEO of New England Electric System, which owned several nuclear plants in the region, began making the case for carbon pricing as a response to climate change.

Other partisans of nuclear power also recognized the relevance of climate alarms. This included Alex Flint, a staffer for Senator Pete Domenici of New Mexico. Flint started working for Domenici as a teenager and eventually rose to a position overseeing the billion-dollar budgets of the nation's nuclear weapons laboratories, including Los Alamos and Sandia. (Other Domenici staffers irreverently referred to his office as "the glow-in-the-dark team.") By the mid-nineties, Flint told me, scientists at the labs had convinced him "that the climate was changing, and we had a very serious problem."

In 2000, following a traditional trajectory for well-connected congressional staffers, he moved over to the private sector as a lobbyist and quickly recruited an impressive list of nuclear-industry clients, including Exelon Corporation. John Rowe, the apostle of carbon pricing, had just created Exelon by merging two giant utilities with extensive holdings in nuclear and coal plants. Rowe proceeded to sell off the coal operations, because, as he later explained, "I thought climate legislation would come sooner or later and that I'd rather have my money in the nuke fleet." At the same time, Exelon spent heavily on lobbying in Washington. Within ten years of its founding, the company had invested more than $35 million in such efforts. Unfortunately for Rowe, the oil and gas industry had even deeper pockets and was viscerally opposed to any price penalty on its copious emissions. But Rowe's investment still yielded gratifying returns, most notably in the 2005 Energy Policy Act. The bill authorized $13 billion in tax credits, plus additional loan guarantees, for new commercial reactors. This enormous bounty was crafted by none other than Alex Flint, who had returned to public service as the staff director of the Senate Committee on Energy and Natural Resources. (He then moved back to private employ the following year to head the Nuclear Energy Institute's governmental affairs office.) Money authorized under the act began to flow in 2007, when Congress appropriated $18 billion in loan guarantees for new reactors and another $4 billion for uranium enrichment. The largesse sparked hopes of a "nuclear renaissance" as utilities announced plans for new reactors.

By then, climate change had moved to the forefront of public discussion. Obama spoke eloquently of the threat during his 2008 campaign and urged a cap-and-trade initiative to curb carbon emissions. His close ties to Chicago-based Exelon were highlighted by bountiful campaign donations from Rowe and other executives, as well as the prior service of his chief strategist

David Axelrod as a consultant for the company. One Exelon lobbyist boasted of serving "the president's utility." But Exelon was not alone in securing presidential favor. In February 2010, Obama announced $8.3 billion in loan guarantees for two new reactors known as Vogtle 3 and 4, to be built in Burke County, Georgia. "We will not achieve a big boost in nuclear capacity," declared the president, "unless we also create a system of incentives to make clean energy profitable." As is traditional with the placement of such industrial facilities, the new reactors were to be constructed adjacent to a poor Black community. The neighborhood, Shell Bluff, was already racked by cancers that residents ascribed to existing nuclear facilities. Not surprisingly, they vehemently opposed the project. "We voiced our opinion," one local resident told CNN. "We didn't want them, but we're just the little peons." The president, they said, "doesn't know we're down here.

Eleven years later, the Vogtle plants are still under construction. Originally slated to be finished in 2017, they may now be ready in 2023. Costs have soared from $14 billion to $27 billion, a hefty slice of the overrun being borne by electricity customers in Georgia. Next door in South Carolina, ratepayers are still seeing onerous supplements on their monthly bills for two plants that were abandoned in 2017 because of soaring costs and the bankruptcy of the main contractor. In November 2020, Kevin Marsh, the former CEO of the South Carolina utility SCANA, pled guilty to fraud in concealing the $9 billion cost of the uncompleted reactors. He is now serving a two-year prison sentence.

Passing off additional costs to utility customers would appear to be a standard business model. It tends to require the complaisance of state legislators, who can demand and receive a high price for their favors—unseemly transactions that call into question the notion of "clean" nuclear energy. In November 2016, senior executives at Ohio's FirstEnergy hatched plans to shunt more of the operating costs of their two nuclear plants onto individual customers. As later detailed by an FBI criminal complaint, the scheme involved lubricating the election of a cooperative Republican legislator named Larry Householder as

Speaker of the Ohio House of Representatives. To this end, $61 million moved via a series of dark money cutouts to Householder, who used the funds both for personal needs and for financing his campaign and those of allies who could supply the necessary votes for the rate increase. It proved a sound investment. Householder was duly elected Speaker and proceeded to pass a bill in 2019, with bipartisan support, that authorized $1 billion in rate supplements to bail out the company's two Ohio plants. (One of these, Davis-Besse, outside Toledo, has a hair-raising safety record, including a hole in the reactor vessel and cracks in its concrete containment shell.) Although the bill canceled existing mandates for renewable energy, proponents were eloquent in their concern for the climate. Representative Jamie Callender, for example, who got just under $25,000 from FirstEnergy and served as a primary sponsor of the bill, spoke piously of the need to encourage "zero carbon emissions." A FirstEnergy spokesman applauded Callender and other sponsors "for their efforts in recognizing the important and vital role nuclear energy, along with many other clean energy sources, plays in providing clean, safe, and reliable carbon-free energy to Ohioans."

Unfortunately for the plotters, the FBI had monitored their deliberations. Following disclosure of the bribery scheme, public outrage led to a repeal of the bailout. Householder, indicted along with four associates, denies the charges and has yet to go to trial. FirstEnergy, none of whose employees faced criminal charges, agreed to a $230 million fine, and its generating unit was spun off under the name Energy Harbor. ("We call it Pirates' Cove," joked the Toledo attorney Terry Lodge, who has been litigating cases related to Davis-Besse since 1979.)

While Energy Harbor saw its scheme collapse, Exelon has suffered no such setback in pursuit of bailouts through similar means. A federal investigation revealed that an Exelon subsidiary lavished favors in the form of jobs and contracts on associates of Illinois House Speaker Mike Madigan, long the most powerful politician in the state, and was rewarded with beneficial legislation, most notably a $2.35 billion subsidy enacted in 2016, for two money-losing reactors that the company had discussed closing. The subsidiary agreed to pay a $200 million fine, which was more than balanced by the $694 million subsidy signed into law by J. B. Pritzker in September 2021, a response to Exelon's threats to close two other aging plants—one of which appears to have generated a significant cancer cluster in its neighborhood. Though the Sierra Club opposes nuclear energy, the Illinois chapter supported that legislation because of the measures it included to phase out coal and gas sources. The Illinois bailout is far eclipsed, however, by the federal largesse promised by the Biden administration's infrastructure and climate legislation. An analysis by the Nuclear Information and Resource Service suggests that 54 percent of the $41 billion will be split between just three companies, with Exelon set to receive $15 billion. (Energy Harbor is the runner-up, with $5 billion.)

For all the hopeful talk about new technology, however, the industry's principal concern is to keep aging reactors running long after their original life spans, even where this poses serious safety risks. In a process known as embrittlement, for example, vital components such as containment vessels crack following decades of neutron bombardment, leading to the release of lethal radiation. Nonetheless, the Nuclear Regulatory Commission appears happy to grant extensions: plants originally designed to last forty years are being authorized to run for sixty or eighty in total. Point Beach 2, a reactor on Lake Michigan that the NRC itself listed in 2013 among the most embrittled plants in the country, is applying to be relicensed to operate for eighty years. The reactor and its twin, Point Beach 1, have been cited for safety violations and equipment malfunctions more than 130 times. At the NRC, there is even discussion of allowing plants to run for a century, long after their designers and builders are dead. "None of these extreme extensions have addressed critical 'knowledge gaps' for the reliability of major irreplaceable and inaccessible systems," said Paul Gunter of Beyond Nuclear, a tireless watchdog group working to challenge the extensions. In his view, the industry is being allowed to head blindly into the unknown, with no idea how or when age-related cracking and embrittlement will lead to component failure and potential meltdown.

❧

Prosperous and 70 percent white, West Hills, California, is one of the communities that have sprouted near the Santa Susana Field Laboratory in the decades since the 1959 meltdown. Unlike the poor, sick, and embittered residents of Shell Bluff, people living in West Hills had until recently only the barest inkling that nuclear power in the neighborhood might have had unwelcome consequences. "Almost no one knew about the Santa Susana Field Lab, or they thought it was an urban legend," Melissa Bumstead, who grew up in nearby Thousand Oaks, told me recently. In 2014, Bumstead's four-year-old daughter, Grace, was diagnosed with an aggressive form of leukemia. "This has no environmental link," her pediatric oncologist told her firmly. Childhood cancers were rare, and this was just cruel luck. Then, while taking Grace to Children's Hospital Los Angeles, Bumstead ran into a woman who recognized her from the local park where their young daughters played. The woman's child had neuroblastoma, another rare cancer, as did another from nearby Simi Valley, whom they encountered while the children were getting chemo. Back at home, someone on her street noticed the CHILDHOOD CANCER AWARENESS sticker on Bumstead's car and mentioned that another neighbor had died of cancer as a teenager. Bumstead began to draw a map detailing the cluster of cancer deaths in small children just in the previous six years, but stopped working on it in 2017. "I had such severe PTSD when I added children onto it, my therapist told me to stop." But it is still happening, she said, mentioning the unusual number of bald children she had noticed in local elementary schools in recent years, as well as the far-above-average rate of breast cancer cases recorded in the area. A cleanup of the field lab was due to be completed in 2017, but it has yet to begin.

I called Bumstead because I had been struck by the fact that TerraPower's Natrium reactor resembles in its basic features the long-ago Sodium Reactor Experiment at Santa Susana. (*Natrium* is Latin for sodium.) "That's exactly what we had!" Bumstead exclaimed when I mentioned that liquid sodium is integral to TerraPower's project. "The meltdown was in the sodium reactor." As her comment made clear, such liquid sodium technology is by no means innovative. Nor, in an extensive history of experiments, has it ever proved popular—not least because liquid sodium explodes when it comes into contact with water, and burns when exposed to air. In addition, it is highly corrosive to metal, which is one reason the technology was rapidly abandoned by the US Navy after a tryout in the *Seawolf* submarine in 1957. That system "was leaking before it even left the dock on its first voyage," recalls Foster Blair, a longtime senior engineer with the Navy's reactor program. The Navy eventually encased the reactor in steel and dropped it into the sea 130 miles off the coast of Maryland, with the assurance that the container would not corrode while the contents were still radioactive. The main novelty of the Natrium reactor is a tank that stores molten salt, which can drive steam generators to produce extra power when demand surges. "Interesting idea," Blair commented. "But from an engineering standpoint one that has some real potential problems, namely the corrosion of the high-temperature salt in just about any metal container over any period of time."

TerraPower's Jeff Navin assured me in response that Natrium "is designed to be a safe, cost-effective commercial reactor." He added that Natrium's use of uranium-based metal fuel would increase the reactor's safety and performance. However, Blair told me that such a system had been tried and abandoned in the fifties because the solid fuel swelled and grew after fissioning.

In a March 2021 report for the Union of Concerned Scientists, the physicist Edwin Lyman likewise concluded that there was little evidence that reactor designs like Natrium's would be safer than water-cooled models. "When I read about many of the current proposals," Blair said, "it is almost as if they are unaware of all the work that has gone before." Citing the Navy's abandonment of sodium reactors, he suggested that companies such as TerraPower "are unaware, or intentionally choose to ignore history." He recalled that Admiral Hyman Rickover, who ran the Navy's nuclear program for three decades, would personally command the sea trials of every new nuclear submarine. In that spirit, he suggested, "they should only license a small modular reactor on condition that the head of the corporation that built it takes up permanent residence within a quarter mile of the plant."

As the sodium saga indicates, the true history of nuclear energy is largely unknown to all but specialists, which is ironic given that it keeps repeating itself. The story of Santa Susana follows the same path as more famous disasters, most strikingly in the studious indifference of those in charge to signs of impending catastrophe. The operators at Santa Susana shrugged off evidence of problems with the cooling system for weeks prior to the meltdown, and even restarted the reactor after initial trouble. Soviet nuclear authorities covered up at least one accident at Chernobyl before the disaster and ignored warnings that the reactor was dangerously unsafe. The Fukushima plant's designers didn't account for the known risk of massive tsunamis, a vulnerability augmented by inadequate safety precautions that were overlooked by regulators. Automatic safety features at Santa Susana did not work. This was also the case at Fukushima, where vital backup generators were destroyed by the tidal wave.

No one knows exactly how much radiation was released by Santa Susana—it exceeded the scale of the monitors. Nor was there any precise accounting of the radioactivity released at Chernobyl. Fukushima emitted far less, yet the prime minister of Japan prepared plans to evacuate 50 million people, which would have meant, as he later recounted, the end of Japan as a functioning state. Another common thread is the attempt by overseers, both corporate and governmental, to conceal information from the public for as long as possible. Santa Susana holds the prize in this regard: its coverup was sustained for twenty years, until students at UCLA found the truth in Atomic Energy Commission documents.

Most striking of all is the success of official campaigns asserting that even the most serious accidents have caused little or no harm. The spectacular scale of the Chernobyl disaster, with its mass evacuations and radioactive clouds wafting across borders, made it difficult to downplay health effects. Yet, as Kate Brown, a historian of science at MIT, details in *Manual for Survival: An Environmental History of the Chernobyl Disaster*, the International Atomic Energy Agency and the World Health Organization helped promote the notion that the disaster's health effects had been minimal. In 2005, the UN settled on a figure of 4,000 deaths among those most exposed in Ukraine, Belarus, and Russia—a number at the low end of a strikingly wide range, Brown observed. The IAEA had earlier reported "no health disorders that could be attributed directly to radiation exposure." It was only when Keith Baverstock, a scientist with the World Health Organization, defied a superior and publicly disclosed a sharp increase in extremely rare thyroid cancers among Belarusian children that there was some grudging acceptance of the disaster's deadly consequences. Even so, Baverstock says, he was threatened with firing unless he withdrew his findings; others in receipt of WHO funding claimed the jump in cases was merely the result of intensified screening.

Brown spent ten years in archives across Ukraine, Belarus, and Russia, disinterring records of what happened to the millions of people exposed not only to the invisible cloud, but to its residue in the landscape from which they drew their food. That residue had global reach—a truck carrying Ukrainian blueberries to the United States from Canada was so radioactive it was stopped at the border. Traveling around affected areas, some far from the plant itself, Brown encountered evidence of communities shredded by radiation, such as women who sorted wool from sheep slaughtered in the radiation zone. Toting bales of radioactive wool, Brown has said, "was like hugging an X-ray machine while it was turned on over and over again." Many got sick and died. Yet amid the tens of thousands of pages Brown perused, just one obscure official document furnished a hard figure for Chernobyl-related deaths: 36,525. That was the number of women in Ukraine who received pensions because their husbands had died as a result of the disaster—a toll far in excess of anything reported by Western officials. But that stark number must represent only a small fraction of the total. "That's just Ukraine," she told me, "which received only 20 percent of the radiation. There's no comparable figure for Belarus, which got far more."

While Brown mined records of Chernobyl's effects on humans, Timothy Mousseau of the University of South Carolina and his Danish colleague, Anders Møller, spent decades studying its consequences on the landscape around the plant. "It's not a complete void of life. It's much more insidious than that," Mousseau told *Harper's Magazine* in 2011. "Because everything's still there, it's just being modified at some low level." Birds, animals, and plants suffer the baneful effects of radiation to some degree. Early on, Mousseau was struck by the near absence of spiderwebs, normally abundant in forests. Studying the area around Fukushima, he saw many of the same results. This conclusion was not popular with the Japanese authorities. "One reason we don't know as much about Fukushima as we should," he told me, "is that the Japanese—the government, academia, the corporation, it's all the same thing—really discouraged research. I was certainly pressured not to publish my findings. It was in the form of sticks and carrots, carrots being, 'Wouldn't it be nice to have an institute for studies of Fukushima, and by the way, you really don't want to publish those papers that you've written recently.'" He published them anyway.

In light of the evidence of post-Chernobyl thyroid cancer, researchers mounted a major effort to screen children in the area around Fukushima. Year after year, the numbers steadily ratcheted up, eventually reaching twenty times normal levels. (As with thyroid cancer in Belarus, officials from UN agencies claimed the rise in cases was merely the result of intensified screening.) Meanwhile, local authorities began a campaign to discourage children from getting screened, advising them of "the right not to know." The campaign had some success, and the number of participating children dropped. Not coincidentally, from 2016 on, the number of reported child thyroid cases started to decline.

"The right not to know" about the effects of nuclear power is currently embraced far beyond Fukushima. In the face of escalating alarm about climate change, the siren song of "clean and affordable and reliable" power finds an audience eager to overlook a business model that is dependent on state support and often greased with corruption; failed experiments now hailed as "innovative"; a pattern of artful disinformation; and a trail of poison from accidents and leaks (not to mention the 95,000 tons of radioactive waste currently stored at reactor sites with nowhere else to go) that will affect generations yet unborn. Arguments by proponents of renewables that wind, solar, and geothermal power can fill the gap on their own have found little traction with policymakers. Ignoring history, we may be condemned to repeat it. Bill Gates has bet a billion dollars on that.

Harper's Magazine, January 2022

Postscript. The boom in power-gorging data centers on the back of the AI frenzy launched in late 2023 brought the nuclear revival to undreamed of heights. The data centers' potential power requirements far exceeded anything conventional electricity generators, certainly not renewables such as wind or solar, could supply, prompting widespread assertions that nuclear, notably the fabled small nuclear reactors, could come to the rescue. Tech companies hurried to make deals with reactor companies, with one even contracting to take power from a refurbished Three Mile Island Unit One. Needless to say, none of the obvious underlying problems discussed here were discussed, or even mentioned amid the general and ignorant enthusiasm.

Larry Householder was convicted at trial and sentenced to twenty years in prison.

20

Elder Abuse

Nursing Homes, the Coronavirus, and the Bottom Line

At the beginning of 2020, Canterbury Rehabilitation and Healthcare Center, a nursing home in Richmond, Virginia, housed 160 elderly residents, roughly half of whom were African American. Most of them were there courtesy of Medicaid, the government program that finances health care for those with little or no money. By mid-May, 80 percent of Canterbury's residents had been infected with the novel coronavirus. A third of them were dead.

Sharon Mitchell, a sixty-two-year-old former dental receptionist, was one of the casualties. She had been at Canterbury for two years, her son Ronald told me, following a stroke brought on by the shock of losing her longtime receptionist job. She had been healthy enough to have poststroke rehabilitation therapy at home, but therapists refused to travel to the public housing project where she lived, deeming it too dangerous. So, after much discussion, the family elected to send her to Canterbury (then known as Lexington Court), where Medicaid would cover poststroke treatment.

Even before the pandemic, the facility had a poor reputation. In 2018, a staff nurse was convicted of attempting to rape a seventy-two-year-old Alzheimer's patient. In October 2019, a report from the Centers for Medicare and Medicaid Services (CMS) cited major staffing shortages and almost three times the number of "health deficiencies" as the national average. By Ronald's account, Canterbury was "a bad place, a very bad place." On his weekly visits, his mother told him of "people going to the bathroom on the floor in the hallways" and described Alzheimer's patients wandering into her room at night. "Her clothes were stolen; her jewelry was stolen," he told me. The therapy, it turned out, consisted of biweekly sessions in which she was asked to spin a wheel with her hand for fifteen minutes. He was shocked when his mother told him she was given a shower just once a week: "'Thursday's my shower day,' she told me. Otherwise they gave her a wipe-down with a baby wipe every two days."

Unsurprisingly, Sharon routinely contracted hygiene-related urinary tract infections, which led to seizures that sent her to nearby St. Mary's Hospital. During one of these hospitalizations, a year into his mother's stay, Ronald spotted blood on one of her socks. Pulling it off, he found that her big toe was infected—it had been neglected by the staff for so long that "the flesh was all eaten away; I could see the bone." Gangrene had invaded her leg, which eventually had to be amputated above the knee. Immobilized thereafter, Sharon spent most of her time in bed. She was often dehydrated because she could not hold a cup, Ronald said, "but they wouldn't help her drink, or put her on an IV."

Ronald saw his mother for the last time in February, before visitors were barred as a precaution against the coronavirus, which had already attacked a nursing home outside Seattle. Two months earlier, Canterbury had been acquired by Tryko Partners, a fast-growing private equity concern, which operated it through an affiliate, Marquis Health Services. A Marquis spokesperson told me that by the time of the COVID-19 outbreak, "in-house staffing was at its highest point in years," and that wages had been temporarily doubled. But so far as Ronald was concerned, "Nothing had changed. Nothing." On March 18, a Canterbury patient was diagnosed with the virus. Sharon also tested positive soon after, and was moved into a quarantine unit the center had set up. When Ronald called her after the move, she told him she needed a drink of water. "I stayed on the line for an hour and a half while she pressed the bell for a nurse, but no one ever came," he said. When he complained, Canterbury staff told him they had just two nurses looking after forty patients. (A Canterbury spokesperson excused the inadequate staffing on grounds that it met CMS guidelines.) Three weeks later, Sharon was dead. "My mom died all alone," Ronald told me, bitter at the neglect—the dehydration, the pro forma therapy, the gangrene—that he is convinced led to her death. "She was only sixty-two. She was capable of getting better. She didn't deserve to die like that."

Months into the pandemic, it has become clear that the majority of people infected by the coronavirus suffer mild or no symptoms and recover quickly. Despite the panic and economic devastation, the risk of death or serious illness from the virus for most people is relatively small. For people of color, it is worse. According to one study, Black Americans were more than twice as likely as white Americans to die of COVID-19 complications. But it is worst of all among those with health issues, particularly the elderly. At the height of the pandemic in New York City, for example, fewer than 1 percent of people who died while infected with COVID-19 were confirmed to have lacked an underlying illness.

Inevitably, then, the virus has found its most ideal conditions in the warehouses storing America's elderly population. No one knows the current death toll. As of early July, CMS put the number at 33,509, but the count covered only federally regulated nursing homes, not assisted-living communities. The homes, moreover, were not required to report deaths that occurred before May 8, although the agency said it was confident that "the vast majority" did so. One in five nursing homes didn't bother to report their numbers at all. A *New York Times* study in late June put the number of deaths in US nursing homes at a staggering 55,000, but even this figure did not necessarily include all of those who became infected in a home but died in a hospital, as was the case for Sharon Mitchell. In some states, the vast majority of COVID-19 deaths were in homes: 64 percent in Massachusetts, 68 percent in Pennsylvania, 77 percent in Minnesota. In New Jersey, one in every ten people housed in nursing homes or assisted-living centers died. This was a helpless population, helpless because so often confined in a state of neglect and squalor. But despite or perhaps because of their conditions, they were worth a lot of money. In effect, they were being harvested for profit.

The business model is simple. It depends in part on the personal funds—including insurance policies—of patients or their families, but in larger part on the government programs dedicated to caring for the elderly, Medicare and Medicaid. "It's a shell game," explained Doris Gelbman, a Charlottesville, Virginia, attorney who specializes in elder law. "In the first go-round, a patient is covered by Medicare, which pays for treatment and rehabilitation—but only for a limited time. When the Medicare runs out, the patient can either go home, or pay for long-term care." This can drain away a lifetime of savings in short order, and once it does, Medicaid starts picking up the bill. But Medicaid will only spend a limited amount per patient. (In most of Virginia, including Richmond, the cap is $6,422 a month.) "The only way the home can make it worthwhile and meet their profit target is to cut corners," said Gelbman. "And that's why you have low-paid, untrained, and overworked staff."

Like a flash of lightning, the virus has illuminated a corner of society and the economy that normally festers in obscurity. I asked Mary Evans, a former senior consultant for several leading nursing-home chains, whether she was surprised at the havoc that COVID-19 had wrought in the industry. "It's not surprising at all," she said. "It was only a matter of time until something like this happened." Evans recounted a litany of horror stories, including a Maryland home where unattended patients had uncut toenails "curling around and growing into their feet." "It's a nightmare," she said. "You see why I don't do this anymore."

The practice of segregating the elderly in profit-making old-age homes was born in the mid-twentieth century. There were also homes for the elderly in Victorian times, but they were not yet seen as a financial opportunity. The hugely popular nineteenth-century American poet Will Carleton (a frequent *Harper's Magazine* contributor) became famous with his 1872 poem "Over the Hill to the Poor House," which relates the story of a widow left without property and abandoned by ungrateful children who consign her to the miseries of institutional care: "Over the hill to the poor house, I'm trudgin' my weary way/ I, a woman of seventy, and only a trifle gray." As with the British poorhouses described by Dickens, the grim conditions of their American counterparts reflected the prevailing belief that poverty was in itself a moral failure, and thereby merited appropriately austere treatment. Investigation of one notorious Massachusetts facility revealed, among other atrocities, the deliberate starvation of inmates and the sale of their corpses to medical schools. Most aging Americans avoided this fate by relying on their children to care for them, often sealing the deal with a promise of inheritance. Gelbman summarized this common arrangement: "A daughter would stay home, not get married, and look after the parents as they got old and infirm while her siblings went off and raised families of their own. But in return, she got the house."

As the Princeton historian Hendrik Hartog explained in his book *Someday All This Will Be Yours*, this custom persisted into the 1940s, at which point Social Security began replacing the family in providing care and shelter for the elderly. In 1950, an amendment to the 1935 Social Security Act established direct federal payments to privately owned homes, which until then were mostly charities or mom-and-pop operations. (Owing to searing memories of the poorhouses, government aid to any "inmate of a public institution" was explicitly barred.) A for-profit industry was born. Initially the federal subsidies were small, though still enough, according to Mary Mendelson's 1974 muckraking exposé, *Tender Loving Greed*, to "whet the appetite" of hustlers who perceived "the exciting profit potential in the nursing home." These opportunities would expand dramatically in 1965, when the creation of Medicare and Medicaid turned a trickle of federal largesse into a torrent. Medicare financed health care for anyone over sixty-five, and would pay for up to a hundred days in a nursing home for patients recovering from hospital treatment. Medicaid, in addition to providing medical aid to the poor of any age, also provided for unlimited stays in nursing homes. Naturally, hustlers were poised to take full advantage of the near limitless supply of taxpayer money. An Orthodox rabbi named Bernard Bergman built up a nursing-home empire worth some $25 million (while employing Rocco Scarfone, a senior member of the Columbo Mafia family to supervise his flagship nursing home) before being tried and jailed in 1976 for siphoning off Medicaid payments into his own private accounts.

Such examples notwithstanding, the arrival of Ronald Reagan's business-sponsored administration in 1981 saw a determined effort to dismantle nursing-home regulations deemed irksome by the industry, such as requirements that patients be adequately fed. Retreating in the face of public outcry, his administration adopted the alternative and equally effective course of failing to enforce said regulations. By the following year, according to a report by Kathleen Hughes of Ralph Nader's Center for Study of Responsive Law, the inspection budget for the agency that oversaw Medicare and Medicaid was so diminished that nursing home inspections had essentially ceased.

The terms of trade established in the years after 1965—in which cutting costs was favored over improving service—appear to be more or less unchanged. The industry has "no pricing power," Omotayo Okusanya, a managing director for equity research at Mizuho Securities, explained. "It lives on whatever the government opts to pay." The art of successful management is thus: "one, control costs, and two, control the patient mix," meaning ensure that a facility optimizes its ratio of Medicare to Medicaid patients. "Medicare pays more," said Okusanya—sometimes more than it should. Life Care, a large chain of nursing homes whose Kirkland, Washington, facility saw the first major COVID-19 outbreak, was fined $145 million by the Justice Department in 2016 for "rehabilitation therapy services that were not reasonable, necessary, or skilled." Such practices are not uncommon. Genesis HealthCare, the largest chain in the United States, paid more than $53 million in 2017 to settle lawsuits by federal law enforcement alleging that its subsidiaries "submitted false claims for services that were grossly substandard and/or worthless."

In an arrangement that is fairly typical for the industry, Genesis operates homes and manages their services, such as therapy or hospice, but does not necessarily own the buildings or the land they occupy. Until recently, many of the company's properties belonged to Sabra Health Care REIT, a $3 billion real estate investment trust. Created to facilitate investments in property in the same way mutual funds enable investment in stocks, these companies are relieved of all corporate tax liability provided that at least 90 percent of their income is paid out in dividends. Initially, REITs were only permitted to own businesses that passively collect rent, such as office buildings. Health care facilities, including nursing homes, were excluded from REIT ownership. That changed in 2008, thanks to an intervention by Senator Orrin Hatch of Utah, a trustworthy friend of the nursing home industry. In July of that year, as financial tremors began to shake Wall Street, Congress passed the Housing and Economic Recovery Act. This measure did little to stem the impending crisis, but buried deep in the legislation was a provision inserted by Hatch, at the urgent request of the REIT industry, permitting them to buy up nursing homes and other health care properties. Demand was brisk, given the growing pool of elderly Americans—known in the industry as the "silver tsunami"—and has remained so. REITs now own over 2,000 of the nation's 15,000 nursing home and assisted-living properties, and their interest in larger properties means their percentage of the total beds is even larger. This makes them especially powerful players in the industry, with returns running significantly ahead of those in other areas of the property market. REITs lease their homes to operating companies such as Sabra and Genesis that are, in theory, entirely independent. Should the operator fall on hard times or into bankruptcy, their losses do not affect the property owner. As Charlene Harrington, a professor of sociology and nursing at the University of California, San Francisco, told me, "It's all about real estate."

Genesis itself is under the ownership of private equity, the twenty-first-century answer to Rocco Scarfone. Private equity is the mechanism by which financiers take over a firm using borrowed money and extract as much cash from the purchase as possible—under the guise of "restructuring" it in the form of dividends and fees—before finally discarding the remains either to another buyer or in bankruptcy court. Mitt Romney's Bain Capital, for example, applied this technique to the once-flourishing Toys "R" Us, destroying the business in a few short years. Beginning around 2004, private equity firms began devouring nursing homes at an accelerated pace. Today, these unregulated groups own or operate one in every ten senior facilities in the country.

The consequences for residents have not been happy. A study published just before the coronavirus onslaught under the auspices of New York University's Stern School of Business asked, "Does Private Equity Investment in Healthcare Benefit Patients?" In studiously guarded language, the answer was no. Patients, on the other hand, certainly benefit investors. Delving into Medicare data, the researchers found that private equity firms had discovered a variety of ways to recruit more patients, thereby bumping up revenue by 8 percent, which, together with staff cuts, boosted the annual take from an average 110-bed home by more than three-quarters of a million dollars. While the average profit margin before taxes for a publicly traded company prior to the 2020 crash was around 10 percent, Evans, the former nursing-home consultant, recalled that the figures for nursing home firms had more often been between 18 and 25 percent. "They're very cagey about disclosing this, but that's what they were shooting for," said Evans. "They'll say, 'Oh, we care about medical care and medical quality,' but when push comes to shove, they'll say, 'We're losing money hand over fist,' which means they're not making their projections. They cry poor so they don't have to give their employees raises. They operate with barely enough staff. But they make a lot of money."

One of the principal monsters in the private equity world is the Carlyle Group. In 2007, Carlyle acquired HCR ManorCare, a nationwide nursing home chain. Four years later, after ManorCare's debt load had grown from $1 billion to $5 billion, Carlyle hived the company's real estate holdings off into a separate company, which it sold to a health care REIT called HCP for $6.1 billion, earning its investors $1.3 billion. Under the deal, Carlyle leased the homes back from HCP and continued to extract hefty management and consulting fees from ManorCare, ultimately garnering at least $80 million.

The consequences for the aged and infirm patients subjected to this exercise in financial engineering were sickeningly predictable: crushed by payments on the debt that Carlyle had piled on, as well as $39.5 million in monthly lease payments to the

REIT, ManorCare vigorously slashed costs by cutting care for its 25,000 residents. A 2018 *Washington Post* investigation of the whole sorry saga found that health code violations reported by Medicare inspectors at ManorCare facilities jumped by at least 26 percent in the years after Carlyle's purchase. Its debt having climbed to $7.1 billion, ManorCare went bankrupt. (CEO Paul Ormond managed to get away with a compensation package worth $117 million.) Welltower, a $21 billion REIT, bought the real estate at a cost that worked out to $57,000 per bed, a profitable investment given that less than two years later it sold three of the nursing homes for $67 million, or $156,000 per bed. Today, the analyst Okusanya rates Welltower a "buy."

The strategy employed by Tryko Partners, the private equity operation that runs Canterbury Rehabilitation and Healthcare Center, where Sharon Mitchell spent her last years, appears to be similar to Carlyle's. Among the thirty other homes it owns is Brentwood Rehabilitation and Healthcare Center, in Danvers, Massachusetts, which it bought for $3.8 million in 2013. By 2015, according to a detailed investigation by Paul Leighton in the *Salem News*, the facility had been rated "much below average"—the lowest possible category—by Medicare inspectors, who described filthy conditions, overworked staff, and neglected patients. Norman Rokeach, the CEO of Marquis Health Services, Tryko Partners' health care affiliate, told Leighton that understaffing was due to employees calling in sick or being otherwise unable to work. The $400,000 loss that Brentwood posted in 2015 might have excused the staffing problem but for the fact that Brentwood was meanwhile paying $1.3 million in rent to companies owned by Rokeach and other Tryko principals— effectively draining the struggling facility of resources. (A spokesman at the time claimed, "We're moving in the right direction. We're proud of what we're doing here.") Four years later, Brentwood is still rated "much below average." As of mid-June, thirty of its residents were reported to have contracted COVID-19, twenty-two of whom had died.

The pandemic has apparently done little to disturb the industry's business model. As media reports this spring chronicled soaring numbers of deaths in nursing homes, another ascending graph denoted booming stock prices for nursing home corporations. After having bottomed out just after mid-March, around the time Sharon Mitchell was diagnosed with the coronavirus, they had been on an upward trajectory ever since. On April 15, the day Mitchell died, the Janus Long-Term Care ETF (market symbol OLD), which reflects the market performance of companies involved in long-term care, was up 38 percent from its low. By June, it had climbed almost 70 percent. Clearly, the crisis was by no means bad for nursing homes, at least not for the 70 percent that are for-profit.

As Okusanya told me, success in the nursing-home business lies in "getting the Medicare-Medicaid mix right." In March, nursing homes suddenly got a significant boost in Medicare patients. Owing to (another) miscalculation by modelers overestimating the severity of the pandemic and the consequent shortage of hospital beds, New York, Pennsylvania, New Jersey, and other states ordered hospitals to off-load medically stable patients to nursing homes, including people who had been diagnosed with and treated for COVID-19. The nursing homes were required to accept them, and in New York, Governor Andrew Cuomo forbade homes from testing new arrivals. The results were disastrous, as carriers broadcast the virus throughout overcrowded facilities. Once this was publicized, Cuomo and other state executives came in for well-deserved abuse. But for nursing home owners, there was a silver lining. In October 2019, Medicare instituted a change to its payment systems that made it more profitable for nursing homes to accept Medicare patients from hospitals. According to one analysis, data from April "clearly shows COVID-positive patients generated higher rates than non-COVID patients"—$699 per patient per day, an increase of 9 percent over February's numbers. Patients were evicted to make room, the New York Times reported, many of whom wound up in "homeless shelters, rundown motels, and other unsafe facilities," though this has long been a common practice in the industry. Some homes turned into coronavirus-only facilities, including Country Villa South, an eighty-seven-bed Los Angeles home. Well before the pandemic's arrival, its owner, Rockport

Healthcare Services, was sued for allegedly dumping patients without notice to make way for more lucrative replacements. All part of getting the mix right.

As the rising number of nursing home deaths began generating ugly headlines, industry officials were quick to adopt the roles of both victim and supplicant. "The truth is that nursing homes have not failed America. The public health system has failed nursing homes," announced Mark Parkinson, the former nursing home entrepreneur and governor of Kansas who commands the industry's chief lobbying operation, the American Health Care Association. "Long-term care facilities are doing everything possible to stop the spread of this virus. But we need help."

That help was soon on the way in the form of the $2 trillion CARES Act. "Here Comes the COVID-19 Cash," Okusanya wrote in a note to his clients. Nursing homes initially stood to receive $1.5 billion, and further bailout assistance boosted that sum to $5 billion by the end of May. "There are no strings attached," Seema Verma, the CMS administrator, confirmed at a White House press conference. "So the health care providers that are receiving these dollars can essentially spend that in any way that they see fit." This was in addition to help provided to the industry in the form of dismantled oversight and regulations. Toby Edelman, an attorney with the Center for Medicare Advocacy, described how CMS had "waived the rule [stating] that homes cannot discharge a patient without notice," thereby making it easier for nursing homes to dump low-paying Medicaid residents in favor of Medicare patients requiring treatment for COVID-19 at the recently boosted rates. Indignantly, Edelman dismissed recent CMS data indicating that only 3 percent of nursing homes have infection problems (such as the urinary tract infections that sent Sharon Mitchell to the hospital), even as figures from a Government Accountability Office report had revealed dangerous rates of infection at four out of every five homes between 2013 and 2017. "Are we supposed to believe that infections have suddenly almost disappeared?" Edelman asked. Normally, nursing homes are monitored by ombudsmen, licensing agencies, and, most importantly, patients' relatives. Under lockdown, all that went away. "There's no oversight," concluded

Edelman. "No infection surveys, no ombudsmen, and no families visiting. I'm really frightened about what's going on."

Free from outside scrutiny, the nursing home industry has been working hard to ward off any future penalties for its treatment of patients during the crisis. This effort has already been handsomely rewarded in a number of states, most notably New York. Deep in Cuomo's 2020–21 budget is a paragraph providing that, for the length of the COVID-19 crisis, any health care facility or health care professional shall have immunity from any liability, civil or criminal, for any harm or damages alleged to have been sustained as a result of an act or omission in the course of arranging for or providing health care services.

This neatly lets corporate owners and executives off the hook for any and all mistreatment of their patients. (As reported by David Sirota in *Jacobin*, Cuomo and the New York State Democratic Committee received no less than $2.3 million from the hospital and nursing home industries in his frantic effort to ward off an electoral challenge from Cynthia Nixon in 2018. Their faith was apparently not misplaced.)

These immunity provisions, or "get-out-of-jail-free cards," as Gelbman described them to me, soon spread far beyond New York. As of early July, twenty-one states had adopted immunity laws, each identical to Cuomo's decree. Uncoincidentally, governors in those states had been in grateful receipt of a total of $44 million in campaign contributions from the nursing home and hospital business since 2017. Meanwhile, in Washington, Senate majority leader Mitch McConnell was pressing for corporate immunity from coronavirus-related federal lawsuits. Aghast at the prospect of the nursing home industry escaping accountability, advocates for the elderly rose in protest: "The magnitude of the crisis in nursing homes is directly related to years of cost cutting and understaffing, in an effort to maximize profits for nursing home owners and operators," a coalition of 250 advocacy organizations wrote Senate leaders. "To allow facilities to face no repercussions for these actions, while asking nursing home residents to pay with their lives, is a perverse outcome that cannot be tolerated." Nevertheless, as of late June, McConnell remained unmoved, promising a "hard line" and "strong legal protections" for corporations against COVID-19 lawsuits.

The wreckage wrought by the pandemic among the elderly in the United States has by no means been unique. At least half the deaths attributed to COVID-19 across Europe have occurred in nursing homes. In some countries the toll has been far higher— as much as 75 percent in the United Kingdom and 64 percent in Norway. A Dutch nursing home worker posted a video of himself walking past empty room after empty room, exclaiming, "All the people here died of corona. This whole corridor is dead. Dead." The same pattern has persisted in Sweden, where the deceased have been almost all elderly. The high death rate in Sweden has been eagerly cited as evidence that the country's failure to lock down brought inevitably lethal consequences. But Swedes in general escaped relatively lightly, while at least half of those who died were in nursing homes. Another 26 percent were elderly Swedes being attended to at home by overextended care workers shuttling between clients without proper protective equipment, inexorably spreading infection. All of this, though financed by government and local authorities, was managed by for-profit companies. This was true across much of the continent, including in Britain, where nursing homes were privatized by Margaret Thatcher in 1990 and where many have since fallen into the hands of private equity. This pattern suggests that the heavy death toll among the elderly might be traced to one main source: the neoliberal privatization craze that has swept the Western world over the past forty years.

However, an arid statistical table published last year by the World Health Organization suggests a more fundamental truth. It tabulates the number of nursing home beds per hundred thousand people in each European country. Sweden scores very high—1,276 per hundred thousand. Britain is also high, at 847. The same computation puts the United States at 515. Greece, on the other hand, whose citizens tend not to put their elderly relatives in homes and still regard their care as a family responsibility, scores a mere 15. The disparities in casualty rates are equally striking. In terms of deaths per hundred thousand, Sweden's rate is 53; the United Kingdom comes in at 66; and the United States has 39. Greece, meanwhile, despite having the largest proportion of elderly people in Europe, has so far escaped with a mere 2 deaths per hundred thousand. One might almost conclude that the death toll that has so traumatized and destabilized much of Western society in 2020 was not wrought principally by the coronavirus, but by nursing homes.

Ideally, we might emulate Greek family relationships and arrangements (or move to Greece to grow old) and abandon the institutional care approach in favor of a model where the bottom line is not the driving priority. Cedars Healthcare Center is a 141-bed home in Charlottesville, Virginia. It shares many characteristics with the hardest-hit facilities—a population averaging about eighty years old, many of whom are African American and almost all of whom are on Medicaid. Yet as of mid-June, it had not had a single COVID-19 infection. When I asked how this could be, chief nurse Amy Ryan took me through the relatively straightforward measures the facility adopted in early March, following news of the initial nursing home outbreak in Kirkland. Cedars discouraged staff from working shifts at other homes, correctly anticipating that such movement would spread the infection. It stockpiled sufficient supplies of protective equipment such as masks. Crucially, it also adjusted the air-conditioning system to prevent circulation throughout the buildings. I asked whether any of these measures had required much labor or investment. "Not really," she replied. "It was all pretty straightforward. Just getting ready in good time."

It was hard to see why these precautions could not have been more widely adopted. But there was another factor involved, one less likely to be duplicated. Cedars is part of CommuniCare, a company still owned and run by its founder, Stephen Rosedale, together with his sons, in Cincinnati. Many of the measures adopted by Cedars, such as modifying the air-conditioning, were instituted by headquarters early in March. So far, the chain has largely been successful in curbing COVID-19. Twelve of its eighty-seven homes escaped infection entirely, including some in poor, high-risk neighborhoods. However, it seemed to me that the most important factor was that Rosedale believes that it is important to see things from the perspective of residents and the staff who care for them. Rosedale and his sons have all spent time working as certified nursing assistants, the bottom of the chain of command, very far removed from the financial engineering background of industry supremos.

Of course, nursing home residents and workers have not been the only vulnerable groups affected by the pandemic. Prisoners, obviously at risk but confined nonetheless, have suffered greatly, as have meatpacking workers, chained to the assembly lines thanks to Trump's endorsement of greedy corporate pleas that the country would otherwise face a meat shortage (even as exports to China soared). Such are the routinely callous effects of our economic system. But the treatment of the aged stands out. As Simone de Beauvoir once wrote: "By the way in which a society behaves toward its old people, it uncovers the naked and often carefully hidden truths about its real principles and aims." The virus, it could be said, has made these truths self-evident.

Harper's Magazine, September 2020

21

Blood Money

Taxpayers Pick Up the Tab for Police Brutality

Over the past three years, the city of South Tucson, Arizona, a largely Latino enclave nestled inside metropolitan Tucson, came close to abolishing its fire and police departments. It did sell off the library and cut back fire-truck crews from four to three people —whereupon two-thirds of the fire department quit—and slashed the police force to just sixteen employees. "We're a small city, just one square mile, surrounded by a larger city," the finance director, Lourdes Aguirre, explained to me. "We have small-town dollars and big-city problems."

Almost half the population of South Tucson is below the poverty line, resulting in tax revenues so modest that the loss in sales tax from the closure of a local restaurant can significantly impact the overall take. But although the painful cuts may have saved the fire and police departments, one budget item could not be cut, can never be cut: the $600,000 in annual payments, two-thirds of it interest, on the city's bonds.

The origin of this obligation goes back to a July night in 1977, when twenty-four-year-old José Sinohui was driving his pickup down South Sixth Avenue and passed officer Christopher Dean, who was confronting a crowd of unruly youths outside a fast-food restaurant. For reasons that were never satisfactorily explained, Dean drew his gun as Sinohui cruised by and fired seven .45-caliber bullets at the truck, one of which hit Sinohui in the back and killed him.

Following years of angry protests in the community, a judge ordered the city to pay Sinohui's family $150,000 in compensation, a sum steep enough to cause South Tucson to lose its $1 million liability insurance coverage. Consequently, in 1980, when a jury awarded $3.5 million to the paralyzed victim of another police shooting, Roy Garcia, himself an officer who was wounded when a fellow policeman blasted away at a schizophrenic man barricaded inside a house, the city could not afford a down payment on the award and was forced into bankruptcy. After protracted negotiations with Garcia, the city finally opted to borrow the money. Turning to Wall Street, South Tucson solicited its first small contribution from the multitrillion-dollar municipal bond market, floating a bond worth some $1.9 million. No one ever asked the local taxpayers to vote on whether they wanted to be saddled with this obligation.

Having committed future generations to paying off this initial debt, the city council later compounded matters by resorting to so-called scoop-and-toss borrowing—paying off old bonds with the proceeds from new ones, like putting credit card debt onto another credit card. The obvious drawback to such a scheme is that each time repayment is pushed back, the amount of interest owed grows larger. With the first refinancing, in 1987, the debt grew to $4.5 million. Again, no one outside the city council was asked to vote on the measure, nor on the next trip to the Wall Street ATM, in 1990, nor on subsequent refinancings, in 1991, 1998, 2003, and 2007. With each rollover, South Tucson was obligated to cough up extra cash in the form of fees to underwriters, lawyers, bond insurers, credit-rating agencies, printers, the bank ensuring that bondholders received their money, the firm that furnished each bond with its identifying number, and other fees. Today, the seed planted by that long-ago shooting generates an annual harvest of $600,000 in interest and principal repayments to bondholders—the second-biggest item, after the police department, on the city budget. By the time the debt is paid, Aguirre informed me sadly, South Tucson will have paid $6.3 million in interest alone, out of a grand total of $13.9 million. That will not happen until 2037, fifty-three expensive years after the first trip to the bond market.

Policing is an extremely safe occupation, ranking far behind logging, commercial fishing, roofing, groundskeeping, and other civilian jobs in terms of fatality rates. Nonetheless, police culture appears to be imbued with the notion that officers' lives hang by a thread at all times, thus justifying a violent response to anything they perceive as a threat, such as the eighty-seven-year-old Georgia woman hit with a taser this August thanks to a knife she was carrying to cut dandelions. Prosecutors and jurors generally accept this dubious presumption of constant peril, so officers can usually avoid punishment by testifying that they feared for their lives.

Accordingly, although police kill, on average, about 1,000 people a year, of the eighty officers charged with homicide between 2005 and 2017, barely more than a third were convicted. But even when juries or prosecutors balk at criminal charges or guilty verdicts, victims or bereaved relatives are increasingly able to exact some financial satisfaction when overwhelming evidence is available. In part, this is due to technology. Ubiquitous smartphone, dashboard, and body cameras, as well as DNA-based checks on forensic evidence, which can reverse past frame-ups, have caused compensation payments to rise. A 2015 *Wall Street Journal* study found that the ten biggest police departments in the country had over the previous five years spent a collective $1.02 billion to settle cases that included shootings, beatings, and wrongful imprisonments.

Such payouts are generally thought to not only compensate for suffering but to serve as punishments for the perpetrators and deterrents to future bad behavior. This assumption certainly seems to be shared by ordinary citizens serving on juries in such cases. "They can't get away with this," declared Andrea Diven, a juror in a 2017 Chicago trial that awarded $44.7 million to a man shot and seriously wounded by a drunken officer with a record of violent behavior. "It's something that's embedded, and it needs to change." She and a fellow juror emphasized to reporters that the enormity of the award was intended to send a message to the city to do something about errant police behavior. (The four cents awarded by a Florida jury in 2018 to the fiancée and three children of Greg Hill, shot by police through his garage door following complaints about his loud music, was presumably intended as a different kind of message.)

In theory, Diven's supposition that the huge award should have a beneficial effect was well grounded. The concept of retribution for injustice is enshrined in Section 1983 of the US Code, which states that any person depriving another of his or her civil rights "shall be liable to the party injured in an action at law, suit in equity, or other proper proceeding for redress." (The law derives from the 1871 Civil Rights Act, introduced by President Grant to implement the Fourteenth Amendment and, more specifically, to crush the Ku Klux Klan.) According to UCLA law school professor Joanna Schwartz, the law, as it relates to police brutality, is expressly directed at individual officers, in the hopes of improving their behavior in future. "That certainly has been the way in which the courts have talked about the effects of litigation," she told me. "Their underlying notion is that these lawsuits are not only going to compensate [victims] but also to deter police from doing it again." So deeply ingrained is this concept in legal theory that in recent years the Supreme Court has relied on the concept of "qualified immunity," which essentially gives a pass to misbehaving public officials, especially law enforcement, so long as it can be argued that they were behaving "reasonably." The idea, Schwartz says, is that courts will let officers off the hook out of concerns that "the financial threat, as well as the threat of litigation, will cause people to decide not to become officers, and will cause them to be overly timid while they're on the job."

In reality, Schwartz argues, the idea that delinquent cops are ever threatened with personal financial sanctions is "fiction." As she concluded after studying thousands of cases from 2006 to 2011 in eighty-one law enforcement agencies large and small, individual officers paid just 0.02 percent of the $735 million awarded in suits against those departments. Furthermore, as she noted in a 2014 article, they paid nothing in punitive damages "even when officers were disciplined, terminated, or prosecuted for their conduct." (As it happens, Christopher Dean, the officer who kicked off South Tucson's problems, was a rare exception, and was ordered to pay $50,000 to the Sinohui family.)

Although individual officers are rarely on the hook, the police forces they belong to sometimes do pay a slice of the cost. But this money usually comes from a portion of their budget expressly set aside for that purpose, so, as Schwartz demonstrated in a later study, payments have no impact on department operations. If lawsuits end up costing more than is set aside in these special budgets, the city pays the excess, not the law enforcement agency. All too often, as in South Tucson, governments put it on the municipal credit card by issuing bonds.

In a blistering June 2018 report, the nonprofit Action Center on Race and the Economy coined a memorable term: "police brutality bonds." Over the course of several years, ACRE researchers unearthed and detailed the increasing amounts that cities across the United States have had to borrow at interest to pay for pain and suffering inflicted by police. As with the South Tucson case, the costs can hang over a community like a curse for a very long time.

Beginning in 2004, for example, the city of Bethlehem, Pennsylvania, levied a tax on its citizens to pay off what was officially described as "the Hirko settlement debt." Twenty-one-year-old John Hirko Jr. had been killed in 1997 by a local SWAT team who raided his house after an informant suggested that he was a drug dealer. Wearing no insignia identifying them as police, the raiders tossed a flash grenade through a window only moments after knocking, and shot Hirko multiple times, mostly in the back. The house, set aflame by the grenade's explosion, burned to the ground. Although a local prosecutor ruled that the young man's death had been justifiable homicide, the jury in a federal suit brought by Hirko's family concluded that his civil rights had been violated. Then, just as the jury was about to begin deliberations on damages, the city hurriedly agreed to grant the family $7.39 million, almost a quarter of the annual budget. Not having the money at hand, the city issued a bond and levied an extra property tax specifically linked to the settlement and known locally as the Hirko tax. Ultimately, the city paid off the bond in 2015 with a final payment of $876,960. But this brought no relief to Bethlehemites, as the city government decided to keep the tax anyway, and used it to make interest payments on newer bonds it had issued in the meantime.

Other examples cited in ACRE's survey include Fullerton, California, where in 2011 six police officers beat a homeless man to death with their fists and batons over the course of nine minutes and forty seconds. Even though an Orange County jury accepted the defense's argument that the officers acted in accordance with their training, the city agreed to a $1 million payment to the victim's mother, which came from the proceeds of a larger bond issued by the city. Hammond, Indiana, issued a bond in 2008 to pay Larry Mayes $4.5 million in compensation for the nineteen years he spent behind bars for a rape he did not commit. (He had originally demanded $1 million for every year he spent unjustly incarcerated.) As in other such cases, the city's costs for locking up an innocent man went far beyond the amount of the award. In the formal legal statement regarding the sale, the city noted that it would be issuing "a second series of bonds ... in an amount not to exceed $1,190,000, in order to reimburse the City for certain legal and related costs incurred as a result of this litigation."

Even without such fees, borrowing money can be a very expensive way to pay for police misbehavior. Chicago, for example, raised $709.3 million in the bond market between 2010 and 2017 to settle claims such as the $5 million awarded to the family of Laquan McDonald, shot sixteen times—all but one while he already lay wounded on the ground—by police who then faked evidence to justify the killing. Commenting on the city's hefty settlement tab, John Mousseau, a bond specialist who is the president of the money management firm Cumberland Advisors, calculated that with interest, "the final cost will be more than double that." In fact, ACRE concluded, Chicago taxpayers will end up paying a staggering $1.7 billion on just these settlements.[1]

---

[1] According to ACRE's research, Chicago resorts to brutality bonds far more than any other city. Los Angeles ranks second, having borrowed $71.4 million. New York City does not appear on the list, but only because data isn't available for the means the city employs to pay settlements, which amounted to $308.2 million in 2017 alone.

A high interest rate is a presumptive indicator that high-risk investors will not get their money back, which would be the case if Chicago went bankrupt. According to Bhatti, however, that view is completely unjustified. "The credit-rating system itself, when it comes to municipalities, is completely out of whack, given that the default rate is less than point-zero-zero-one percent for municipalities to default on bonds," he told me. Furthermore, "Chicago, under state law, is not allowed to file for bankruptcy. Chicago cannot go bankrupt. So it means that actually Chicago is a very safe investment. Literally, if the state does not allow you to go bankrupt, that means that the city has to find a way to pay the money." Despite being such a safe investment, though, cities are still at the mercy of credit-rating agencies, whose arbitrary power determines just how much money Wall Street will be able to extract.

As to who is actually supporting Chicago's finances, including the brutality bonds, it is shockingly clear that poor people, mostly Black, shoulder an undue burden. ACRE bluntly termed this a "transfer of wealth from communities—especially over-policed communities of color—to Wall Street and wealthy investors." Chicago, with its huge portfolio of brutality borrowings, presents a striking demonstration of this transfer at work. Not only do poor Chicagoans bear the brunt of police misconduct itself, but as tax-payers they must share in compensating the victims. In fact, they are actually taxed more onerously than their wealthy neighbors across town (who are, of course, less likely to be shot or brutalized by law enforcement). This striking example of racial injustice was laid bare in a detailed 2017 investigation by the *Chicago Tribune*, which revealed that the Cook County tax assessor's office, which oversees Chicago, had for many years been routinely overvaluing homes in poor neighborhoods and undervaluing properties in wealthy ones. As a result, homeowners in lower-income neighbor-hoods such as North Lawndale and Little Village had been paying double the property tax rate levied on the more affluent residents of areas such as the Gold Coast or Lincoln Park.

Further compounding this disparity is Chicago's heavy reli-ance on parking tickets and traffic fines as a source of revenue, collecting nearly $264 million in 2016—7 percent of the city's operating budget. A recent *ProPublica* investigation revealed that poor Black neighborhoods furnished most of that sum, not least because of the proliferation of cameras to detect red-light violations in these areas. The take for city coffers is additionally boosted by residents who have trouble finding the money to pay initial fines, which then balloon with late fees and even more fines, forcing many to choose between losing their driver's license and going bankrupt. Fines for failing to display city vehicle stickers —which now cost $200, thanks to a steep hike introduced by Emanuel in 2013—are a major cause of bankruptcy among Black residents of Chicago.

But there is another, and even more insidious, way in which poorer city residents pay for the behavior of lawless law enforcement. Schwartz quotes a former Chicago city attorney who told her, "When you had to budget more for [police] tort liability you had less to do lead poisoning screening for the poor children of Chicago. We had a terrible lead poisoning problem and there was a direct relationship between the two. Those kids were paying those tort judgments, not the police officers."

Screening for lead poisoning is a discretionary expense, which can be and often is deferred in favor of what are considered more urgent demands on the budget. Payments to bondholders, on the other hand, are absolutely mandatory: the unpalatable alternatives being default, bankruptcy, and "restructurings" of city finances and services by stony-hearted outside overseers. ACRE, which highlights the attorney's quote in its report, cites further examples of how Chicago has cut essential services, such as mental health clinics, a disproportionate number of which have been shut down in the predominantly Black South Side. Given that at least one in four—and perhaps as many as half—of all fatal police shootings involve victims with untreated mental illnesses, according to the Treatment Advocacy Center, this would seem a particularly shortsighted, not to say heartless, economy. School cutbacks (the school system is independent but relies on the city budget for funds) have equally disastrous consequences for poor Black communities. In 2018 alone, Chicago has shuttered four different South Side high schools. As Miracle Boyd, a student protesting the closure of her school, put it, "Whether you kill us slow or kill us fast, you still kill us."

There is therefore a tragic paradox underlying the entire process by which brutality bonds are issued and paid off. Investments in after-school programs, mental health clinics, and violence-prevention initiatives are sure ways to reduce violence and crime, and thereby reduce the perceived need for aggressive policing. But these services get slashed when their budgets are diverted to pay for the consequences of police misbehavior—costs that are exacerbated by resorting to bonds, and the inexorable interest payments they require. Police departments' budgets, however, tend not to suffer in these cutbacks. Law enforcement spending across the nation has actually been steadily rising over recent decades. Thirty-eight percent of Chicago's budget is consigned to law enforcement—$1.46 billion—a proportion exceeded only by Oakland, California, where 41 percent of the city's spending goes to the police. (Tiny South Tucson's current sixteen-person force consumes 40 percent.)

Overall, the United States spends $100 billion a year on its police, and another $80 billion on incarceration—three times what was spent on police and corrections forty years ago. At the same time, of course, violent crime rates have until recently been steadily dropping, a phenomenon that has had no discernible effect on the level of policing or mass incarceration—notoriously larger, by an order of magnitude, than other countries', even those with higher crime rates. Given the phenomenon of brutality bonds, it could therefore follow that high police budgets are, in effect, a worthwhile investment as far as bondholders are concerned. They are a bet placed on increased levels of police violence that generate lawsuits and payouts, which ultimately lead to profitable investment products. Renewal of the process is further guaranteed by cutbacks required to service the debt, thus ensuring that underlying societal problems will endure and generate even more investment opportunities.

Ironically, efforts at reform—one driver of high police budgets—can actually boost the cost of police misbehavior for cities. Egregious cases will often generate a wide-ranging federal investigation by the Department of Justice that can stretch over years, identify deep-rooted problems in the relevant police force, and eventually lead to a consent decree by which the city agrees to clean up its officers' act. But such agreements tend to be expensive. A DOJ investigation into the Cleveland police, for example, identified a pattern of using unreasonable force, including shootings, tasings, and beatings, often of the mentally ill. The ensuing agreement to end such behavior, city officials calculated, would cost as much as $45 million over the next five years. The city, which had already borrowed $12.1 million at hefty interest rates on the bond market to pay for settlements, has had to go deeper into debt to finance the cleanup, including $800,000 for mandated police body cameras. Along with the added debt, the cost of reforms necessitated cutbacks in city services, including those dealing with opioid addiction and mental health.

If these costly reform programs led inevitably to improved policing, the expense might be justified. But the record indicates this is not always the case. The effects of Cleveland's agreement with the Justice Department, for instance, were only temporary. Although police behavior, as measured by declines in lawsuits and settlements, tends to improve overall while such an agreement is in force, studies have suggested that it begins to deteriorate again once the decree is lifted.

This is not to say that efforts to improve police behavior are invariably fruitless. Requiring officers to exhaust all other means to resolve a situation before opening fire reduces killings by 25 percent, according to Campaign Zero, a nonprofit founded in the wake of the 2014 police killing of Michael Brown in Ferguson, Missouri. Rules banning strangleholds bring down killings by 22 percent. The culture of individual police departments, in terms of leadership and training, clearly makes a difference. Between 2013 and 2016, for example, police in Buffalo, New York, killed zero people, while police in Orlando, Florida—a city similar in population, demographics, and crime rates—killed fifteen. Schwartz pointed out to me that insurance companies, which smaller cities tend to rely on as cover for police settlements, have gotten results by threatening to pull coverage unless a police department demonstrates that it has taken actual steps toward improving its behavior. ACRE suggests, among other proposals for reform, that police officers should have to take out malpractice insurance, just as doctors do, and that local governments should be transparent as to which officers are provoking settlements, how much they are costing, and who pays. Fundamentally, though, the problem is that the costs of errant policing are cloaked, if they are mentioned at all, in the opaque legalese of bond offerings or tax bills. No official document links police violence to a lack of lead-poisoning screening for children, or to the interest payments to Wall Street that will take priority for years and decades to come.

When I called John Mousseau of Cumberland Advisors to discuss the question of brutality bonds, I asked him whether that was really the way we should be paying for police misbehavior. "How do you justify taking the mistakes of today and giving them to the citizens of tomorrow to pay off?" he replied. It was a rhetorical question, but the answer was clear: it's the way we do business.

Harper's Magazine, November 2018

22

The Hindutva Lobby

How Hindu Nationalism Spreads in America

In the summer of 2023, California legislators approved a bill banning discrimination on the grounds of caste. Defined in the bill as "an individual's perceived position in a system of social stratification on the basis of inherited status," caste is a central feature of life for hundreds of millions of people in India and beyond. The measure had been championed by California's Dalit community. Once known as "untouchables," Dalits occupy the bottommost rung of the Hindu hierarchy, and they have traditionally been confined to menial occupations on the fringes of Indian society, purely because of their birth.

Dalits in California report that this ancient system has been imported to the United States, where it remains prevalent in the Indian diaspora, including among those in the tech industry. "They say that in California this doesn't exist," declared the measure's sponsor, State Senator Aisha Wahab. "If it doesn't exist, then why do we have so many people advocating for the need of this bill?" (As if to corroborate Wahab's allegations, Google had canceled a planned talk in 2022 by the Dalit activist Thenmozhi Soundararajan, in reaction to the vehement objections posted on internal Google message boards that denounced her as "Hinduphobic"—a common defense against claims of casteism.) Despite furious opposition from leading figures in California's Hindu tech community—such as Asha Jadeja Motwani, widow of the engineer who helped craft the original Google search algorithm—by September the measure had passed both House and Senate with overwhelming bipartisan majorities and was sent to Governor Gavin Newsom for his signature. While Newsom deliberated, Dalit activists, led by Soundararajan, waged a monthlong hunger strike outside the state legislature. Then, in October, Newsom announced that he was vetoing the bill. It was unnecessary, he claimed, because any discrimination was already covered by existing civil rights laws.

Newsom's decision took many by surprise, but others knew better. A month earlier, the ambitious governor, widely considered a future Democratic presidential candidate, flew to Chicago, where Joe Biden's campaign had convened major donors for a meeting of the Biden Victory Fund PAC. Among them was Ramesh Kapur, a wealthy Massachusetts entrepreneur, whose voice and checkbook carry weight in the firmament of Democratic Party fundraising. In Chicago, Kapur made it clear to Newsom that he faced an important choice: if he ever hoped to secure Kapur's support, he had better make the right decision on the caste bill. Kapur was hoping to encourage competition between Newsom and Kamala Harris, whose mother was Indian. "I raised money for her when she ran for the Senate and the presidency," Kapur told me. (His goal, he said, is to elect the first Indian American president—"hopefully before I get reincarnated!") "If you want to be our next president," Kapur bluntly informed the governor, "veto the bill."

Newsom received an equally unequivocal message from Ajay Jain Bhutoria, another major Biden fundraiser who had served as deputy finance chair of the Democratic Party. "We used very strong words," Bhutoria, a Silicon Valley entrepreneur, later recounted on Twitter, telling him that definitely he has a bright future in national politics ... But at the same time, if there's a mistake made on his side, he loses the support of the community. And I think he got the message very loud and clear."

The ultimatum was decisive. Kapur said that Newsom emailed him three hours before going public: "I'm going to veto it." Newsom's move dashed the hopes of all who had fought for the bill, but it seems likely to reap him rich rewards. "Now that he has made that decision, he has become the champion of the Hindu cause," Kapur told me over the phone from California, where he was busy organizing the first in a series of fundraisers for the governor in Silicon Valley, Chicago, and New Jersey. "Newsom is hot in the Indian American community!"

Since July, Indian Americans have found a better champion. Days after Joe Biden dropped out of the presidential race, Kapur himself happily told me that "the whole community is excited, and united" around the news of Kamala Harris's growing stack of endorsements. As the 2024 election shapes up to be the most expensive ever, with campaigns set to raise and spend at least $15 billion, doors are opening for an emerging lobby of Hindu donors up and down the ballot.

The Indian American diaspora has been growing ever since passage of the Immigration and Nationality Act of 1965 allowed non-Europeans to settle en masse in the United States for the first time since the twenties. Given that visa approval was in part skills-based, the influx of immigrants from India was weighted toward the well-educated, who were more likely than not to hail from one of India's "upper castes." This trend persisted after 1990, when legislation expanded access to temporary work visas; since then, the Indian American community has grown to some 4.6 million people, two-thirds of whom are Hindu or consider themselves close to Hinduism. The community has flourished economically, notably in the tech industry, where Indian American CEOs proliferate, including the current bosses of Microsoft, Google, and IBM. A 2019 Pew Research Center study reported that 75 percent of Indian American adults had a college degree, and that the median annual household income was $119,000. According to a 2020 Carnegie Endowment study, Indian Americans enjoy a standard of living twice that of average Americans. Politicians naturally see potential rich pickings in such a group. Josh Novotney, a Pennsylvania Republican political operative and lobbyist put it to me this way: "It's extremely important in politics to always build relationships in new communities for both fundraising and for votes, and to also know what's going on. So if you have the ability to tap into a community like that, it is very valuable."

Domestic constituencies with strong overseas attachments have long been part of the American political landscape. The most obvious example is the pro-Israel lobby, feared and embraced across the political spectrum, with its deepest attachments in the Democratic Party. This year may be different. Since October 7 —coincidentally the same day that Newsom announced his veto—the ongoing slaughter in Gaza has brought electoral peril for the Democrats. Polls report withering support across important components of the coalition that brought Biden to victory in 2020, especially among the Muslim community, which gave him up to 85 percent of its votes in that election, according to some polls. Although Hindus were less supportive of Biden than Muslims were in 2020 (25 percent went for Donald Trump, according to certain estimates, a slight uptick from 2016), some see their votes as the perfect replacement for the Democrats' faltering Muslim coalition.

"We can make the difference!" Kapur exclaimed, brandishing a state-by-state breakdown of Hindu and Muslim populations to show that his fellow Hindus could deliver votes as well as money. Muslims outnumber Hindus in America, 3.5 million to 3 million. But in key swing states, the numbers Kapur presented to me, drawn mostly from 2014 data, almost balance out: Pennsylvania is home to 130,000 Hindus and 150,000 Muslims. In Georgia, the state's 172,000 Hindus outnumber its 123,000 Muslims, while the 110,000 Hindus in Michigan provide some counterweight, Kapur implied, to the quarter-million Muslims, many of whom are outraged by the Biden administration's support for Israel. In Nevada, Hindus outnumber Muslims by almost three to one, while in Virginia, Hindus have an edge of 200,000 to just under 170,000. During the 2021 Virginia governor's race, both the Democratic candidate, Terry McAuliffe, and the Republican, Glenn Youngkin, paid attention to this voter pool and dutifully visited Hindu temples, but Youngkin reportedly made the stronger impression—he "listened deeply" to their concerns, as American Hindu Coalition chairman Shekhar Tiwari put it, especially their complaints about local schools' efforts to promote diversity by modifying admissions policies at their expense. Youngkin was not the first Republican to cultivate and enjoy Hindu support. In 2015, the Chicago billionaire industrialist Shalabh Kumar set up the Republican Hindu Coalition, which describes itself as "modeled after the highly successful Republican Jewish Coalition"; Steve Bannon was an honorary co-chair of the group. Kumar and his wife poured money into Trump's 2016 election campaign, which was making major media buys in swing states. Trump even recorded a message in Hindi.

Kumar has reportedly extolled Indian prime minister Narendra Modi as his idol, but Modi has received hardly less fulsome tribute from Biden and Harris. Throughout his term, Biden and his administration fortified ties with Modi as an ally as relations with China grew ever more sour. Welcoming him to the White House last June, Biden effused about "two proud nations, whose love of freedom secured our independence, bound by the same words in our Constitution—the first three words: we the people." He went on to pay tribute to the Indian diaspora as "a bridge between our nations," citing the record number of Indian Americans serving in Congress (known as the "Samosa Caucus"), and remarked, "We see the pride of the community in our incredible vice president." He hailed Harris as "the proud granddaughter of an Indian civil servant." When Harris hosted Modi at a luncheon during the same visit, she recalled her childhood visits to what was then Madras, and celebrated Indian Americans' impact on the economy. "As we look toward the future, the United States and India, the world's oldest and largest democracies, instinctively turn to each other and are increasingly aligned," she said. "Prime Minister Modi, you and I have both dedicated our careers to the noble work of public service."

The praise for Modi as a fellow champion of shared democratic values was ironic, not least because US intelligence and Justice Department officials were meanwhile concluding that officials in Modi's government had actively plotted to murder a US citizen, a Sikh nationalist leader, on American soil. According to a detailed and well-sourced *Washington Post* exposé, the plot was directed from the highest levels of Indian intelligence, with the apparent blessing of officials close to Modi himself—all while Modi basked in Biden's lavish encomium. (The Indian government has denied involvement.) In years past, there had been no such welcome mat for Modi in Washington. From 2005 to

2014, before he became prime minister, he was banned from even setting foot in the United States thanks to his alleged role, when he was chief minister of the northwestern state of Gujarat, in the incitement of a murderous anti-Muslim pogrom in 2002 that killed upwards of a thousand people, some of whom were burned alive. Modi's visa was restored only after he was elected prime minister in 2014 on the Hindu-supremacist program known as Hindutva that has defined both his entire political career and his extremist party, the Bharatiya Janata Party (BJP).

Under Modi's rule, millions of Muslim voters have become vulnerable to disenfranchisement through tendentiously applied citizenship laws. The majority-Muslim state of Kashmir has had its constitutionally guaranteed autonomy revoked, and its population has suffered harsh repression. Many of India's 200 million Muslims live in fear of violent attacks, including lynchings, while bulldozers demolish their homes and mosques. (Hence the alarm among Muslims in Edison, New Jersey, home to nearly 30,000 Indian Americans, when Modi supporters headed a 2022 Indian Independence Day parade with a bulldozer plastered with pictures of a leading Islamophobic BJP politician.) In this year's Indian election campaign, Modi upped the ante, telling a roaring crowd at a rally in April that the opposing Congress Party would give resources to Muslims first. "They will gather all your wealth and distribute it among those who have more children. They will distribute among infiltrators," he told them. "Do you think your hard-earned money should be given to infiltrators? Would you accept this?" As it turned out, Modi's rabid rhetoric proved less appealing in the face of popular discontent over economic hardship and widening inequality. The BJP lost dozens of seats in the election and gave up its outright majority in Parliament. Nevertheless, he retained power and has shown little sign of abandoning his nationalist agenda. Significantly, Amit Shah—his closest political ally and an extreme hard-liner who has referred to Muslim immigrants as "termites" who should be "thrown into the Bay of Bengal, one by one"—was reappointed as minister of home affairs.

Modi's nationalist program was shaped by the Rashtriya Swayamsevak Sangh (RSS), a paramilitary group founded in the twenties. Its agenda of Hindu supremacy directs antipathy toward India's Muslim minority, deeming the population an alien presence that subjugated Hindus in a series of historical conquests. As M. S. Golwalkar, an RSS leader for more than thirty years, wrote in 1939: "To keep up the purity of its race and culture, Germany shocked the world by her purging of the country of the Semitic races—the Jews. Race pride at its highest has been manifested ... a good lesson for us in Hindustan to learn and profit by."

Race pride, or Hindu supremacy, has endured as the nationalists' core ideology, resting on an evocation of a mythical past in which Hinduism reigned supreme in India for thousands of years before Muslim incursion. As Modi, according to the *Times of India*, told a cheering audience of Indian Americans in Houston during his June 2023 visit: "India has regained the confidence that had been snatched from it during the thousand-year-long foreign occupation."

Following independence and partition, India adopted an explicitly secular constitution that offered protections for religious minorities and other groups, and that banned discrimination by caste. But the RSS refused to recognize it, instead pursuing its own agenda through an alphabet soup of related groups collectively known as the Sangh Parivar. Then, in 1980, the RSS set up a political wing, the BJP, where Modi emerged as a leading light. The party soon found a potent issue in a sixteenth-century mosque in Uttar Pradesh supposedly occupying the site of the mythical birthplace of Rama, a principal deity in the Hindu pantheon. In 1992, the BJP fomented a riot in which a frenzied mob tore down the offending building. Ensuing pogroms killed some 2,000 Muslims.

Over the following two decades, Modi solidified control of the party, finally scoring a definitive victory in the 2014 parliamentary elections. Later that year, his visa restored, he came to the United States and addressed an ecstatic crowd of 19,000 cheering Indian immigrants in Madison Square Garden. "You all have earned a lot of respect in America through your conduct, values, traditions, and ability," he told them. "The Indian democracy witnessed an unprecedented turn of events, and you played a crucial role in the final outcome."

In fact, the RSS and its BJP offshoot had been looking to mobilize overseas for a long time—at least since 1953, when an RSS leader exhorted the movement's activists to launch a "world mission to propagate the Hindu notion of the world as a single family." In the United States, groups such as the Hindu Swayamsevak Sangh (HSS)—the international wing of the RSS—and the World Hindu Council of America, whose parent organization was set up by RSS leaders in the Sixties, have hundreds of branches. In 2003, not long after the Gujarat anti-Muslim pogrom generated global condemnation of Hindu extremism, a group of second-generation Indian American professionals founded the Hindu American Foundation (HAF). Its purpose, according to the attorney Suhag Shukla, one of the group's co-founders and its executive director, is to combat misperceptions of Hindus in America. "Whether we look at the way that Hindus are portrayed in things as basic as social studies, teaching materials—the whole of Indian society is flattened to something that's almost like an archaic museum piece that's been unchanging," Shukla told me. "That's not an accurate reflection of what Indian society is or has been."

But the new organization was closely connected in word and spirit to the RSS and its spin-offs. For example, the HAF co-founder Mihir Meghani, a California physician, had been an activist with the World Hindu Council of America. In 1998, the BJP's official website featured Meghani's essay "Hindutva: The Great Nationalist Ideology," in which he paid tribute to the mobs that destroyed the mosque in 1992. The essay derided the edifice as a "dilapidated symbol of foreign dominance," whose demolition thereby released "thousands of years of anger and shame, so diligently bottled up." (Meghani has since denounced the essay.)

Evidently, countering what Shukla has called "negative reductive stereotypes" includes an aggressive defense of Indian government actions. In 2019, the progressive Democrat Pramila Jayapal (herself Indian-born) introduced a resolution in the House urging the Indian government to end mass detentions in Kashmir; after the HAF successfully lobbied to defeat it, the group announced that HINDU AMERICAN ADVOCACY WORKS! in a press release celebrating the defeat of the "anti-Hindu, anti-India resolution." Away from Washington, the HAF works to promote its causes on the local level, such as in the campaign against the California caste-discrimination bill. "I personally edited the letters of a number of top-level CEOs that were writing to Governor Newsom saying, This is not going to be good for Californians," Shukla told me.

The fight against what are deemed unwelcome stereotypes extends to American classrooms. In 2016 in California, Hindu-nationalist groups claimed that sixth-grade textbooks were biased against Hindus and demanded they be revised to give a kindlier depiction of the caste system, and to downplay the role of patriarchy in India. The California Department of Education caved, voting unanimously to incorporate the proposed changes for nearly a dozen textbooks. The episode echoed a similar dispute a decade earlier, in which a group of South Asian academics protested the whitewashing of Indian history in state textbooks. One of those scholars, Michael Witzel, a professor of Sanskrit at Harvard, was attacked at the time as a "Hitler" by those who were leading the charge to amend the materials.

Attacks on academics are a recurring feature of the assertive Hindu nationalist agenda, in which any scholarly analysis of ancient Indian history or the roots of Hinduism that challenges the nationalists' preferred version promptly elicits menacing personal vitriol. Thus the Rutgers professor Audrey Truschke, a specialist in premodern Sanskrit texts and South Asian history, has required armed police protection during lectures and public appearances for fear of animus against her critiques of the nationalist agenda. She summarizes the Hindu supremacist worldview as "simply fascist," a characterization which has garnered her a lawsuit from the Hindu American Foundation, pegged to her endorsement via Twitter of two Al Jazeera articles critiquing the HAF and related nationalist groups. The suit was dismissed by a US District Court judge in 2022, but the attacks on Truschke continued. "I wake up and read my hate mail," she told me in April. "Death threats, misogynist attacks, anti-Semitic attacks—even though I'm not Jewish—threats to rape my daughters. It would probably be unsafe for me ever to return to India." Nevertheless, she continues to speak out: "I want to show them I'm not scared."

The rise of Hindu nationalist influence in the United States inevitably invites comparison with the pro-Israel lobby, an acknowledged source of inspiration. As Shukla explained to me, Meghani "had already been doing a lot of work with the Jewish community," learning from its success in shaping and promoting a favorable narrative. As Israel's political influence comes under increasing challenge, it still enjoys vociferous support from the Hindu nationalist community.

In this year's Democratic primary for Pennsylvania's twelfth congressional district, for example, Representative Summer Lee, a progressive Democrat and unequivocal defender of Palestinian rights, was opposed by a local councilor, Bhavini Patel. Pro-Israel groups had spent $5 million in the 2022 election in a failed attempt to defeat Lee. This time AIPAC stood aside, but Patel was backed not only by a "Moderate PAC"—funded to the tune of $800,000 by the Republican billionaire Jeffrey Yass, a staunch supporter of Israeli causes—but by leaders in the Hindu nationalist lobby. Meghani himself co-hosted a Patel fundraiser in January. (Ramesh Bhutada, another of the hosts, is vice president of the HSS.) "We are making really strong efforts within the Jewish community, within the Hindu community, to encourage people registered as independents and Republicans to reregister as Democrats for the primary," Patel declared at the January fundraiser. Support for Israel, and denunciations of the progressive Squad, were major themes of her campaign. "If we don't get Bhavini elected, we're gonna have ten to twenty years of someone like Ilhan Omar or Rashida Tlaib," Meghani told donors during the fundraiser. "This is our chance." The effort, as it turned out, fell short; Lee scored a crushing victory in the April primary, owing in large part to her strong local popularity and success in delivering benefits for the district while in office.

These uncompromising campaign interventions go back further. In July 2020, a Chicago City Council alderman introduced a resolution urging the city government "to reject violence in the name of any faith." It cited attacks on India's Muslims and compared Modi's program to the "bigoted policies" of Trump. City councils across the country routinely pass such worthy but toothless resolutions, but this one quickly drew well-organized opposition from not only the American Jewish Committee but also the Islamophobic think-tank Middle East Forum. A group set up by the Illinois Hindu activist Bharat Barai, an oncologist who had hosted Modi on earlier US visits, spread word that the resolution was inspired by "extremists" linked to Hamas and spoke to a professional lobbyist to work for its defeat. The mayor's office, under pressure from the Indian Consulate General, watered down the resolution. Drawn-out negotiations produced an anodyne version shorn of references to Trump and Muslim lynchings, merely decrying discrimination. Even this was not enough. When the truncated measure finally came up for a vote, it was defeated decisively.

Barai has exerted influence far beyond Illinois. In 2013, he discerned the potential of an ambitious young politician from Hawaii, Tulsi Gabbard, who had been elected to Congress for the first time on a progressive platform in 2012. Though not of Indian descent, Gabbard identified as Hindu—her mother was a convert. Those on the left who would cheer her opposition to US military interventions paid little attention to the implications of her religious affiliation, but it was enough to loosen purse strings. Along with other notable figures in US-based groups, Barai began making sizable donations to her campaigns. When asked by the journalist Pieter Friedrich why he backed a progressive after previously supporting a Tea Party congressman, Barai replied: "It doesn't matter to me whether it is a Republican or Democrat."

Barai's push for Gabbard was a shrewd investment, especially at a time when Modi's right-wing agenda and the violence of his supporters was attracting unwelcome attention in the US Congress. In November 2013, a bipartisan group of House members introduced a resolution warning that "strands of the Hindu nationalist movement have advanced a divisive and violent agenda that has harmed the social fabric of India." Gabbard struck back, declaring it "critically important that we focus on strengthening the ties between the two nations, and I do not believe that [the resolution] accomplishes this." Her stand reaped dividends all around. The HAF applauded her opposition to the "anti-India" resolution, while, according to Friedrich's analysis of Federal Election Commission data, pro-Modi donors poured no less than $123,000 into her 2014 reelection campaign—almost a quarter of her total war chest. At her wedding in 2015, attended by a host of Sangh luminaries, an attendee read out a letter of congratulations allegedly from Modi himself.

Other politicians in receipt of Barai's largesse continue to flourish in the mainstream, notably the suburban Chicago congressman Raja Krishnamoorthi, to whom Barai and his wife have donated at least $32,000. A leader in the Samosa Caucus and endorsed by the HAF, Krishnamoorthi spoke at a gathering of RSS-related US groups, as part of a 2019 Chicago celebration of the founding of the RSS, on a stage adorned with a portrait of the Nazi sympathizer Golwalkar. He faces no serious challenge for his seat this year, but has nonetheless raised a pot of at least $16 million. He has emerged as an outspoken hawk regarding China, serving as the senior Democrat on the House Select Committee on the Chinese Communist Party, while co-sponsoring the bill to bar Chinese ownership of TikTok, which has been banned in India since 2020.

Representative Ro Khanna, first elected in 2016 in a district that includes most of Silicon Valley, has taken a subtler approach. Making his name as a progressive, especially as an articulate critic of Pentagon spending and foreign wars, he has been sharply critical of the Hindu nationalist agenda, calling in 2019 for "every American politician of Hindu faith to reject Hindutva." But Khanna appears to have since shifted his position. Four years after his denunciation of Hindutva, he urged to have Modi address a joint session of Congress during his June 2023 state visit, an event boycotted by several of his fellow progressives. That same year, he and Krishnamoorthi sponsored legislation to fast-track weapons sales to India.

Along with Patel, the Hindu American PAC has this year endorsed not only a host of Democrats running for congressional and state offices, but also Republicans, such as the Georgia congressman Rich McCormick, hailed by the group for his stand on "Hinduphobia and Pakistan-supported terrorism against Indians in Kashmir." (Not coincidentally, McCormick's district includes, in his words, "almost a hundred thousand" immigrants from

India, including "one out of every five doctors.") David Brog is another Republican endorsed by the PAC as a candidate for the Nevada state assembly. A distant cousin of former Israeli prime minister Ehud Barak, he is the co-founder of the hugely influential Christians United for Israel and a fervent advocate for a "Jewish–Hindu alliance ... there's no community in America with whom we share more than the Hindu-American community."

Had there ever been doubts about the significance of the Hindu community in American politics, they have surely been allayed by the tumultuous events of this year's election cycle; overall, the political effort of this lobby's influence is bipartisan. Vivek Ramaswamy, scion of an upper-caste immigrant family from Kerala, vied for the Republican nomination. Now, a "proud granddaughter of an Indian civil servant" is the Democratic presidential nominee, and Usha Chilukuri Vance, herself the daughter of Indian immigrants, may be headed for the vice presidential mansion as Second Lady. There can be little doubt that this community, endowed with wealth, organization, and potent political connections, will continue to grow in influence, becoming its own political bulldozer.

Harper's Magazine, October 2024

23

Playing Dead

On April 25, the same day that FBI agents arrested a Wisconsin judge and ICE deported a cancer-stricken four-year-old US citizen to Honduras, I arrived in Grand Island, a city of some 50,000 in the heart of rural Nebraska, for a People's Town Hall. It was part of a series of such events promoted by the national Democratic Party to channel grassroots outrage over the Trump administration's unbridled assaults on the fabric of American government, an outrage most forcefully demonstrated by the massive crowds turning out for the Fighting Oligarchy rallies—which started in Nebraska—assembled by Bernie Sanders and Alexandria Ocasio-Cortez. Congressional Republicans, who had experienced an unwelcome taste of popular discontent at their own formerly placid town halls, were now under orders from party headquarters to avoid such encounters. "If they won't talk to their own voters, then Democrats will," announced Ken Martin, the newly installed chair of the Democratic National Committee. "That's why we'll be hosting People's Town Halls in all fifty states across the country, starting now with vulnerable GOP-held target districts."

Grand Island, for its part, hardly qualifies as vulnerable. It sits in Nebraska's vast Third Congressional District, where the Republican representative Adrian Smith was re-elected for a tenth term in 2024 with just over 80 percent of the vote. But like most of his peers, he had largely been shirking meetings where he was likely to face protest. The DNC venue, festooned with placards proclaiming benefits before billionaires, was packed to capacity with more than 300 people. Most but not all were Democrats. "I didn't know there was a Democratic Party in Nebraska—I'm an independent," a man in the line for the ample buffet said loudly. "We should be on the streets!" shouted an elderly gentleman bearing a striking resemblance to Sanders. Debby Thompson, a retired English professor, had jettisoned her postretirement plan to write a history of plastics and, the day after the election, had connected with her local county Democratic Party. "I went to a meeting because I thought, I can't do this alone. I want to do something," she told me. As with many of those stirred to action by Trump's return, her activism was not confined to party-led organizations. She had also set up a local branch of Indivisible, the progressive group born in the days of Trump 1.0 that, along with Sanders, has been mobilizing protests this time around. She was now helping lead regular demonstrations in her hometown of Hastings, twenty-five miles away.

The day before the town hall, Republican Senator Pete Ricketts of Nebraska, a multimillionaire whose family owns the Chicago Cubs, had ventured to hold a town hall in Kearney, home to a campus of the University of Nebraska—a rare exception to his party's policy of lying low. Thompson had gone along with her friend Joyce Moore, a retired elementary school teacher. Ricketts, she told me, had been dismissive of voters who peppered him with questions about the so-called Department of Government Efficiency's cuts to services and threats to benefits. "Folks from south-central Nebraska were asking Ricketts important questions, and his replies were, in essence, either that we were wrong or that we should just trust Congress and the president," she said. Moore, the vice chair of the local Democratic Party in nearby Adams County, recalled feeling politically isolated when she moved to the state six years ago. "People in Nebraska just fall into being Republican," she said. The Democrats, in her experience, had been involved in "state politics and things, but there wasn't the motivation, fear, anger"—the emotions she felt were now spreading across the state. A protest that she and Thompson had helped organize in Hastings the previous week had attracted seventy-five people despite its being Easter weekend. "We had people from little towns all around us," Thompson told me, driven by angst over Trump's tariffs, threats to the state's agricultural exports, and looming Medicaid cuts—a presumptive body blow to rural hospitals. "There's a lot of people out there that just want to feel like they're doing something because they are so frustrated and upset with the way things are going."

Introducing the town hall, the Nebraska Democratic Party chair, Jane Fleming Kleeb—now also a vice chair of the DNC—extolled the advances local Democrats had made since she took the job in 2017. "We had 504 Democrats who were elected across the state. We now have 1,027 Democrats who were elected across the state. We're making massive progress," she said cheerfully. She then introduced the evening's featured speaker, Representative Ro Khanna of California, a rising star of the progressive wing of the Democratic Party who co-chaired Sanders's 2020 presidential campaign. Khanna is one of a number of progressive congressional Democrats encouraged by the party to appear in red-district town halls in an attempt to rebut impressions that the party is quiescent in the face of Trump's onslaught. As a representative of much of Silicon Valley, the heart of his northern California district, he stressed that despite the many billionaires among his constituents, he nevertheless won re-election on a platform of taxing the rich. In what sounded at times like a presidential stump speech, Khanna denounced the Republican push to cut taxes for the wealthy as perilous for the deficit, and warned of Republican threats to Medicaid, mentioning their grievous effect on rural hospitals. He referenced Abraham Lincoln, hailed the generation that won World War II, and stressed the need to understand AI in order to "build wealth in the community." Evoking the arrest of the Wisconsin judge, he fervently denounced the administration's assaults on the rule of law: "The most patriotic thing in America is standing up for the Constitution!" he said, drawing sustained cheers from the crowd.

But the audience wanted answers. "What, if anything, can the Democratic members of Congress do to get back to the work they should be doing—the power of the purse, checks and balances, setting tariffs?" demanded Moore. "I'm curious about what you and your colleagues are doing to stop the funneling of American dollars into a genocide in Palestine?" queried a lady at the back of the hall, eliciting loud applause. Another person decried the government's support for Russia instead of Ukraine, prompting somewhat louder applause. A Latino questioner made a heart-felt plea on behalf of undocumented immigrants threatened with deportation to countries they'd left decades ago. A bank employee asked about Trump's evisceration of banking regulations and his promotion of crypto.

Though eloquent in detailing the dire effect of Trump's edicts, Khanna had little to offer in the way of immediate solutions. On tariffs, he suggested that Democrats in Congress should seek out and work with Republicans "who suddenly realize how irrational the tariff policy is." He denounced Trump's private crypto ventures while touting Bitcoin as a "store of value" for young people. Responding to the genocide question, he cited his vote against sending "offensive weapons to Netanyahu," while suggesting the (chimerical) two-state solution for Palestinians as the proper policy goal. Khanna also ventured the occasional jab at his own party's leadership, such as Chuck Schumer's contentious decision to support the Republican continuing budget resolution and the failure of any prominent Democrat to stand with the Haitians in Springfield, Ohio, when they were accused of eating dogs and cats.

After the event, I asked Thompson what she thought of Khanna's performance. Some of his answers were "better than others," she said, but for her, that wasn't the point of the evening. "Really, we wanted to register our discontent with the disastrous Trump administration and with our complicit senators and representatives," she said. "It also helped to gather with like-minded people for a recharge." Whether the party that had organized the event could harness any of that energy, however, was an open question.

The hundreds of thousands of Americans packing into meetings and rallies around the country in the first traumatic months of the year found comfort in the company of others. But for the most part, their hopes for redress lay with the Democratic Party. They may be forlorn indeed; according to a poll conducted in part by the Associated Press in May, only a third of Democrats feel optimistic about their party's future. "The Democratic Party is hollowed out," Tory Gavito, president of Way to Win, a group organizing progressive donors, told me. "It's one of the most vicious cycles I've ever been through. You have Schumer and the old-school crew [who say], 'Just let the Republicans flame out on their own and we can elect a ham sandwich in the next cycle.'" She also highlighted efforts to push the antiregulation, free-market "abundance agenda," promoted by the *New York Times* columnist Ezra Klein, which was "going great among a class of Silicon Valley donors."

Meanwhile, she pointed out, the success of the Fighting Oligarchy rallies has shown that the populist wing of the party is generating enormous energy. "This left-right paradigm only matters to the elites," Gavito said. "It doesn't actually matter to the voters. Everybody's cherry-picking their ideological views. You can have a mom anti-vaxer still want to have history taught in schools. So ideology is not linear in that way."

The scrambling of left and right was clearly demonstrated in Nebraska last year, when the most significant threat faced by Republicans came not from the Democrats, but an independent named Dan Osborn. An industrial mechanic and former union leader who rose to prominence leading the 2021 strike against the cereal giant Kellogg's in Omaha, Osborn ran against a Republican senator, Deb Fischer, on an anti-corporate, pro-worker platform that also called for gun rights, tight border controls, abortion rights, immigration reform, legal marijuana, raising the national minimum wage, and lifting the cap on Social Security contributions. To the alarm of Republicans, he surged in the polls, ultimately coming within less than seven points of beating Fischer and forcing the party to divert significant cash to shore up support for her. "In my campaign, I never talked about Trump or Harris," Osborn told me. "I talked about education for their kids, about crumbling infrastructure, how Fischer was letting the railroad companies off the hook on safety. I said to people, 'What do you need?'" Strikingly, Osborn outpolled Harris by nearly 20 percent. "The Democrats are still doing the same thing they did in 2024," he said, "just 'F Trump.' They died on that hill."

A similar approach paid off in northern Michigan for Betsy Coffia, a former social worker and journalist who flipped a rural statehouse district from red to blue in 2022. Last year, even as Democrats lost control of the Michigan House, she increased her margin of victory and flipped six red precincts while making no secret of her support for reproductive rights and gun safety. Like Osborn, she talked about winning over voters by addressing issues they cared about, rather than obediently following a script devised by strategists for the Michigan House Democratic caucus campaign. "I went rogue," she told me over the phone as she returned to her office from the state capitol. "There was a lot of pressure to go with the consultants' one-size-fits-all generic messaging, which was really just hammering abortion rights," she said—rights that had already been protected in Michigan. "I didn't feel like that was what I was hearing and seeing from my constituents." Accordingly, instead of investing money to broadcast the consultants' generic message, she spent it on her own messaging, tailored to the expressed needs of her district, such as funding for rural busing. "I got into some trouble for doing that," she said. "But I was right!" She had no kind words for a national Democratic leadership that was seemingly "super-focused" on winning the 2026 midterms. "I think it's appalling how people are like, 'This will help us in 2026,' when your country's being taken over by an authoritarian bully. The Democratic Party has not been up to the moment, and that's not going unnoticed by a lot of very loyal Democrats in my community."

Ken Martin's DNC aims to address some disaffections like Coffia's; as he wrote in a guiding memo in April, the party will "organize early, organize always, organize everywhere, and win anywhere." The People's Town Halls were evidence of this ground game, as is the money Martin is funneling to state-party leadership and away from more consultant-heavy strategies. But instead of presenting a united front, the DNC has since been riven with infighting, sparked by the efforts of David Hogg, the twenty-five-year-old school-shooting survivor and progressive activist, to displace incumbents with a younger generation of Democrats while he was serving as vice chair.

Kleeb, the DNC vice chair, agrees that the party has fallen short. She has seen upsurges of discontent in rural Nebraska before. Part of a ranching and farming family, she fought long and hard against the Keystone XL Pipeline, the bitterly contested project to move oil from Canada across the state. When that fight was at its height, she recalled, people had "turned out in massive numbers for town halls. They deeply care about protecting their community, whether it's their rural hospital or their water supply." But the Democratic Party had shown little to no interest in local organizing—or even showing up. "We've lost all this ground in rural communities because we have stopped talking with them, showing up, being in their communities, knowing who the opinion leaders are, because so many of our Dems got old and kind of moved on, and we didn't ever replace them."

In Kleeb's experience, there had been paltry financial support from national headquarters for local parties across the country. Money at the DNC was diverted to feed an ascendant class of consultants versed in the mysteries of "voter analytics." Powerful Democratic donors had diverted funds from party-organized voter-registration drives, insisting that this important task be left to nonpartisan outside groups that enjoyed tax-deductible funding. When I first met Kleeb, in February 2017, she had just taken over Nebraska's Democratic Party. We had both recently been at the DNC meeting in Atlanta, where the party establishment squelched the election of the popular progressive congressman Keith Ellison as party chair in favor of former labor secretary Tom Perez. Former governors and senators, Kleeb said, were "calling state chairs and officers who had votes and saying, 'We really need you to go with Team Perez.'" Perez did not disappoint his establishment backers, populating key party positions with corporate-friendly consultants and lobbyists.

Eight years later, Kleeb, now fifty-two, has risen in the party as a close ally of Martin and the head of the Association of State Democratic Committees. At a meeting of Nebraska Young Democrats the day after the Grand Island event, I heard her reminisce about her own beginnings in politics, including organizing programs for the homeless and working with AmeriCorps—another institution Trump has stripped for parts. She recalled how, when she headed the national Young Democrats during the George W. Bush years, activists sported stickers featuring the slogan NOT MY PRESIDENT. "That was a symbol of resistance back in the day," she said. Now simply being anti-Trump isn't enough. "I think young people, just like older voters, want to know what the Democrats are going to do." Among other programs she would

like to see Democrats adopt, she cited expanding public education to cover pre-K through community college; Medicare for
All, making it easier for farmers and ranchers to get insurance;
and taking action on climate change. The Young Democrats in
the room listened attentively, some expressing fears that they
faced a more immediate crisis. "If we really meet the moment,"
murmured a graduate student at the University of Nebraska, "it
will bring on martial law."

Kleeb remained upbeat, giving me an enthusiastic report on the
changes Martin was bringing to the DNC. The Republicans had
adopted the infamous Project 2025, the far-right agenda being
implemented under Trump, so the DNC is constructing a Project
2029, with a principal focus on protecting voting rights, Kleeb
said. Meanwhile, the DNC has quietly deployed legal teams to
prepare for "worst-case" scenarios, such as Trump interfering
with the 2026 elections or attempting to run for a third term in
2028. More immediately, Martin is now pumping money in the
direction of the long-neglected state parties. "A million dollars
a month—that's twenty-one percent of the DNC budget," Kleeb
told me, with parties in red states getting extra. Martin has also
talked of adopting a "holistic" approach, in which Democrats
will wage a "perpetual campaign" not only in all fifty states, but
also in every county and precinct.

Martin's principal opponent in the DNC chair race, the
Wisconsin Democratic leader Ben Wikler, had secured the energetic support of party-establishment heavyweights, including
House minority leader Hakeem Jeffries, Nancy Pelosi, Chuck
Schumer, and the tech billionaire and major Democratic donor
Reid Hoffman, who reportedly donated $250,000 to Wikler's
campaign. But it was the state parties, with which Martin had been
working for eight years, that provided the crucial votes to ensure
his convincing victory. His rhetoric skews populist, decrying, for
example, "candidates on the Democratic side who take money
from people who don't share our values ... We should only take
money from people who share our values" and exclude union-
busting corporations and polluters. Among other reforms, Martin
has pledged to displace powerful consultants who have long fed
off the party. "Most of them are going to be gone because they

provide absolutely no value or service," he has said. "The only thing they care about is lining their own pockets versus winning." That might include those who rose to power back during the Obama and Hillary Clinton eras and who secured major roles in the 2024 race. Harris's campaign chair, Jen O'Malley Dillon, for instance, co-founded her firm, Precision Strategies, after serving as DNC executive director early in Obama's first term. The company waxed rich on Democratic campaigns during Obama's second term and through Trump's first, after which O'Malley Dillon managed Biden's 2020 effort, served as his White House deputy chief of staff, and chaired his 2024 campaign until party leaders belatedly forced him aside. She then stayed on to lead Harris's campaign, in the course of which Precision Strategies garnered handsome rewards from both Harris's operation and the DNC. Gambit Strategies, a firm that received $122 million from the Harris operation, was co-founded by Megan Clasen, a veteran of Hillary Clinton's 2016 presidential bid; Bully Pulpit International, recipient of $101 million from Harris, is headed by Andrew Bleeker, formerly lead digital-marketing strategist for Obama's 2008 campaign. The most lucrative area for consultants lies in paid media (campaign advertising on TV and online), for which the media- and production-buying specialists reap commissions. Media Buying & Analytics, owned by the Atlanta firm Canal Partners Media (itself founded by the veteran Georgia Democratic operative Bobby Kahn), took in at least $281 million from the Harris campaign.

The concentration of power over party messaging in powerful Washington-based firms evidently contributed to the party's losses among minority groups, whose own interests and concerns often go unreflected in TV spots. The 2024 election saw a fatal erosion of Democratic support among Latino and Black voters. According to Chuck Rocha, a consultant who has focused on the Latino community, by his own count only 10 out of 250 Democratic consultant firms are Latino or Black majority-owned, one of which is his own. All too often, Rocha told me, Spanish-language campaign ads were simply translations of generic English-language spots, as opposed to messages specifically crafted to appeal to Latino communities. Colin Rogero, a consultant who worked with the Biden-Harris campaign, later complained that efforts to pitch the candidate to Latino voters fell short because campaign officials debated "back and forth about whether or not we should take on these tough issues, because we might upset this person or that person."

Among those potentially upset by taking on "tough issues," such as clear populist messages and criticism of Israel's ongoing massacre in Gaza with US weapons, were those supplying the big money. Mark Cuban, a billionaire Harris donor, hinted that he had gotten a staffer fired for suggesting that Harris supported a tax on unrealized capital gains. Haim Saban, the billionaire who forked over $7 million in the early aughts to build a new DNC headquarters in Washington, has expected and certainly received satisfactory Democratic policies on Israel, as reflected in the party's adamant refusal to allow a Palestinian American to speak at its 2024 convention, and the continuing support by a majority of congressional Democrats for arming Israel's onslaught. Not coincidentally, Democratic congressional candidates received the bulk of AIPAC funding in 2024: 58.6 percent, as opposed to the 38.5 percent allotted to Republicans.

Whatever his intentions, the party machinery inherited by Martin will be difficult to reform. James Zogby, a member of the DNC for the past thirty-two years who spent sixteen of them on its executive committee, applauds Martin's strategy as "a needed shift in resources from the national party, where money largely went to consultants." But Zogby—who once told me his mission is to be "a pain in the ass" for the DNC—also provided stark insights into the inner workings of the institution. "Think the Bulgarian Communist Party circa 1955," he said sourly, describing a tightly controlled, top-down structure. "There has never been a discussion about budget or priorities. It's an opaque process that is run by consultants and law firms, and the party members are kind of props. We go to meetings and sit there to look like there's actually a decision-making process, but there's not." Ordinary members, he said, "do not have opportunities to ask questions" at the biannual meetings, nor could they easily introduce resolutions. Even the executive committee's more frequent meetings haven't featured much, or any, general discussion.

(On a conference call with DNC members the weekend after Biden's catastrophic debate with Trump, then–DNC chair Jaime Harrison reportedly turned off the chat function and refused to take questions.)

Martin may aspire to refashion the party's worldview, but he is confronting decades-old inertia that may well be impossible to overcome. "They still have a model of victory that's based on the Obama coalition," said Zogby, "but there's no Obama in the picture." He recalled an executive committee meeting in the wake of the 2014 midterm elections, which had brought massive Republican gains. "The party pollster came in and said, 'We did well, even though we lost. We kept our coalition together. We won the Black vote, the Latino vote, the youth vote. We just didn't win enough of them. So we've got to put more resources into it.'" Mindful of white working-class voters who had defected to the Republicans in large numbers, Zogby spoke up. "We've been losing ground in Pennsylvania, Ohio, and Michigan, and as a result those states are going to be passing anti-union, anti-women laws, and it's going to affect everybody," he recalled saying. "And [the pollster] shot back at me and said, 'We're not going to be throwing money away, wasting it on people who aren't going to vote for us.'" This attitude was further articulated by Schumer in July 2016, at a time when Trump's appeal to working-class resentments was drawing massive crowds. "For every blue-collar Democrat we will lose in western PA, we will pick up two, three moderate Republicans in the suburbs of Philadelphia. And you can repeat that in Ohio, and Illinois, and Wisconsin."

After three elections and a further withering of Democratic support among blue-collar communities, as well as among Black and Latino voters, Schumer appears to remain confident that Trump, embarking on his malign assault on the constitutional order, will ensure future Democratic success. James Carville reiterated the same point in the *New York Times* Opinion section this past February, suggesting that it's time for Democrats to "roll over and play dead. Allow the Republicans to crumble beneath their own weight and make the American people miss us." Zogby described a Schumer address to the DNC early this year laying out the Democrats' strategy: to "keep bringing Trump's numbers down so that when it got into the low forties they would be able to win control of Congress."

Even with party popularity trending at subterranean levels, there is scant indication that elected Democrats in Washington are deviating from business as usual: Schumer opted to support a Republican continuing resolution on the budget after saying he wouldn't. A number of Democratic senators have voted on a consistent basis for Trump's Cabinet nominees. Senator John Hickenlooper, of Colorado, who voted for ten of them, explained that to do otherwise might "piss people off." Senator Elissa Slotkin, of Michigan, a party-establishment favorite who trumpets her service in the CIA and talks a lot about deploying "alpha energy," reverently invoked Ronald Reagan and George W. Bush in the party's official response to Trump's address to Congress in March. Deriding Sanders's rallying cry to "fight oligarchy" on the grounds that those outside elite institutions may not know what it means, Slotkin has advised Democrats to say they oppose "kings" instead. ("I think the American people are not quite as dumb as Ms. Slotkin thinks they are," responded Sanders.) Despite growing outrage at the cruelties of Trump's deportation program, Hakeem Jeffries had reportedly sought to discourage congressional Democrats from journeying to El Salvador in solidarity with illegally imprisoned Kilmar Abrego Garcia, though he has denied it. Twelve Democratic senators and forty-eight House members voted for the xenophobic, Republican-sponsored Laken Riley Act, which enables the deportation of undocumented immigrants merely accused of assorted offenses, and gives individual states standing to sue the federal government for enacting immigration policies they do not like.

Despite the huge and enthusiastic crowds cheering on Sanders and Ocasio-Cortez at their rallies, many Democrats are still focused on squashing threats from the left. "You have to look at the Democratic Party as an army that has been fighting a counterinsurgency campaign against guerrillas, who are the leftists and progressives calling for justice, equity, health care for all," said Robert Saleem Holbrook, a Black progressive activist in Philadelphia. "They know how to fight the left, but they don't know how to fight Trump."

History indicates that the prime imperative of party organizations is to maintain control over the party, and thus they are most energized by threats to their control by insurgents. But establishment counterinsurgency campaigns are not necessarily successful. After all, Republican party leaders fought hard to control the Tea Party uprising that ultimately spawned MAGA and Trump's total dominance of the GOP, and failed.

In May, the DNC's credentials committee recommended that Hogg's election be voided on account of a procedural challenge, requiring him to rerun his race, after which he announced he would not stand for reelection. Hogg had aroused fury both inside the DNC and among other Democratic authorities with an initiative to raise money for his own outside group to mount primary challenges against "dead-weight" incumbent Democratic members of Congress; in response, Carville dismissed him as a "contemptible little twerp." Hogg remained unrepentant. He told me that he is fighting for "generational change" and recruiting candidates who will take on such entrenched interests as Big Oil and the National Rifle Association. "The DNC has pledged to remove me, and this vote has provided an avenue to fast-track that effort," he announced after the committee vote. Hogg ultimately opted not to run for re-election as vice chair, announcing that he would continue to challenge "the culture of seniority politics that brought our party to this place" from outside the DNC.

Interested to hear more from the much-abused congressional leadership, I consulted a senior Senate Democratic staffer with a keen appreciation of battleground races, who agreed to speak on background. In contrast to the jeremiads I heard from Zogby and others, his outlook was upbeat. "I don't think we need wholesale change in the Democratic Party," he told me. In his view, 2024 "was an extremely close election ... Harris was handed the hardest thing to do in politics ... She just had to run so hard," he said, giving voice to the view that Harris could have done better had she had more time (despite the fact that her initial lead over Trump evaporated during the final three weeks of the campaign). The staffer had no patience for the notion that a candidate with more populist appeal would have fared better. "Some of my Democratic friends love to say, 'If you just get way out there on progressive issues, there's a bunch of people in the rural areas that are going to come your way or in the suburban areas that are going to come your way.' And I just have never seen that." Instead, he insisted, Democrats should focus on "the economy," which is "only going to get worse," thanks to Trump's disastrous policies, which will inevitably raise prices and cost jobs.

The party's hopes and attention, the staffer told me, are intensely focused on Virginia, where the former congresswoman Abigail Spanberger is running for governor in November. Spanberger trades heavily on her national-security credentials as a former CIA employee; she has made centrism her calling card, with a fondness for working with Republicans and blaming progressive messaging for Democratic defeats. Her rhetoric in the current campaign indicates little promise of causing serious offense to corporate interests, which will be reassured by her pledge to refuse to sign any bill repealing the state's anti-union right-to-work law. In the view of the Democratic staffer, she is the ideal candidate, owing to her "very strong following, really good grassroots fundraising, good level of support from traditional Democratic donors." Spanberger leads in the polls and fundraising, while the Virginia Republicans are riven with internal disputes, so she is likely to win, and popular revulsion over Trump's destructive initiatives may propel the party to wins in the 2026 midterms. But such victories will likely reassure party elders resistant to change, thereby leaving in place the same party that fought and lost the 2024 election, complete with its attachment to Israel and military spending.

Despite the reforms instigated by Martin to buttress local organizers like Kleeb, and the populist energy revealed by the Sanders and Indivisible mass meetings, party strategy will still probably be centered on the rallying cry of "F Trump," which failed to secure victory in 2024. In the absence of an audit of the defeat (though Martin has promised one), a consensus has emerged that the fault lies entirely with Biden and his clique for having selfishly insisted on running despite his evident senility. That explanation has the merit of letting everyone else off the hook; but the grim roster should include the vacuous Harris, the inept and avaricious consultants, the endorsement of the Gaza genocide that alienated a significant number of young voters, and the lack of any convincing communication of what the party stands for.

Meanwhile, the bulk of Americans struggle with mounting debt, deficient health care, crumbling infrastructure, and decaying public services and education. Martin may pledge to energize the grass roots with support for state and local parties, but those with long memories may recall that the former DNC chair Howard Dean promised a similar effort in the early aughts, only to see it wither within a few short years. It would certainly be noble if the party were to reject cash from those "who don't share our values," but might that include Blackstone, the private equity giant previously active, for example, in fighting rent-control initiatives and mass-evicting tenants? The company was Schumer's leading contributor from 2019 through 2024. Or AIPAC, whose interventions in Democratic primary campaigns to defeat incumbents have far exceeded the wildest dreams of David Hogg? Martin may be funneling extra funds to state parties, but what happens to them there is another matter. Rocha complained to me that the same consultants who harvested the bulk of the $2 billion spent by the Harris campaign are now working for leading Democratic candidates in the 2026 and 2028 races.

Back in Nebraska, Kleeb's efforts have borne fruit with a massive swing in Omaha, where a Democrat, John Ewing Jr. defeated a three-term Republican mayor in May. Meanwhile, Osborn is mulling another independent campaign for Senate on a populist platform, this time against the incumbent Ricketts. Osborn told me that he will call out the dominance of wealthy and corporate donors across both parties—and refuse to accept any corporate PAC donations. Given that in 2024 he won nearly 20 percent more votes than Harris with an explicitly anticorporate platform, and given the Democrats' oft-professed desire to "reconnect with the white working-class vote," his willingness to take on issues that weigh most heavily on Americans' minds might provide a better lodestar for Democrats than centrist platitudes.

For those still striving to understand what it is that those lost voters really want, the truth is out there, sometimes revealed in surprising places. I talked with Margie Omero, a seasoned pollster and veteran of many Democratic races who, in recent months, has been conducting focus groups with working-class voters, most of whom voted for Trump. Despite Democrats' hope and expectation that Trump's economic mismanagement will crater his working-class support, she reports that many voters accept his promise that, although his policies may create pain in the short term, there will be tremendous gain down the road, "a golden future."

"Well," Omero asked them, "what's on the other side?" What long-term gains might Trump deliver? The focus groups' answers were telling indeed. "People say things that Trump isn't promising, like universal health care and addressing income inequality," she said. "People are filling it in with what they want, what they need."

Harper's Magazine, August 2025

Afterword

The Big Lies

This book's initial chapter detailed the first time an invading army rampaged through Washington, DC, burning the edifices of government and cowing a terrified populace. Early in his second term, Donald Trump took steps to repeat the exercise, not as the tragedy suffered at the hands of British troops but as a malign farce stage-managed by domestic forces. In the summer of 2025, desultory groups of National Guardsmen and women, along with detachments of normally chair-bound crime warriors from the offices of assorted federal law enforcement agencies, began patrolling select and normally crime-free areas of the nation's capital, such as Union Station and the National Mall. As with so many of Trump's pronouncements and edicts, the show of force was promoted with a lie: that Washington, DC, was overrun by roving bands of criminals. An abundance of statistics confirmed that local crime rates were steadily declining and had been for some time. The infinitely cruel assaults on immigrant communities by the rapidly expanding force of ICE agents was similarly premised on the lie that immigrants were disproportionately criminal, whereas all evidence confirmed that they are in fact disproportionately law-abiding. The true purpose of these attacks on civil liberties was clearly to incite fear, fear among the citizenry at large of a Trumpian drive for a military-police state and actual terror among ICE's targets at the prospect of being forcibly wrenched from their homes and families and "disappeared" either into exile or, all too likely, local and foreign dungeons.

The ongoing assaults on civil liberties, real and potential, were received with protest but no effective resistance by Congress or the courts, calling to mind the aphorism, coined by former federal judge Robert Cindrich, that in the last resort "the Constitution turns out to be no more than a gentleman's agreement," tossed into the fire whenever a president opts to dispose of it. The threat highlighted in Chapter 2—"The Enemies Briefcase"—that presidents have an armory of draconian emergency powers at their disposal was being fully realized. The deployment of troops on the streets of American cities, the assaults on immigrants, including the deportation of legal residents, the whimsical imposition of tariff trade barriers, the militarization of the southern border, the designation of foreign drug-dealing enterprises ("cartels") as terrorists, mining and energy production on federal lands were all deployed by the invocation of one or other alleged emergency power granted to the executive branch, in some cases long ago. Trump's punitive tariffs against Canada, for example, were justified as a response to illegal exports to the US of the fentanyl narcotic by our northern neighbor. Signing one such emergency declaration, Trump declared: "You know what that allows you to do? That means you can do whatever you have to do to get out of that problem. And we do have that kind of an emergency."

Among the "problems" dispelled by Trump with strokes of his pen was of course the aforementioned gentleman's agreement, which expressly assigns control of spending, the "power of the purse," to Congress. But Congress proved to be a broken reed, unable, or at least unwilling, to assert its prerogatives. Presumptively, the other branch of government, the judiciary, should also serve to impede unchecked presidential power. Indeed, a plethora of lower court judges attempted to do just that, ruling against Trump's illegal deportations, his diversion of money duly allocated by Congress for disaster relief and foreign aid, his summary firings of federal workers and other measures that would surely have shocked James Madison. However, the judges' efforts were largely nullified by a Supreme Court solidly packed with a Trump-friendly majority thanks to his three appointments during his first term. Thus, although Trump railed against "liberal judges" the overall effect has been to enhance the power of the judiciary at the expense of Congress. Although Trump's first term had been marked by serial failures, such as the attempt to end Obamacare, or exclude Muslims, or overturn the 2020 election, his one great success was the installation of that unshakably subservient Supreme Court majority. As a retired senior federal judge remarked to me, "Trump II would have been impossible without Trump I."

Trump's justifications for his emergency edicts were lies, but they were big lies, the utility of which had been defined by Adolf Hitler: "[I]n the big lie there is always a certain force of credibility," he wrote in *Mein Kampf*, "because the broad masses of a nation are always more easily corrupted in the deeper strata of their emotional nature than consciously or voluntarily; and thus in the primitive simplicity of their minds they more readily fall victims to the big lie than the small lie, since they themselves often tell small lies in little matters but would be ashamed to resort to large-scale falsehoods." Trump of course does not eschew small lies, such as concern his golfing or academic honors, but the overall approach, as succinctly enunciated by his former campaign manager Steve Bannon, has been to "flood the zone with shit."

The assaults on immigrants and Black urban populations—for who else was Trump evoking when he talked about "roving gangs"?—fulfilled an important political goal for the president. Racism and enmity toward alien outsiders are traditional features long embedded in American society and have been an important component of his carefully cultivated populist MAGA base. In further expression of xenophobic sentiments, the administration seemed bent on discouraging foreigners from setting foot in the United States at all by, among other measures, charging would-be visitors a hefty fee for tourist visas. Other initiatives designed to satisfy MAGA appetites included the drive to suppress programs aimed at reversing racial and gender discrimination, demonized as DEI and "woke," along with faltering gestures promoted as an end to widely unpopular military adventurism abroad. MAGA remains very much the public face of Trumpism, as in Bannon's right-wing nationalist populism. But although MAGA was one animating force in the Trump regime, its spokespeople essentially performed the role of observers and commentators. Tellingly, when Justice Department anti-trust director Gail Slater appeared poised to oppose a proposed multi-billion tech industry merger, a genuinely populist initiative, she was swiftly undercut by lobbyists closely linked to the Trump family.

Meanwhile, the overlords of Silicon Valley (vehemently denounced by Bannon as "100 percent oligarchs" who "believe in technofeudalism") have enjoyed a commanding role in substantive policymaking. The tech industry's overriding priority has been the hard-wiring of artificial intelligence technology and infrastructure, not to mention its scam-ridden sibling crypto, into the heart of the US economy. Achieving that goal requires an unprecedented expansion of energy production and distribution across the country to power the clusters of gargantuan data centers central to the project. Introducing his "AI Action Plan" at an industry gathering in Washington in July 2025 (his appearance immediately preceded by the hymn "How Great Thou Art" and Sinead O'Connor's "Nothing Compares 2 U"), Trump bestowed his unalloyed blessing on the project. He spoke of his efforts to drive down the price of oil in order "to have very inexpensive electricity so that you can power up the plants. You're going to need more electricity than any human beings ever in the history of the world." This was certainly correct. In Virginia, for example, Dominion Energy, the dominant utility (and political power) in the state, was preparing to meet demands for power supplies to the AI industry's data centers that amounted to a tripling of electricity currently used in the state for all purposes. One data center "campus" proposed for Virginia would alone demand the power of four large nuclear power stations, more than the current usage of ten smaller US states.

Overall, Trump endorsed plans to strip the AI industry of regulation, punish states who dared impose their own regulations, accelerate the deployment of AI across all areas of government, shred regulations on nuclear power and fossil fuel generation, and do away with copyright restrictions irksome to the AI industry, while restricting speech in AI by forbidding references to DEI and other ideologically unwelcome topics. Employers would be given enhanced power to control workers. In sum, Trump was giving the full backing of the federal government to a gigantic bet on a technology promising a quantum leap in economic potential. As of mid 2025, the promised benefits were proving slow to appear—95 percent of companies employing AI reported no appreciable gains in revenue—but such warning signs appeared to have minimal effect on the overall policy. Further evidence abounded of the tech oligarchs' influence on the Trump regime, most obviously in the position of J. D. Vance as vice-president. Vance, who owes his political career to Peter Thiel, a presiding authority in the Silicon Valley oligarchy. Thiel bankrolled Vance's foray into venture capitalist finance and then his successful 2022 Senate campaign in Ohio, serving throughout, by Vance's own account, as his mentor. Others speaking for the tech elite at the heart of the administration include Thiel's friend and associate David Sacks, the White House "AI and Crypto Czar" and a co-author with Michael Kratsios, Thiel's former chief of staff, of the Action Plan described above. It is also worth noting that major tech companies, including Microsoft and Thiel's Palantir, have been profitably stalwart supporters of Israel's extermination program in Gaza, support which has doubtless carried more weight with the Trump administration than complaints from some MAGA elements.

While promising golden rewards for the economy at large, the most immediate payoff sought by Silicon Valley clearly lay in government largesse, principally to be found in the defense budget. Thiel himself, as noted elsewhere in this book, long ago set out to bring the military-industrial complex back to Silicon Valley, with his own companies at its very center. The fruits of this endeavor were glaringly obvious in the money that flowed to to Palantir from the Pentagon in the first few months of Trump's second term, at least $300 million as of August 1, with the promise of much more to come, including a potential $10 billion from the US Army for supervision of the military's entire software management system as well as a large share of the contracts for Trump's quixotic Golden Dome missile defense program. Palantir and other defense tech industry stockholders could find further grounds for optimism in the position of Thomas M. Williams as the Office of Management and Budget official overseeing all defense programs. Williams's wife Cara, a former Palantir employee, held, as of August 2025, at least $2 million and as much as $10 million in Palantir stock options.

While Thiel's influence was evident in White House policymaking and the money flowing therefrom, fellow oligarch Elon Musk was the initial face of Trumpism in power, directing DOGE, the entity created to shred and emasculate the "administrative state" as directed by the federal bureaucracy. Largely recruited from the tech world of Silicon Valley, and imbued with its ethos of "move fast and break things" to bring the (purported) energy and efficiency of the industry to the business of government, his minions raged through federal departments. Yet, once Musk fell out with Trump and departed Washington, along with his principal lieutenants, the influence of DOGE fell away. Boasts of shrinking the federal deficit turned out to be empty. Even at the Pentagon, a byword for waste and inefficiency, DOGE could claim a mere $10 billion in savings, 1 percent of the defense budget. Many of those summarily dismissed were hurriedly summoned back. As of the end of July, an estimated 148,000 people had left government service, just over 6 percent of the total federal workforce. Included in that number were tens of thousands who had accepted offers of early retirement but were still being paid full salary and benefits. Very little had changed, apart perhaps for an increase in government inefficiency thanks to the departure of some skilled and experienced officials.

On the other hand, an important if unspoken Trump promise has been entirely fulfilled: a tidal wave of corruption. One hundred days into his second term, Senator Elizabeth Warren issued a list of one hundred instances of corrupt dealings by Trump and his underlings, including such acts as paying for the White House Easter Egg roll by soliciting corporate sponsors who had business pending with the federal government; the launching of a Trump crypto meme coin just prior to his inauguration, as well as one under the name of his wife, Melania; hosting a private dinner for the top 220 investors in his meme coin; and pardoning a crypto scamming firm and its executives who had been fined $100 million for illegal dealings. Trump's favor, corporations and other institutions soon learned, could be earned with promises of cash. Universities forked over hundreds of millions of dollars in recompense for permitting antisemitism, i.e. legitimate protests over Israel's massacres in Gaza. Media corporations bowed to demands for millions of dollars to ward off meritless lawsuits. The country of Qatar greased the wheels of Trumpian favor with the gift of a $400 million jet. "I'd be a fool to say no," said Trump.

A former close friend of Trump's recalled to me that he had once confided his ultimate ambition: to be the world's first trillionaire. Eight months into his second term, a painstaking investigation by *New Yorker* writer David Kirkpatrick into the amount garnered by Trump and his family while in office tabulated a running total of $3.4 billion. So, he had a long way to go, but it was still only 2025.

August 2025

Acknowledgments

Fulsome thanks are due to all those who encouraged and counseled me on the preparation of this collection, notably Leo Hollis and Kelly Burdick at Verso Books. Equal gratitude is owed to Rick MacArthur and his tireless team of editors at *Harper's Magazine*, as well Daniel Soar at the *London Review of Books*, Kelley Vlahos at *Responsible Statecraft* and Freddy Gray at the *Spectator*. Most of all I thank my wife Leslie, my most unstinting supporter and perceptive critic, who first encouraged me to publish this book.

Index